THE K-EFFECT

The K-Effect

ROMANIZATION, MODERNISM, AND THE TIMING
AND SPACING OF PRINT CULTURE

Christopher GoGwilt

FORDHAM UNIVERSITY PRESS   NEW YORK 2024

Copyright © 2024 Fordham University Press

All rights reserved. No part of this publication may be reproduced, stored in a retrieval system, or transmitted in any form or by any means—electronic, mechanical, photocopy, recording, or any other—except for brief quotations in printed reviews, without the prior permission of the publisher.

Fordham University Press has no responsibility for the persistence or accuracy of URLs for external or third-party Internet websites referred to in this publication and does not guarantee that any content on such websites is, or will remain, accurate or appropriate.

Fordham University Press also publishes its books in a variety of electronic formats. Some content that appears in print may not be available in electronic books.

Visit us online at www.fordhampress.com.

Library of Congress Cataloging-in-Publication Data available online at https://catalog.loc.gov.

Printed in the United States of America

26 25 24   5 4 3 2 1

First edition

for Siu Li

Contents

Introduction: Conrad's "timely appearance in English"   1
The K-effect, 6 • Conrad's "timely appearance in English," 13 •
The K-effect circa 1911, 21 • Overview of the Book, 25

1   The English Case of Romanization: From Conrad's
    "blank space" to Joyce's "iSpace"   31
    Defining Romanization: The *Oxford English Dictionary*
    and Joseph Conrad, 32 • Conrad's Accusative Case:
    Lord Jim and *Nostromo*, 51 • Joycean "iSpace"
    and the Conradian "blank space," 59

2   The Russian Face of Romanization:
    The K in Conrad and Kafka   72
    Language, Script, and Reform in the Russian Empire, 77 •
    Under Western Eyes, *A Personal Record*, and "Prince Roman,"
    83 • Kafka and Conrad: The Character and Function of K in
    Central Europe, 102

3   The Chinese Character of Romanization:
    Conrad and Lu Xun   117
    The Chinese Script Revolution and Romanization, 118 •
    Conrad's Chinese Characters: *Almayer's Folly* to *Victory*,
    127 • Conrad and Lu Xun: The Interface of Chinese
    and Roman Characters, 144

4 Sanskritization, Romanization, Digitization 157
Sanskritization, 165 • Sanskritization and Romanization in the OED and in Pramoedya Ananta Toer, 174 • Digitization, 179

ACKNOWLEDGMENTS 191

NOTES 195

BIBLIOGRAPHY 217

INDEX 227

THE K-EFFECT

Introduction:
Conrad's "timely appearance in English"

The following book investigates the history of romanization and its ongoing effects in shaping modern print media. "Romanization," simply put, is the phenomenon of writing or printing something using roman letters.[1] Most of us are so used to the way this organizes our reading practices, we are likely to overlook the different temporal and spatial scales of reference it implies: the phonetic spelling out of individual letters and words; the historical development and geographical spread of the roman alphabetic writing system; and the relatively recent proliferation of different forms of transliteration into roman letters. The task of this book is to consider how romanization works at all these different levels simultaneously, with particular attention to the way the recent global turn toward romanization complicates our understanding of the temporal, spatial, geographical, and historical dimensions of print culture.

At the first level, there is the phonetic function of roman letters, the way the spatial arrangement of letters shows how to pronounce a word in spoken time (so the lettering of the English word "ketchup," for example, scripts what the International Phonetic Alphabet renders "ketʃ.əp"). This already implies two related, but different things: the transcription of speech into writing; and the transliteration from one script, or writing system, to another. The phonetic function is clearly related to the historical emergence and geographical spread of the roman alphabet, although this has led to exaggerated claims about the uniqueness, prestige, and dominance of the roman alphabet. At this level of history, the roman alphabet (conflated with the phonetic alphabet, or simply *the* alphabet) appears synonymous with the history of print culture. At yet another level, the recent proliferation of romanization systems, beginning around the end of the nineteenth century, complicates the claim to roman alphabetic singularity and uniqueness. At the scale of this more recent phenomenon, romanization repositions the history of roman alphabetic writing systems within a much broader and more volatile, changing hierarchy of languages and scripts (as the word "ketchup," indeed, bears the historical traces of transcription and transliteration across a variety of Malay and Chinese languages and scripts). As the roman alphabet comes to serve a multiplicity of languages, coexisting alongside multiple scripts, the phonetic function of roman letters is supplemented, supplanted, and in some cases fundamentally displaced, by hybrid, non-phonetic features, some of which appear new (as with the alphanumerical digital coding of letters), some of which are more characteristic of other writing systems (notably the graphemic elements of Chinese characters), and some of which have long characterized those features of print culture so closely associated with roman letters. All together, these constitute a transformation in global histories of writing and print literacy. Even the simplest definition of romanization implies all at once: the timing and spacing of letters on the page; the history and geography of alphabetic writing; and the changing face of global print media.

To examine the phenomenon of romanization at all these levels, I draw on the insights of linguistic analysis, transnational modernist studies, and a close attention to the work of Joseph Conrad, read in global and comparative perspective. This book triangulates its argument through these three different lenses in order to highlight a phenomenon that remains undertheorized, even as it structures the very medium of the linguistic theories, modernist examples, and Conrad texts under discussion. Before proceeding, this Introduction will outline some of the challenges facing any attempt to account for the phenomenon of print romanization.

Linguists offer a number of rich resources for understanding the ancient origins of the roman alphabet, its development and worldwide spread as a dominant writing system, and the complexity of its function in transliterating languages and scripts.[2] The transliterating function of the roman alphabet is an especially important, if underexamined, feature of global modernization. Sociolinguists have provided various accounts of the historical proliferation of different systems of romanization over the turn from the nineteenth into the twentieth centuries.[3] These include a range of contrasting examples of script conversion to roman letters such as the state-sponsored, top-down conversion from the Ottoman Perso-Arabic script in Turkey in 1928, and the more gradual, less centralized conversion from Arabic script to romanized print in Indonesia. There are also examples of proposed reforms that did not lead to script conversion, for example, in Japan and China; and examples, too, of orthographic reforms, standardizing or modifying existing variations of roman alphabetic writing systems, as with Cyrillic and most European variants of the roman alphabet. Yet a full comparative linguistic accounting of the phenomenon of romanization seems remote (if not impossible) in part, because the linguistic frame of reference for giving such an account is itself conducted within a predominantly romanized scriptworld. There is no simple way to overcome what linguists have critiqued as the "Latin alphabet fetishism" underlying some of the most comprehensive and comparative studies of the world's scripts.[4] The linguistic challenge of accounting for the timing and spacing of the print medium we currently inhabit, remains the problem of a science of writing, framed by its own entanglement in the historical and geographical reach of romanization.[5] "Grammatology," the term coined by I. J. Gelb for the comparative study of the world's writing systems, thanks to Jacques Derrida's *Of Grammatology*, has come to name the philosophical limitations posed by any such study. In the words of Madeleine V.-David, cited by Derrida, "Undoubtedly the fact that we are 'alphabetic' writers . . . conspires strongly in hiding from us . . . essential aspects of the activity of writing."[6] For this reason, linguistic and sociolinguistic perspectives, while essential for this book's argument, are not sufficient to explain the linguistic, literary, and cultural phenomenon of romanization.

Linguistic and sociolinguistic perspectives can be complemented, as I endeavor to do here, by paying attention to modernist writers experimenting with the aesthetic effects of the written word. Scholars of transnational modernism offer a variety of different accounts as to how multilinguistic and multimedia forms of modernist aesthetic experimentation intersect with linguistic changes, policies, and reforms related to romanization.[7] The translingual practices of writers such as James Joyce, Franz Kafka, or Lu Xun illuminate how analysis of aesthetic form may be as important for understanding the effects of romanization as historical accounts of language policies, debates, and script reforms. Recent studies, moreover, have extended the comparative linguistic and cultural reach well beyond the traditional European focus of twentieth-century modernist studies, promising richer attention to the interrelation between multiple languages and multiple scripts informing global modernism. Yet no comprehensive comparative account exists to explain the role played by romanization in the transnational production and exchange of art, literature, and criticism at the beginning of the twentieth century. As with linguistic studies, the very frame of reference for global modernist studies has been set in place by the historical circumstances of standardizing systems of print romanization.

Emily Apter has drawn attention to the importance of Atatürk's 1928 romanization reforms in making Istanbul the academic setting for exiled German philologists (notably Auerbach and Spitzer) who influenced the later twentieth-century discipline of comparative literature in the United States.[8] Besides the case of Istanbul, one might also consider a range of other examples: Moscow, where late Tsarist and early Bolshevik language policies impacted the emergence of Russian formalism; and Tokyo, where debates about romanization served to mediate the formation of early twentieth-century Chinese modernism.[9] Seemingly more peripheral circuits of transnational modernism may also be important to consider. The case of Indonesian modernism is an example that has helped shape the argument of this book. By contrast to the state-decreed alphabet reform in Turkey, the more decentralized adoption of romanized print Malay in Indonesia provides an important counterpoint for genealogies of contemporary, comparative literary studies.

One of the major challenges facing both linguistic and literary approaches, is the sheer multiplicity of languages and scripts involved in assessments of the phenomenon of romanization. This is especially challenging given the English-language bias that tends to dominate scholarship in both linguistic and literary studies. The blind spots fostered by the dominance of English are reinforced by (and indeed related to) the blind spots fostered by the dominance of romanized writing systems. There is no single roman alphabet,[10] and the multiplication of romanization systems demands attention to a wide range of European and non-European languages involved in the development of those systems, as well as their interaction with a wide variety of different scripts besides roman letters. Yet linguistic, literary, and media studies are all prone to conflating dominant forms of writing with a singular alphabet; and the singularity ascribed to the roman alphabet is often itself conflated with the twenty-six letters of the English alphabet. This book seeks to address those blind spots as an essential part of its examination of the phenomenon of romanization. To do that, it takes as its main point of reference the work of a single English-language writer, Joseph Conrad.

Joseph Conrad (1857–1924) is uniquely suited to a study of romanization because his decision to write novels in English emerges from such a rich and complex crossing of multiple languages across multiple scripts. Of Polish origin, born in northwestern Ukraine, a linguistically diverse part of the then Russian Empire, Conrad came to writing fiction late in his life, adopting a form of English shaped by the experience of his first career as a British merchant marine sailor, traveling throughout the world. Readers, critics, and other writers have, from the start, turned to Conrad's texts for the way that they set English within a multilingual context. There is, indeed, a rich array of languages informing Conrad's English: not only Polish and French (in which he was more fluent than English), but also Russian (which he claimed not to know), Malay (so important for the Malay settings of many of his novels and stories), Chinese (also important for the Malay settings), not to mention those African languages notoriously excluded from *Heart of Darkness* (as Chinua Achebe has memorably argued in his indispensable critique of that novella).[11]

The variety of languages and scripts that appear in Conrad's fiction invites attention to the role of romanization in particular sociolinguistic reforms over the extended turn from the nineteenth to the twentieth century: the role of romanization in the standardization of English; the role of romanization in Russian script reforms (both in the late Tsarist period and in the early years of the Russian revolution); the shift from Arabic to roman script in the writing of Malay and the formation of *bahasa Indonesia*; and the multiple romanization systems involved with the script reforms shaping contemporary Chinese. Conrad's fiction is therefore a useful point of reference, since it invokes a range of different geographical areas where romanization reforms were either enacted or attempted: Britain and the United States (debates about script standardization); Central Europe and Central Asia (with Cyrillization and romanization); Southeast Asia (the shift from *jawi* or Arabic to *rumi* or roman script); and China (where multiple script reforms preceded the formation of the current *pinyin* romanization system that coexists with standard, simplified, written Chinese characters). If Conrad's fiction points to the multiple stories that need to be told about the role of romanization in different parts of the world, and across different languages and scripts, it is also important for emphasizing the connections between those rather different stories of script reform. Not only is there no single story to be told here, but Conrad's fiction also emerges from the difficulty in bringing those multiple stories together; the difficulty in telling how different languages and scripts cross over into the same reading experience. The narrative form of Conrad's novels registers the spacing and timing of roman letters on the printed page as the site of changing hierarchies of language and script in modern print media.

Conrad's fiction invites consideration of the effects of romanization at all those levels that I noted at the outset: in the spelling out of words and sentences; in the narrative assumptions implied by the historical and geographical spread of roman alphabetic writing systems; and in the broader context within which the changing hierarchies of language and script effect a transformation in print culture. The timing and spacing of roman letters embedded in Conrad's multilingual practice, in the work of his narratives, and within the context of global romanization reforms and media transformations, offers a necessarily partial perspective on the sociolinguistic phenomenon of romanization, as well as the relevance of aesthetic responses to the phenomenon in transnational avant-garde modernism. For that very reason, Conrad's fiction provides a comparative point of reference for considering the perspectival distortions of other modernist writers, and for assessing the linguistic phenomenon of romanization, its history, its geographical and political reach, and its ongoing influence on the temporal and spatial appearance of print media. The logic of this partial, skewed, but revealing perspectival distortion is what this book explores as the *K-effect*.

The K-effect

When a name or a place is transliterated into English from another script (say, Muhammad or Chekhov; Khartoum or Beijing), the effect of romanization remains largely hidden. The main purpose, after all, is to render the sound of the name as clearly as possible in roman letters. Yet if romanization seeks to make a foreign word familiar, the effect is also, in part, the reverse. The transliteration seeks to capture, in the look of the roman letters, the sound and the look of the name or place as originally rendered in the foreign script. "Muhammad" (مُحَمَّد)—"Chekhov" (Чехов)—"Khartoum" (الخرطوم)—"Beijing" (北京): the appearance of each of these names also harks back to the foreign Arabic, Cyrillic, or Chinese script from which they are transliterated. It is this double-effect of romanization that I explore in this book. I call it the K-effect for a variety of reasons, primarily to highlight the recurring effects of the letter K throughout Conrad's fiction, which might then stand as an abbreviated example for the double-effect of romanization at work in Conrad's fiction, transnational modernism, and global print media more generally.

One striking illustration of this K-effect is found in the *Oxford English Dictionary*'s (OED) entry for the letter K (see Figure 1). Explaining the phonetic function of the letter, the OED first situates English usage within the history of the letter's formation in the Roman alphabet, "taken from the Greek *Kappa* K, originally Ж, from Phoenician and general Semitic *Kaph* ꓘ." The early Latin displacement of the letter K by the letter C helps explain why English has relatively few "native K words" (as the OED puts it), K having served medieval scribes as a "supplementary letter to C" in rendering the "'hard' or k sound of C before *e*, *i*, or *y*" in transliterating "Greek or other foreign words." This already suggests the effect of the letter K in marking a distinction between "foreign" and "native" words. The effect becomes even more apparent when the OED turns to more recent history: "The native K words . . . are a small company. But their number is greatly reinforced by the foreign words of recent adoption, many of them very imperfectly naturalized, with which this letter is crowded." Behind this claim about the way that the letter K marks a distinction between "native" and "foreign" words, there are many assumptions to which I will return later. The entry, as a whole, showcases all the different levels implied in definitions of romanization. Indeed, in explaining the phonetic function of the letter

K.

K (kēɪ), the eleventh letter of the alphabet in English and other modern languages, was an original letter of the Roman alphabet, taken from the Greek *Kappa* K, originally ꓘ, from Phœnician and general Semitic *Kaph* 𐤊. Its sound in Greek and Latin was, as in English, that of the back voiceless stop consonant, or guttural *tenuis*. But at an early period of Latin orthography, the letter C (originally representing Greek *Gamma*) was employed for the k sound, and the letter K itself fell into disuse, except in a few words, notably the term *Kalendæ* and the prænomen *Kæso*, where the traditional abbreviations Kal. and K. kept up the memory of the archaic spelling. But, with the exception of such archaisms, C became the regular Latin symbol of the k sound, and, as such, was substituted for Greek Kappa when Greek words were latinized, as in Κίμων, Κῦρος, *κόμμα*, *Cīmōn*, *Cȳrus*, *comma*. In late Latin, when the sound of C before a front vowel had become palatalized, or passed over to (tʃ), as in Italian *cento*, *città*, the same fate befell the C of latinized Greek words, such as *Cyrus*; but later Greek words in living (esp. Christian) use such as *kȳrie eleïson* (*κύριε ἐλέησον*), which retained the Greek pronunciation, continued to be written with K. To Latin scribes of the sixth, seventh, and eighth centuries, K was thus known as a supplementary letter to C, of use in Greek or other foreign words which had the 'hard' or k sound of C before *e*, *i*, or *y*. Hence it was naturally put to use in the writing of Old High German, Old Saxon, Old Frankish, Early Italian, and some dialects of Old French, in which a k sound came before *e*, *i*, or *y*. In writing these languages, C was usually employed, as in Latin, before *a*, *o*, *u*, or finally; but in practice there was considerable overlapping, with the final result that, in German, K ousted C, and is now the proper letter for this sound in that language, as well as in Dutch and all the Scandinavian tongues; while, in French,

merged in *i*), and before *n* (:—OE. *cn*-), where it is no longer pronounced in Standard English, though retained in some dialects. Medially and finally, *k* is used after a consonant (*ask*, *dark*, *twinkle*), or long vowel (*make*, *hawk*, *like*, *speak*, *week*); after a short vowel, *ck* is used instead of *cc* or *kk*, but the unstressed suffix, formerly *-ick* (*musick*), is now *ic*, though, when a suffix in *e* or *i* follows, *k* reappears (*traffic*, *trafficker*, *trafficking*).

The native K words, being thus confined to Ke-, Ki-, Kn- (with one or two from the dialects in Ka-, Ky-), are a small company. But their number is greatly reinforced by the foreign words of recent adoption, many of them very imperfectly naturalized, with which this letter is crowded. These include a few modern European words, Germanic or Slavonic; but they consist mainly of names of animals, plants, trade products, and native offices, from Oriental, African, American, Australian, and Oceanic languages. The number of these words is augmented by reason of the fact that some of those languages have two, or even three, distinct gutturals, for which, in ordinary English spelling, K has to stand; the combination Kh is similarly put for several fricative and aspirated sounds in Arabic, Turkish, Persian, Hindī, and other tongues. (See the individual words, in the etymology of which the actual origin of the letter is stated.) In giving these words English hospitality, it was formerly usual to follow English analogies and write C before *a*, *o*, *u*, *l*, *r*, *h*; but the more recent tendency has been to favour the use of K in these positions also; giving the non-English initial combinations Ka-, Kh-, Kl-, Ko-, Kr-, Ku-, by which the uncouth or barbarous character of the words is more strongly suggested. Thus *cadi*, *Caffre*, *caique*, *Calmuck*, *Can* (*Chan*, *Cham*), *cloof*, *Coran*, *creese*, *cummerbund*, now more frequently appear as *kadi*, *Kaffir*, *kaik*, *Kalmuk*, *Khan*, *kloof*, *Koran*, *kris*, *kamarband*.

In words from Greek also, many prefer to retain

3. In *Chem.* K is the symbol for Potassium (mod.L. *kalium*). It was formerly used to designate a compound of gold (*Syd. Soc. Lex.*). In *Meteorol.* K = cumulus. In *Assaying*, etc. K = carat. In *Astron.* *k* designates Gauss's Constant, the square of which is a measure of the mass of the sun. For *k* in Quaternions, see I (the letter) 6; in *Cryst.* see H 7.

1853 Sir W. R. Hamilton *Lect. Quaternions* 59 Let i, j, k, denote three straight lines equally long, but differently directed [etc.]. 1886 *Encycl. Brit.* XX. 161/2 The fundamental i, j, k of quaternions.

4. K. is an abbreviation, **a.** for some Christian names, as *Kate*, *Katherine*, *Kenneth*. **b.** for *King*: formerly used alone; now usually in comb., as K.B., King's Bench; K.C., King's Counsel, King's College; K.Q., 'King and queen' iron. **c.** for *Knight* (standing alone Kt.); in K.B., Knight Bachelor; K.C.B., Knight Commander of the Bath; K.C.S.I., Knight Commander of the Star of India; K.G., Knight of the Garter; K.C.M.G., Knight Commander of the Order of St. Michael and St. George; K.G.C.B., Knight Grand Cross of the Bath; K.H., Knight of Hanover (*Obs.*); K.P., Knight of the Order of St. Patrick; K.T., Knight of the Order of the Thistle, etc. **d.** *Electro-physiol.* = *Kathode* (also ka.), *Kathodic*, in K.C.C., kathodic closure contraction, K.C.Te., kathodic closure tetanus, K.D.T., kathodic duration tetanus, K.O.C., kathodic opening contraction (*Syd. Soc. Lex.*). **e.** kg. = kilogramme; km. = kilometre.

1614 Selden *Titles Hon.* 5 Where Moses speaks of Amraphel K. of Sinaghr, the Paraphrase of Onkelos hath expresly K. of Babel. 1623 *Shakspere's 2 Hen. IV*, I. ii. 86 Doth not the K. lack subiects? Do not the Rebels want Soldiers? 1818 Cruise *Digest* (ed. 2) V. 213 It was resolved by the Court of K. B. 1826 *Sporting Mag.* XVIII. 391 They are manufactured from scrap iron (the best K. Q., or King and Queen as it is called). 1833 *Byron's Wks.* (1846) 584/2 Any list of K. B.'s or K. H.'s. 1851 Nimrod *The Road* 11 Axle trees of the best K. Q. iron. 1892 *Pall Mall G.* 21 Mar. 7/1 A movable drum weighing 2½ kg. .. a line of 23 km. length. 1898 Besant *Orange Girl* II. xi, Mr. Caterham, K.C., our senior counsel. 1899 Miss G. Palgrave *F. T. Palgrave* 1 Sir Francis Palgrave, K.H., Deputy

Figure 1. *Oxford English Dictionary* entry for the letter K.

K in English usage, it makes a paradigmatic shift in turning from the ancient history of roman alphabetic forms of writing English to the very recent history of romanized transcriptions into Standard English print form. I foreground these different scales of historical reference by referring to the first as Romanization (with uppercase R, to indicate the long-standing adoption of the Latin alphabet as the writing system for a range of European languages), and the second as that more recent proliferation of systems of romanization (with lowercase r, signaling romanization as transliteration). The use of the letter K to mark "foreign words of recent adoption" highlights the double-effect of (lowercase) romanization.

The OED entry is striking for the biases and prejudices it reveals in the romanized transcription of "foreign words of recent adoption." In "giving these words English hospitality," the OED entry goes on to explain that there has been a shift from using an initial letter C to using the more foreign-sounding K "by which the uncouth or barbarous character of the words is more strongly suggested": "Thus *cadi, Calmuck, Can (Chan, Cham), cloof, Coran, creese,* now more frequently appear as *kadi, Kalmuk, Khan, kloof, Koran, kris.*" The change in English orthography registered here, coincides historically with the moment of accelerated adoption of romanized systems of transliteration worldwide (from the writing systems of Arabic, Persian, Russian, Turkish, Malay, Chinese, Japanese, etc.). The prejudice it registers reveals a volatile set of changing assumptions about language, script, and identity. The OED has since attempted to soften the prejudice, using the phrase "the unnaturalized character of the words" in place of "uncouth" and "barbarous."[12] But the original version lays bare how the process of romanized transcription involves a racialized hierarchy of languages and scripts. At work in much more than just the letter K, this K-effect stands as a revealing index for the way that romanization implicates the seemingly technical act of transliteration in a web of national, ethnic, and racial identifications, biases, and prejudices.[13]

This K-effect surfaces in a variety of ways throughout Joseph Conrad's fiction. One notable example is hidden in the romanized transcription of Conrad's own name: the transformation from Józef Teodor Konrad Korzeniowski into Joseph Conrad. Although, here, the transliteration is from one romanized script (Polish) to another (English), the act of transliterating the middle Polish name Konrad (changing the K to C) makes the author's name both familiar and strange for English readers in ways that duplicate (and complicate still more) the double-effect of romanization. Consciously or unconsciously, the effect of the K behind the C of Conrad's name betrays a range of personal, social, linguistic, and historical issues. As I explore more fully in Chapter 2 (the discussion of Conrad's vexed engagement with Russian themes), the hidden K-effect of Conrad's signature is entangled in that same web of national, ethnic, and racial identifications that characterizes the OED's account of the use of K to represent "foreign words of recent adoption." However, this K-effect occurs not only in the case of Conrad's authorial signature. It recurs as the initial letter of many of his characters (Kaspar, Karain, Kayerts, Kurtz, Kirilyo, Prince K). It also surfaces as an often elaborately embellished letter in the margins of many of his manuscripts. Although the recurring letter K is certainly not the only way that Conrad's fiction engages questions of romanization, it offers an aesthetic counterpart to the OED's entry on the letter. The K-effect in Conrad's writing reveals the fuller range of languages and scripts (European and non-European) within which the OED situates the effect of the English letter K. It also encapsulates the double-effect of romanization at all the different levels noted above: the phonetic spelling out of names and words; the narrative arc implied by the historical and geographical spread of roman alphabetic writing systems; and the changing multilingual, multiscript medium of English print.

All these levels are at work in the opening words of Conrad's first novel, *Almayer's Folly* (1895): "Kaspar! Makan!" It is a simple piece of dialogue, introducing the first name of the title character (Kaspar) through the voice of his wife calling him to dinner ("makan" is the Malay word for "to eat"). But the effect of these opening words is far from simple, introducing a problem of translation (from the Malay) and a vexed colonial relation (between the European Kaspar Almayer and his unnamed Sulu wife who is calling him to dinner), all of which will take some time to work out.[14] After a few pages, the reader will be able to infer that Almayer's wife is calling him to dinner; and over the course of the novel the reader will be able to measure (at least some of) the ironies implied by the colonial relation of European to Malay, prefigured by that opening call. But it will take even longer to unravel the plot implications of the disorienting linguistic form of address with which Conrad begins his literary career. As the first in a projected sequence of three novels, *Almayer's Folly* introduces a set of complicated social, political, and linguistic relations that will take Conrad his entire career to work out (since *The Rescue*, the last novel in the sequence, did not appear until 1920). Implied in the combined K-effect of that opening address, moreover, is a still unfolding geopolitical and sociolinguistic rearrangement in the hierarchy of European and non-European languages and scripts. It will take the length of this book to attempt to explain the different cultural and linguistic contexts converging on the phenomenon of romanization condensed in the K-effect of the name (Kaspar) and the Malay word (makan). It is by no means obvious how this opening dialogue registers all of the aspects of romanization that I will be exploring: notably, the historical shift from Arabic (*jawi*) to roman (*rumi*) in writing Malay (Chapter 1); the increasing politicization of language and script reforms across Europe (Chapter 2); the role of Chinese debates about romanization in shaping a global transformation of print media (Chapter 3); and the influence of Sanskrit models of defining the relation between language and script (Chapter 4). Following the delayed decoding of this inaugural Conradian K-effect enables me to explore each of these different cases of romanization in turn.

As with the OED's account of the letter K, Conrad's English transliteration of the Dutch name "Kaspar" and the Malay word "makan" works on multiple levels. Here though, the sociolinguistic effects of romanization are reworked into aesthetic form. The Russian literary theorist Mikhail Bakhtin offers a helpful way to analyze this aesthetic organization of language, most especially in his use of the term "chronotope" (literally time-space) to consider how narratives (above all, novels) organize time and space. "Chronotopes," according to Bakhtin, are the "organizing centers for the fundamental narrative events of the novel ... the place where the knots of narrative are tied and untied."[15] The K-effect in "Kaspar! Makan!" is the very first place where the "knot" of the Conradian narrative begins to get "tied and untied" around what I will be calling the chronotope of romanization. Bakhtin's term allows me to trace how the various linguistic levels at which romanization works, shape the timing and spacing of narrative form.

At the first level (of phonetic spelling), the foreign, non-English appearance of "Kaspar" and "makan" stages an encounter between what the OED calls "native" and "foreign" words in the spacing and timing of English letters. The implied hierarchy of relations between languages and scripts registered in the dialogue and presentation of character, then gets reworked at the level of theme and plot. In *Almayer's Folly* (as I will discuss more fully later) the timing and spacing of roman letters gets thematized in the English lettering of a sign that marks the "folly" of Almayer's business hopes. These decaying letters (the "half obliterated words, 'Office: Lingard and Co.'" [*Almayer's*, 15]) appear on the door of an unfinished house—mockingly named "Almayer's Folly" midway through the novel—that then, at the end of the novel, gets renamed in Chinese script. This trope of English lettering is an especially pointed, ironic elaboration of the chronotope of romanization in Conrad's work, and it recurs much later in his career via the company sign of the defunct coal company in *Victory*. Reflecting ironically on the English print form that is the medium of Conrad's own novelistic practice, it nonetheless does more than merely ironize assumptions about the ascendancy of roman alphabetic writing systems as synonymous with European colonial improvement, progress, and civilization. As with other memorable tropes produced by the chronotope of romanization in Conrad (the appearance of the English book with Russian marginalia in *Heart of Darkness*; or the conceit of a Russian document translated "under Western eyes" in the novel of that title), what is still more important is the way in which it resituates the romanized print form of English within a range of other languages and scripts. The timing and spacing of English romanization will turn out to depend (in ways that it will take me the rest of this book to argue) on the timespace of other languages (e.g., Malay or Russian) in relation to other scripts (e.g., Arabic, Cyrillic, Chinese) within the changing coordinates of global print media.

Making use of Bakhtin's notion of the chronotope, enables me to examine the way in which Conrad's fiction organizes the linguistic phenomenon of romanization at several different levels simultaneously: at the level of the word, at the level of the narrative, and at the level of a global, multilingual, multiscript, and multimedia transformation in the hierarchy of languages and scripts. Connecting all the different levels at which even the most basic sense of romanization needs to be understood, and following the logic of Conrad's chronotope of romanization, leads me to an overarching argument about the double-effect of romanization. Romanization may seem to involve, primarily, the imposition of European forms of language, script, and identity in the service of colonization. Yet it also involves the contest and decolonization of European forms from the perspective of non-European languages, scripts, and identities. Romanization, usually considered synonymous with the imposition of European culture on the rest of the world ("Westernization"), may, in fact, constitute the opposite—the reconfiguration and dissolution of European cultural forms within a non-European, non-Western frame of reference. The K-effect registers this ambivalent legacy, revealing romanization as a process that simultaneously standardizes and destabilizes contemporary global forms of print media. It is a legacy that continues to define the digital scripting of our times.

This book takes as its starting point the case of Conrad, in order to emphasize the role of romanization in changing the face of English within a multilinguistic and multiscript world. This entails positioning romanized print form within a range of what, throughout this study, are called "worldscripts." Worldscripts designate writing systems that have had (and continue to have) a global and historical reach, including roman, Arabic, Cyrillic, and Chinese. The way in which readers and writers tend to inhabit one worldscript to the exclusion of others, has led David Damrosch to formulate the term "scriptworld."[16] Although Damrosch develops this term to apply to the way that worldscripts form the basis for literary systems, my argument is that the phenomenon of romanization unravels any presupposition of a fit between worldscript and scriptworld. Throughout this study, I adapt Damrosch's useful term scriptworld, but with the proviso that it carries a set of cultural, linguistic, and often racial and ethnic expectations, very different from (and often in conflict with) what a worldscript designates. The K-effect, as it surfaces in the OED and Conrad's first appearance in print, emerges from an especially vexed set of conflicts between the universalizing claims of a worldscript to be able to transcribe any and all languages, and the limiting demands of a scriptworld that ties a particular language to a particular form of printed script.

The linguist Florian Coulmas describes two different senses of "script" that might be used to distinguish a scriptworld from a worldscript: "Some scripts are thought by their speakers to be intrinsically related to their language [creating a scriptworld], while others are perceived as serving a variety of languages [as the worldscripts of roman, Arabic, and Chinese serve a variety of different languages]."[17] The phenomenon of romanization reveals a complex, often hidden, and changing hierarchy of global languages and scripts. So, for example, the OED oscillates between presenting K as the letter of a worldscript used variously by many different languages; and then presenting it as the effect of a scriptworld, marking the difference between "native" and "foreign" words. Something analogous is at work in the K-effect of the first words of Conrad's first novel—"Kaspar! Makan!" Among other things, they pose complicated questions about the relation between Arabic and roman script in the writing of Malay (Arabic evoking a long-standing Malay scriptworld of religious and political prestige; romanized print signaling a newly destabilizing form of communication and exchange).

It is striking that Coulmas talks about the way that scripts are "thought" or "perceived" to be intrinsically connected to a single language or serving a variety of languages. His examples suggest clear-cut distinctions—the Korean and Cambodian scripts are examples of the first (scriptworlds); roman, Arabic, and Devanagari are examples of the second (worldscripts). There are, however, many cases where speakers think that their script is intrinsically related to their own language, even though it is perceived by others (and perhaps also at the same time by themselves) to be a worldscript that serves other languages. As the OED entry for the letter K indicates, English presents just such a case in point. That English K-effect is my starting point for examining how romanization reveals a complex and shifting hierarchy of interrelations between global languages and scripts, in which the intrinsic identity of any one, single, scriptworld turns out to depend on a multiplicity of worldscripts. The K-effect of romanization repeatedly demonstrates this—often in an act that is thought or perceived to be a betrayal—in the act of crossing over from one scriptworld to another.

Bakhtin's term chronotope points the way to reading narrative form as part of the study of wider cultural forces, producing "an optic for reading texts as x-rays of the forces at work in the culture system from which they spring."[18] One influential and important example of this is Paul Gilroy's focus on the chronotope of the slave ship as an organizing image for his study of *The Black Atlantic*.[19] For the present study, the term chronotope brings together the importance of romanization as topos and trope in Conrad's work, with a corresponding interest in the temporal and spatial layout of roman letters found throughout transnational, modernist experimentation (both in literature and other artistic media). Sometimes explicit in their self-conscious play on letters, script, and writing systems in general (Joyce's punning experimentation in *Finnegans Wake*; or the language experiments of "zaum" associated with Kruchenykh and Khlebnikov), and sometimes less explicitly so (Woolf's occasional use of alphabetical imagery, for example in the skywriting of *Mrs. Dalloway*), chronotopes of romanization in transnational modernism draw attention to a certain turning point, crisis, or revolution in letters, in the word, and in language (more generally), in which the function of the roman alphabet as a writing system is foregrounded. In certain notable instances, these chronotopes may be directly linked to the changing function of roman letters in relation to other writing systems (e.g., Arabic, Cyrillic, or Chinese). It is in these instances that a broader K-effect comes more fully into view: the combined effect of proliferating forms of romanization and attempts to standardize English within a changing hierarchy of languages and scripts.

The K-effect in this wider, cultural and sociolinguistic sense, points to a contradictory moment in the history of romanization: the simultaneous standardization and destabilization of English as a model for romanized print form in the moment just before the digital conversion of the English alphabet into alphanumerical computer code.[20] The effects of that contradictory historical moment continue to shape the way that we read letters and script in a world now almost entirely mediated by digital code. One place where this is visible is in the title-sequences for television programs and films where credits very often play imaginatively with the appearance and disappearance of roman lettering. Even the space of the traditionally bound and printed book bears the imprint of digital coding in ways that should remind us that print culture has never been as stable as the notion of "print culture" itself suggests.[21] One of the primary archives for this book's grasp of romanization in the timing and spacing of print culture offers an important case in point: the *Oxford English Dictionary*, whose first edition was published in 1933, was originally printed serially in separate fascicles from the 1880s through the 1920s. Later revised editions have reorganized the entire project, now accessible in the online edition, making it an exemplary archival source for tracking the simultaneous standardization and destabilization of English print form, remediated for a digital world.[22]

Conrad's "timely appearance in English"

The Chinese novelist Ha Jin, whose literary acclaim rests on work written in English, notes in *The Writer as Migrant* that Conrad's "timely appearance in English" makes him a "founding spirit," a precursor for those writers, like Vladimir Nabokov and Ha Jin himself, who come to English from other languages (Conrad's Polish, Nabokov's Russian, and Ha Jin's Chinese).[23] Many writers and critics have turned to Conrad for answers to questions of translation, multilinguistic identity, and split cultural affiliations characteristic of contemporary writing. And many of these turn to Conrad, as Ha Jin does, to measure the problem of "betrayal" (of language, nation, culture) vividly illustrated by Eliza Orzeszkowa's attack on Conrad for having betrayed the Polish nation by writing in English. What Ha Jin calls the "language of betrayal," I consider here as a matter of both language and script; indeed, as the effect of an almost fateful entanglement of identity, script, and orthography effecting a transformation in the very medium of print culture. Conrad's "appearance in English," as Ha Jin puts it, is "timely" in the way that it poses this sociolinguistic question of romanization. As Chapter 1 of this book explores, Conrad's appearance in the OED provides a striking example of the role of English in mediating, through romanization, a global interaction and exchange between multiple languages and multiple scripts, over the turn from the nineteenth to the twentieth centuries.

One of the most recognizable signs of the characteristically Conradian "language of betrayal" is his authorial signature. The transformation from his Polish to his English name stands as a graphic reminder of the complex linguistic effects of translation, always at work in his use of English. These effects are repeatedly enacted in readings of Conrad, like those of Ha Jin, Nabokov, or other writers who come to Conrad, whether in English, such as Virginia Woolf, V. S. Naipaul, Chinua Achebe, Ngũgĩ wa Thiong'o, Peter Nazareth, Salman Rushdie, Caryl Phillips, Abdulrazak Gurnah, Arundhati Roy, Jackie Kay, and Leila Aboulela—the list is necessarily truncated—or in other languages, such as André Gide, Thomas Mann, Jorge Luis Borges, Tayeb Salih, Gabriel García Márquez, Pramoedya Ananta Toer, and W. G. Sebald. Conrad himself, repeatedly, returned to what, later in life, he styled as his "neutral pseudonym." In 1901, writing to a Polish historian who happens to share the same name (Józéf Korzeniowski), and in a letter that Ha Jin cites, Conrad puts it this way: "It is widely known that I am a Pole and that Józef Konrad are my two Christian names, the latter being used by me as a surname so that foreign mouths should not distort my real surname—a distortion which I cannot stand."[24] There is good reason to read this K-effect of Conrad's name, as Ha Jin does, in relation to the problem of "betrayal" of linguistic identity. Each time we read a Conrad text (including the rereadings of Conrad's texts that we find embedded in other writers) we encounter this "betrayal." Betrayal is a characteristically Conradian theme: Jim's betrayal in jumping from the *Patna* in *Lord Jim* and Razumov's betrayal of Haldin in *Under Western Eyes* have both been read in relation to Conrad's perceived betrayal of Poland. That theme of betrayal, Ha Jin argues, is felt as a betrayal of language. And that linguistic betrayal, I propose, is also registered as a betrayal in a crossing over from one script to another. The change of name in Conrad's authorial signature encodes this for Conrad and for Conrad's later readers.

Salman Rushdie succinctly captures the complexity of this in *Joseph Anton: A Memoir*. Describing the moment when he was forced to conceal his identity following the *fatwa* proclaimed against him for writing *The Satanic Verses*, he turned to the names "Conrad and Chekhov" to invent an identity—Joseph Anton—that might stand in place of what was perceived to be his own authorial betrayal of script and scripture. Modeled in part on Conrad's own attempt to find a "neutral pseudonym," Rushdie's case involves a much more sensational charge of betrayal than the charge that Conrad betrayed the Polish language, and Rushdie's use of English involved a more sensational crossing over from one scriptworld to another. Yet in foregrounding this rivalry of Islamic scripture and romanized English print (a rivalry that implicitly inaugurates Conrad's career, as well, embedded in the way his first novel is framed by the question of romanized Malay print), Rushdie's attempt to improvise a correspondingly "neutral pseudonym" invents a chronotope of romanization that is very much heir to Conrad, that "translingual creator of wanderers," as Rushdie describes him.[25] Rushdie's chronotope of romanization is the name Joseph Anton, embellishing what is encoded already in the Conradian chronotope of romanization. It conceals behind the Polish and Russian scripts of the first and last names a demonized rivalry between Islamic and anglicized scripts, crossing over all the other scriptworlds (and worldscripts, too), that keep knotting and unknotting Anglo-Indian histories, cultures, and identities.

Fawzia Mustafa has drawn attention to the range of contrasting ways in which the example of Conrad's English has been taken up by later writers, especially in postcolonial African contexts. Comparing V. S. Naipaul's *A Bend in the River* and Abdulrazak Gurnah's *Paradise*, both of which have been read in terms of their rewriting of Conrad's *Heart of Darkness*, she formulates the term "anglophone African difference" to highlight the divergent ways in which later writers reconceive what Conrad's use of English authorizes. Her analysis draws specific attention to the importance of romanized letters and names in Gurnah's *Paradise*, explaining how the "English alphabet" that its protagonist (Yusuf) learns, on his journey to the African interior, reveals a "linguistic infiltration from non-English English speakers."[26] That "linguistic infiltration" marks the "anglophone difference" that inflects the way every rereading and rewriting of Conrad must be seen and heard.

The "anglophone difference" of the K-effect (of Joseph Conrad and Joseph Anton) is apparent from the very first words that Conrad published, and it creates, throughout Conrad's work and beyond, a complex and long-lasting effect of delayed decoding.[27] It is a K-effect that is uniquely part of Conrad's authorial signature in every sense, including the way this Conradian signature is taken up by others reading Conrad, rewriting Conrad, and with the full range of what Mustafa calls the "anglophone difference." Yet it echoes similar effects across languages and literatures. In addition to reading Conrad's "timely appearance in English" in the light of those who come after Conrad (such as Ha Jin, or those Peter Nazareth calls "Conrad's descendants"[28]; and across the "anglophone African difference" between Naipaul and Gurnah), this book also seeks to situate Conrad in relation to transnational modernist writers of his time, and across a range of geographical and sociolinguistic contexts. Key touchstones that this book will juxtapose with Conrad, are found in the experiments of James Joyce (whose work revels in the puns opened up by the perpetual temporal and spatial slippage in English between (uppercase) Romanization and (lowercase) romanization); the K of Franz Kafka's fiction, evoking a Central European sociolinguistic context (Czech and German for Kafka corresponding to the Polish and Russian scriptworlds for Conrad); and the "Q" in Lu Xun's "The Real Story of Ah-Q," marking the place of roman letters within the global and diasporic reach of Chinese writing.

Following a logic inherent in Conrad's work and its reception (inaugurated by the romanized Malay of Conrad's first appearance in English print, "Kaspar! Makan!"), I explore a series of sociolinguistic contexts for situating the phenomenon of romanization, beginning with the case of English, with a focus on the shifting hierarchy of Arabic and roman worldscripts in relation to English and Malay scriptworlds. I turn then to the shadow cast by Russian over Central European debates, with a focus on the way that Cyrillic highlights the multiple systems of romanization, mediating a variety of different European languages and scripts. Thirdly, I address the framing significance of Chinese, with a focus on the mediating role of both roman letters and Chinese characters in the globalization and transformation of romanized print form. I conclude with a reflection on a much broader sociolinguistic and historical survey, presented by the old, forgotten, and idealized model of Sanskrit, whose universal relation to any and all scriptworlds—paradoxically fixed, retrospectively, to the world-script of Devanagari—recurs in the universalizing aims of romanization and digitization. The Conradian K-effect, read in global comparative context, registers these widespread transformations in the standardization, reform, and multimedia transformations of languages and scripts worldwide.

When Ha Jin says that Conrad emerged "at the right time," he suggests that Conrad appeared historically at the beginning of a movement toward a more international, cosmopolitan, and multilingual form of English writing; at a time when English readers were becoming more open to the work of writers from non-English-speaking backgrounds; at a time when English was being opened up by writers who came to English from other languages like Polish, German, or Chinese. This is the moment when English took part in an accelerated standardization of scripts; a moment when language reform throughout the world, and on an unprecedented scale, sought to make the roman alphabet a global, and globalizing, medium for the transcription, transliteration, and translation of all languages, orthographies, and scripts. It is the moment just before the twenty-six letters of the English alphabet provide the basis for the conversion of letters into computer code, the transformation of print culture into digital media. Conrad's "timely appearance in English" coincides with the moment when the prestige of English, linked to the prestige of roman letters, made both seem to be the universal medium for worldwide cultural exchange. This is also, however, an ambiguous moment of opening, of transformation, and of change, whose timing is all at once historical and ongoing.

Ha Jin is also suggestively identifying with Conrad as a figure whose use of English turns on accusations of betrayal. Conrad's turn from Polish to English already suggests how such a "timely appearance in English" is directly related to the way in which "the language of betrayal" works in Conrad—at the level of plot, at the level of the sentence and the word, and in the medium of print. If the turn toward English risks the accusation of betrayal for Conrad, it does so "for those who arrive after him," as well (Nabokov, Ha Jin, Salman Rushdie / Joseph Anton, Naipaul, Gurnah). What historically is opened up by the example of Conrad, then, is the ongoing risk of betrayal for such writers writing in English and across a broad spectrum of postcolonial contexts. That risk is perhaps most obvious when articulated in terms of a betrayal of country, nation, religion, or ethnic identity (Conrad's betrayal of Poland, Nabokov's betrayal of Russia, Ha Jin's betrayal of China, or Rushdie's betrayal of Islam). The linguistic features of this betrayal are also manifested in the act of crossing over from one script to another, in the spelling out of letters on the page, and national, ethnic, and racializing assumptions about the relation between scriptworlds and worldscripts.[29]

To assess the place of English in this historical conjuncture of romanization requires a shift of attention away from the more usual themes of language, nation, and culture, to questions of orthography, script, and print media. *The K-Effect* aims to consider how Conrad appears in a form of English that is actively engaged in mediating between the scriptworlds of languages written in a variety of different worldscripts. On a scale that is all at once much broader, and yet much more narrowly focused than Ha Jin intends, this process of romanization (historically and lexically) crucially determines the "betrayal" of language in Conrad and the Conradian "language of betrayal" facing the company of writers he invokes.

In part, this is a technical matter of orthography—the way that the letters of the roman alphabetic writing system are used to transcribe any spoken word into printed English. But this technical issue also opens up a set of questions concerning transcription, transliteration, and translation across languages and scripts often overlooked in discussions of language, identity, and culture. In orthographic terms, there is little difference between "Konrad" and "Conrad"—although the more marked difference between "Józef" and "Joseph" reveals that the first comes from what linguists call a comparatively more "shallow or surface orthography" (with a lower phoneme-grapheme ratio, where roman letters are augmented with diacritical marks and other signs) whereas the second comes from a "deep orthography" (with a very high phoneme-grapheme ratio).[30] It is this orthographic switching from Polish to English—the disruption of "deep orthography" by effects of "shallow orthography"—that enables the K-effect in Conrad's signature. Tracing the implications of this effect throughout Conrad's texts, and by comparison to other modernist writers, this book extends Ha Jin's perception of the historical appearance of Conrad (his "timeliness") to consider sociolinguistic, aesthetic, and print media dimensions of the work of romanized transliteration.

Precedents for examining the riddle of this orthographic timing and spacing of romanized print culture, may be found in a range of lineages of modernist theory and practice. Jacques Derrida's attention to systematic blind spots in accounting for writing systems is clearly relevant in many ways, from his early work in *Of Grammatology* up to his later meditations on "globalatinization" (*mondialatinisation*, which might alternatively be translated as "global-romanization").[31] Yet Derrida rarely directly addresses the phenomenon of romanization itself. In part, this has to do with the systematic impossibility of accounting for a history of the alphabet within alphabetic writing itself. Derrida's fundamental challenge to assumptions about "phonetic writing" is registered his in use of the words "*espacement*" and "*différance*" which present theoretical versions of what I am characterizing as the "timing and spacing of print culture."[32] His critique of "phonocentrism" presents an indispensable counterpoint to the positivist study of writing systems by I. J. Gelb and other linguists. Because Derridean deconstruction is so rigorously focused on the constitutive instability in the timing and spacing of writing (in every sense), it cannot help but bracket any attempt to historicize the process of romanization.[33]

Derridean deconstruction itself draws on important prior modernist engagements with the orthographic timing and spacing of roman letters: for example, with Mallarmé's experimental placement of letters on the printed page; and with Saussure's interest in the anagrammatical features of writing. There are, indeed, too many examples of this sort of experimentation to enumerate; and, as with Derrida's own project, their relevance for a history of the phenomenon of romanization is not always immediately clear. One especially interesting, and important, recent theorization of the riddle of orthographic space-time is Christina Sharpe's discussion of "anagrammatical blackness" (drawing on Hortense Spillers and Fred Moten): "we can see the moments when blackness opens up into the anagrammatical in the literal sense as when 'a word, phrase, or name is formed by rearranging the letters of another' . . . *Ana-*, as prefix, means 'up, in place or time, back, again, anew.' So blackness anew, blackness as a/temporal, in and out of place and time putting pressure on meaning and that against which meaning is made."³⁴ What Sharpe calls "anagrammatical blackness" (and traces back through a reading of Frederick Douglass) might retrospectively be seen to frame all of the signature effects of Conrad and the way in which Conrad continues to be read today. Reading Conrad "in the wake" of such questions of "blackness and being" requires reading Conrad against the grain, yet, at the same time, unearths an anagrammatical anti-racist logic to the timing and spacing of those most racist of Conradian tropes. Although Sharpe does not explicitly reference Paul Gilroy's use of Bakhtin's term chronotope in his magisterial study, *The Black Atlantic*, her work might be read as a reframing of Gilroy's focus on the organizing chronotope of the slave ships "in motion across the spaces between Europe, America, Africa, and the Caribbean."³⁵ It remains, I think, an open question as to the extent to which Conrad's work is organized around an evocation or an erasure of what Gilroy calls *The Black Atlantic*.³⁶ The question is spelled out in its most offensive form in the title of one of Conrad's most famous books. Like it or not, readings of Conrad follow in the wake of *The Nigger of the 'Narcissus.'* The shadow of the racist epithet in its title continues to demand an anagrammatical, Black reading. The grammar of that racism (and its critical anagrammatical study) is at the root of all of the naming effects in Conrad, all the difficult cases of spelling out letters (as Wait's name proves difficult to spell out in the rollcall for the crew of the *Narcissus*)—indeed, all the chronotopes of romanization organized around the names of ships. Even just the *naming* of Conrad's ships (*Judea, Patna, Nan-shan*), foregrounds effects of romanization that connect both Gilroy's and Sharpe's projects with diasporic, postcolonial, and global readings, to come across all the world's languages and scripts.

The term chronotope, drawn from Mikhail Bakhtin, and refracted through Paul Gilroy's application to the study of *The Black Atlantic*, abbreviates modernist fascination for the orthographic riddle of roman letters. The term itself is just such a chronotope, an arrangement of Cyrillic letters transliterating a romanized transcription from the Greek. I read it, to some extent, anagrammatically as a theoretical term derived from the more general, Russian formalist interest in experiments in linguistics and poetics, such as Jakobson's focus on the grammar of poetry and the poetry of grammar, or Shklovsky's theorization of terms that, like chronotope, are themselves chronotopes of romanization: "priëm" [приём] (device), "ostranenie" [остранение] (estrangement), and the distinction between story and plot, "fabula" [фабула] and "sjužet" [сйужет].³⁷ The decision to emphasize a shared concern for the phenomenon of romanization across a variety of different modernist lineages (and across a range of languages and scripts) is motivated, in large part, by the attempt to foreground the variety and contest among those lineages themselves.

This approach follows from *The Passage of Literature*, where I traced the overlapping and contested interrelation between English, Creole, and Indonesian formations of modernism. That study explored how the "passage of literature" registers a crossing-over between English, Creole, and Indonesian linguistic-literary formations. Every Conradian passage is framed by the Creole and Indonesian modernist formations that appear to come after—but actually precede—its canonically English modernist form. This current study seeks to make explicit that study's implicit emphasis on the romanized print form of the passage of literature. Every passage of text should be read with an eye and ear attending to the multiple, and contested, readings brought to the space of romanized English print (and its "anglophone difference") by speakers from a range of different languages. Here, my focus shifts from language to script; from English, Creole, and Indonesian languages, to the way that romanization is shaped by the languages transliterated from Arabic, Cyrillic, and Chinese scripts. Although the cultural contexts might appear to be rather different, there is an underlying logic linking them. This logic, indexed by the Conradian K-effect, unfolds according to a shifting hierarchy of languages and scripts embedded in the narrative timing and spacing of Conrad's prose and the way it continues to be read today. For the current study, following from my previous work, the most important retrospective, interpretative frame of reference for understanding the contested hierarchy of languages and scripts involved, is the work of Indonesian writer Pramoedya Ananta Toer (1925–2006). Premised on a historical and linguistic grasp of the revolutionary emergence of a form of Malay that became a crucial vehicle in the articulation of Indonesian anticolonial nationalism, Pramoedya's work enables a retrospective rereading of Conrad's English prose, his novel plots—indeed his entire *oeuvre*—in light of the sociolinguistic and literary significance of this emergent form of romanized print Malay.

Conrad's first appearance in print is framed by the language that will become this revolutionary new language of Indonesian, *bahasa Indonesia*. The *print* form of those inaugural words—"Kaspar! Makan!"—registers a shift from the Arabic (*jawi*) script in which Malay was traditionally written, to romanized (*rumi*) print form (used by the largely Chinese-run newspapers published in the form of Malay that Pramoedya Ananta Toer called "pre-Indonesian"). The K-effect of the name "Kaspar," evoking the chiasmus of a shift from C to K across a range of European variants of roman script, is thus embedded within an Indonesian timing and spacing of romanized print form across the three worldscripts of Arabic, Cyrillic, and Chinese. "Kaspar! Makan!"—these opening words encapsulate the riddle of romanized print form at the heart of Conrad's "timely appearance" and whose logic defines the unfolding argument of the present study, moving from the English "case" of romanization, to the Russian "face" of romanization, to the Chinese "character" of romanization, and then considered in the long historical perspective of sanskritization, romanization, and digitization. The logic embedded in the first romanized print Malay words of Conrad's English (a logic of grammar and anagrammatical form) determines the narrative unfolding of Conrad's entire *oeuvre* and the way that it continues to be received today. It exemplifies, too, the chronotope of romanization found elsewhere in modernist writers and artists. And it illuminates the multilingual and multiscript frames of reference for profound transformations in print media over the turn of the nineteenth into the twentieth century.

The K-effect circa 1911

When the OED calls attention to a historical shift in the use of the initial letter K, it marks a temporal and spatial distortion of perspective, central to this book's attempt to account for the phenomenon of print romanization. This K-effect registers a sort of linguistic fault line in the racialized relation of script and identity that runs throughout all the dictionary entries (from the 1880s up through the 1933 supplement, the revised second edition of the late twentieth century, and the ongoing online revisions of the present). The idea that a writing system reflects national, ethnic, or racial identity is a deeply ingrained linguistic assumption. It surfaces in the English word "character," referring to the "set of letters" peculiar to a particular language, and to "the sum of the moral and mental qualities which distinguish an individual or a people" (as the OED itself testifies). The idea that the "character" of a people (whether conceived in national, racial, or ethnic terms) is reflected in the "character" of a script, is what underlies the notion of a "scriptworld." As noted above, there is a variable and shifting sense of how speakers imagine their language to be "intrinsically related" to the script. The K-effect of the OED registers this variable and shifting relation of identity to script, both in the way it spells out the relation between "foreign" and "native" words, and as the complicated temporal and geographical distortion of its own changing archive from the 1880s to the present. The OED's "now" refers, not to one particular moment in the history of the English language, but rather to the convergence of a whole set of changing hierarchies between language and script, and across a range of different scriptworlds and worldscripts. This K-effect marks a volatile and unpredictable racialization in the changing hierarchies of language and script over the turn of the century. There is something more generally analogous and related in the K-effects of Conrad's fiction and those of transnational modernism.

The K-effect of Conrad's authorial signature registers a complex, variable, and changing problem of identity and script everywhere the letter K surfaces in Conrad: not only in his signature, but also repeatedly in the margins of his manuscript and typescript drafts, as well as in the names of fictional characters. As noted above, Conrad claims that he changed his name in 1901, "so that foreign mouths should not distort my real surname." This suggests an important identification with a Polish identity that surely plays a key role in the semiotic play at work everywhere the letter K surfaces in Conrad's writing. As I discuss more fully in Chapter 2, however, there is a marked shift in Conrad's sense of relation to his Polish identity. It is a shift that may be related to changing racial, ethnic, and national stereotypes in English attitudes toward Polish, Russian, and (more generally) Slavic people. Like the shift marked by the "now" in the OED's claim for the changing significance of the letter K, this shift in Conrad's response to being labeled a "Slav" raises a complicated set of questions about the timing of his turn toward addressing his Polish past and writing his Russian novel, *Under Western Eyes*. In the last year of his life, in part referring back to the Polish reminiscences of *A Personal Record*, Conrad wrote to his French translator Charles Chassé, "I have asked myself more than once whether if I had preserved the secret of my origins under the neutral pseudonym of "Joseph Conrad" that temperamental similitude ["references to my Slavonism"] would have been put forward at all."[38] To the extent that this retrospective reflection suggests a particular moment in his career when he betrayed "the secret of my origins," one might identify this as the moment in 1911 when, at the end of the "Familiar Preface" to *A Personal Record*, he added (for the first and last time) the letter K to the initial letters of his authorial signature "JC." The turning point of 1911 (when Conrad completes the two related texts *A Personal Record* and *Under Western Eyes*) conveniently marks a shift in Conrad's work as a whole. Attempting to correct the record of his own Polish or "Slavic" past, he reveals the "secret" of his own national, racial, and/or ethnic identity by revealing the K hidden in his authorial signature. Index of the volatile and shifting racialization of assumptions about language and script over the course of Conrad's lifetime, the addition of the letter K to his signature in 1911 betrays the fault lines (especially around the stereotype of the Slav) that are there from the very beginning of his career. As with the OED, the letter K becomes an index of the volatile and changing relations in hierarchies of languages and scripts.

In a number of ways, this vexed relation to the racialization in the changing hierarchies of languages and scripts is also the shared secret of transnational modernism; and 1911 marks a historical turning point of sorts for the K-effect that this book traces in avant-garde, transnational modernism. The moment when script becomes politicized and racialized—but also the unpredictable effects of that racialization and politicization of script—cannot be situated simply in one place or at one time. Its linguistic effects are manifold and cross all the divides marked by language debates worldwide. Virginia Woolf famously claimed that "on or about December 1910 human character changed" (in her 1924 essay "Mr. Bennett and Mrs. Brown" [also published under the title "Character in Fiction"]). Hidden in this famous formulation, is the shared secret of a volatile shift in the changing character of "character" itself, in that double English sense that combines the idea of a national, racial, or ethnic character, and the written character it is presumed to express. To explore this global shift underlying transnational modernism ("on or about December 1910"—around 1911), each chapter of this book compares Conrad to a different, canonical, modernist writer: the Irish modernist James Joyce (1882–1941); the Czech-German modernist Franz Kafka (1883–1924); and the leading writer of modern Chinese literature, Lu Xun (1881–1936). These writers are chosen as points of comparative reference to emphasize the different sociolinguistic contexts within which their work has become canonical: Joyce's relation to English; Kafka's to German; Lu Xun's to Chinese. In each case, their canonical place is marked by what Lydia Liu (discussing Lu Xun) has called the "translingual practices" inherent in their work and its reception.[39]

For Franz Kafka, writing in German along the linguistic borders within the Austro-Hungarian Empire on the eve of its collapse (at the intersection of German, Czech, Yiddish, and Hebrew), 1911 marks the moment when he explicitly sought to articulate the position of a "minor literature" (famously elaborated by Deleuze and Guattari). The notes "toward a minor literature,"[40] sketched in his diaries from 1911, give shape to that problem of writing in German (on which he reflected in a letter to Max Brod in 1921 on the "three impossibilities" for Jewish writers writing in German): "the impossibility of not writing, the impossibility of writing German, the impossibility of writing differently."[41] As I explore in Chapter 2, the resonant single letter K in Kafka marks the convergence of all of those impossibilities embodied in the challenge of his own fiction (K marking not only Kafka's signature, but also the signature-effect of a series of protagonists, notably in *Amerika*, with its hero Karl Rossman; in *The Trial*, with its central character Joseph K; and in *The Castle*, with its main character, simply K). By contrast to the English case of romanization raised by Conrad's converting "Konrad" to "Conrad," the signature effect of Kafka's K belongs to that convergence of languages and scripts peculiar to the status of German in relation to Czech, Yiddish, Hebrew, and (more distantly)

Russian. What marks a foreign effect in the case of English (for both the OED and for Conrad), for Kafka enacts an estrangement of the laws of language, script, and identity, turning the dominant, major language (German) into the space where a minor literature has been at work all along. In neither case is it a matter of affixing a particular identity to the letter K. Rather, the linguistic, literary, and political effects of romanization make the letter K the mark of a constitutive misfit between language, script, and identification.

The significance of romanization for this shared case of misplaced ethnic, national, and/or racial identification comes to the fore in the example of Lu Xun's "The Real Story of Ah-Q." Here, famously, the roman letter (Q) comes to stand within the Chinese script for the lost, or effaced, Chinese name of the story's character. It has typically been read as Lu Xun's critique of Chinese self-abasement in the face of the foreign: the roman letter Q a mark of that lost Chinese character (in every English sense of the word—identity and script) whose story, "The Real Story," elaborates as part of the problematic emergence of a modern Chinese sense of self, coinciding with the collapse of the last imperial dynasty in the Xinhai revolution of 1911. That date is inscribed in the story, although the story was written later and first published in 1921. The letter Q, of course, is different from the letter K in the English alphabet; and yet it is also marked by a K-effect that underscores the way in which this letter indexes a complex set of problems in transcribing, transliterating, and translating across worldscripts and scriptworlds.[42]

1911 provides a convenient point of reference for situating the moment Ha Jin calls Conrad's "timely appearance in English" within a comparative transnational, modernist perspective. This is not to say that something historically changed "on or about December 1910," again to invoke Woolf. Woolf is not referring (at least not directly) to that sense of the *written* character, the medium through which humans engage in what she calls "character-reading." Yet her concern for the way that modernist writers like Joyce, Lawrence, and herself need new "tools" for describing human nature suggests that the essay's famous formulation is indeed deliberately playing with different senses of the English word "character." And, most notably, the difference between the infinite variability of human nature and the way that a novelist attempts to capture that in a "character" produced by words on the page. It may, at first, seem a stretch to claim that Woolf includes that semantic sense of "character" linking script, identity, and nationality in her invocation of the change in "human character." Yet the terms of her essay's claim for what is happening to "English literature" involve a deliberate balancing between an implied *national* sense of "character" (how to describe Mrs. Brown on the railway) and that "infinite variety" of *human* nature that the novelist seeks to capture.

One of the more striking examples of this balancing act is her brief reference to Conrad:

> Why, then, is it so hard for novelists to create characters which seem real, not only to Mr. Bennett but to the world at large? . . .
>
> Surely one reason is that the men and women who began writing novels in 1910 or thereabouts had this great difficulty to face—that there was no English novelist living from whom they could learn their business. Conrad is a Pole, which sets him apart, and makes him, however admirable, not very helpful . . .

Woolf's dismissal of Conrad here is fascinating (but should be weighed against a rather more positive critical appreciation of Conrad written the same year), and a reminder of the vexed Polish or Slavic stereotype informing the hidden K-effect of his authorial signature. At stake, though, is a conception of "Englishness" that constantly hovers over the keyword "character" that Woolf is exploiting from beginning to end of the famous essay. Woolf's argument is in some ways the diametrically opposed version of Ha Jin's claim about Conrad's "timely appearance in English." While "not very helpful" for the "*English* novelist," according to Woolf, for Ha Jin, Conrad is a "founding spirit" for writers like himself. Yet the reason for excluding Conrad for Woolf and foregrounding him for Ha Jin may ultimately be the same. Conrad's appearance—untimely for Woolf and "timely" for Ha Jin—is for both a question of timing: what Woolf famously characterizes at the beginning of her essay, in her claim that "in, or about December, 1910, human character changed"; and then again what she captures at the end of the essay when she predicts, "we are trembling on the verge of one of the great ages of English literature." For the present study, this concerns the written character of English mediating the romanization of languages and scripts worldwide, engaged in a profound, far-reaching, and still ongoing change in the hierarchy of worldscripts and scriptworlds.

Overview of the Book

Each of the first three chapters of this book is divided into three main sections, following a preamble. In the opening section of each chapter, I outline a set of key sociolinguistic questions raised by the complex global phenomenon of romanization, exploring, in turn, different clusters of language debates. The middle section of each chapter develops a reading of Joseph Conrad's work relevant to that chapter's sociolinguistic focus. The final section of each chapter, pairing Conrad with another modernist writer (Joyce, Kafka, Lu Xun), addresses how romanization emerges as a transnational modernist phenomenon with implications for the transformation of global print media. Each individual section of each chapter might be excerpted and read consecutively together with the corresponding section in the other chapters to produce three rather different arguments: one discussing sociolinguistic debates; one engaged in a critical reading of Conrad's work; and the third focused on transformations in modernism and print media. Readers may prefer to focus on one or another of these three strands of the argument, to the exclusion of the others. In the book's overall conception, however, all three strands are closely intertwined. Its overarching aim is to trace what links the effect of the letter K in linguistic debates about romanization, the effect of the letter K throughout Conrad's fiction, and the effect of the letter K in a comparative study of transnational and multimedia forms of modernist aesthetic experimentation.

Chapter 1, "The English Case of Romanization," examines the prestige of English in coordinating a range of debates about romanization over the turn of the century. It introduces the sociolinguistic phenomenon of romanization with reference to the OED's definition of romanization, and examples of its treatment of Arabic script. While Conrad's text, in some respects, reiterates the OED's colonial presumptions, registering, on the one hand, the historical shift whereby Arabic script is displaced by romanized print form (eclipsed entirely in the online edition of the OED), Conrad's use of Malay registers, on the other hand, the emergence of a romanized print form of Malay that shapes Indonesian, the revolutionary new language of anti-colonial nationalism. Conrad's ironic (and also ambivalent) treatment of English hegemony overseas begins with a contrast between Arabic and roman scriptworlds that shapes the way in which the chronotope of romanization becomes an organizing feature of all of Conrad's work. This chapter examines how Conrad's work, as a whole, is generated by the chronotope of romanization, beginning with the framing function of the opening Malay words of Conrad's first novel and consolidated in his turn away from the Malay fiction as registered in the shift from *Lord Jim* to *Nostromo*.

Chapter 1 concludes with a comparison between the Conradian "blank space" on the map of Africa (from *Heart of Darkness*) and the "iSpace" of Joycean experimentation with the medium of romanized English print form (from *Finnegans Wake*). These chronotopes of avant-garde artistic experimentation present two sides of the same sociolinguistic, historical phenomenon. Both stage English as mediating a profound transformation in print forms worldwide, each anticipating the use of the English alphabet as a template for the later digital conversion of letters into alphanumeric computer coding.

Chapter 2, "The Russian Face of Romanization," turns to the role of the Russian Cyrillic script as an alternative and rival model, alongside the prestige of English, in coordinating language and script reforms over the turn of the twentieth century. The shadow cast by Russia over all of Europe is especially important for Conrad's work, generating some of the most memorable and important chronotopes of romanization. Russian debates over language reform are also inextricably linked to the ferment of modernist theory and practice. The importance of Cyrillic for Conrad's work, and transnational modernism more generally, extends beyond Russian linguistic and cultural contexts, calling attention to a hierarchy of languages and scripts throughout Central Europe, including those that appear in the work of Franz Kafka. The role of Russian in mediating forms of romanization, highlights the complex interdependence and coexistence of multiple languages and multiple scripts, often with unpredictable effects. Most notable, especially at the turn of the century, is the increasing tempo of the politicization and racialization of the ways in which language and script articulate national, ethnic, and racial identities. The racialized politics of script and identity connects the sociolinguistics of script reform in Central Europe and aesthetic modernism in complex ways. The framing example in Chapter 2 is a comparison between Conrad and Kafka, and the national and racial identity betrayed by the signature K-effect in each author's work.

Chapter 3, "The Chinese Character of Romanization," turns from the phenomenon of romanization within the sociolinguistic context of Central Europe to that of East and Southeast Asia. The place of romanization in efforts to standardize modern Chinese script draws attention, not only to the sheer heterogeneity of languages converging in the formation and re-formation of Chinese, but also to its constitutively diasporic coordinates. Conrad's Malay fiction is especially well positioned to highlight this sociolinguistic context. His Malay communities are unimaginable without the Chinese characters who make up the characteristic diversity of their populations (from shipowners to clerks to coolies). Yet Chinese characters constantly appear to disappear (from the very first novel, *Almayer's Folly* [1895] up to *Victory* [1914]). This is true for the characterization both of Chinese people and of Chinese script. Here, I explore how the conflation of Chinese characters as script and as demographic identity frames the very foundations of that sense of community, global trade, and print culture that Benedict Anderson has called "print-capitalism."

Chapter 3's reassessment of "print-capitalism" from the perspective of the Chinese character of romanization, reconsiders the ambivalence of this historical moment, explored already in terms of the ambiguous prestige of English (Chapter 1) and the multiscript shadow cast by Russian (Chapter 2). As with the English case of romanization and the Russian face of romanization, the Chinese character of romanization reveals how the European imposition of roman letters on other languages and scripts has a reverse effect (the K-effect) on those languages and scripts considered dominant. Romanization also involves a destabilization of the very medium of print itself. Europe's long-standing obsession with the medium of the Chinese written character combined with China's revolutionary experimentation with romanization systems, gives particular form to the innovations in writing, media, and technology that characterize the modernist moment. Following what Lydia Liu calls the "ideographic turn," and what Christopher Bush calls "ideographic modernism," this chapter explores how the Chinese character of romanization shapes modernist engagements with new media technologies. Chinese characters are everywhere present, if everywhere effaced, in the mediating role increasingly assumed by the roman alphabet.

This chapter's reading of Conrad's Chinese characters shows how the effacement of Chinese turns out to be an organizing feature of his Malay fiction (framing the relation of Arabic to roman print, discussed in Chapter 1). In part, this has to do with the mediating role of *peranakan* (Indonesian-born) Chinese in the printing of the form of romanized Malay that came to dominate the Dutch East Indies, shaping the medium of "print-capitalism" and the "revolutionary Malay" of what became Indonesian. An extended reading of Conrad's *Victory*, and a comparison between Conrad and Lu Xun, illuminates the importance of this sociolinguistic phenomenon for the multimedia transformation in print culture.

Chapter 4, "Sanskritization, Romanization, Digitization," situates the historical moment of romanization, examined in the preceding chapters, within a succession of three different ways of modeling the history and geography of print technologies. Sanskritization refers to the spread of a Sanskrit form of literacy that Sheldon Pollock has described in terms of the "Sanskrit cosmopolis," a universalizing, political model reproduced in a whole range of scripts throughout South and Southeast Asia. Romanization (with capital R) refers to the history of the development of roman letters as the standardizing, near-universal alphabet for modern literary print form, at least in modern Europe and its colonies. Digitization refers to the recent revolution in media technologies that reproduces all forms of literature, now via computer code. This chapter develops a dialectical grasp of the medium of print through these three forms. It explores how European comparative philology is premised on an idealization of Sanskrit that forgets the way that Sanskrit modeled itself through multiple scripts. The reversal, whereby Sanskrit is privileged according to an identity of language and script, becomes a foundational principle for European comparative philology. This grammatological blind spot, as revealed in the work of Wilhelm von Humboldt and Ferdinand de Saussure, emerges from a practice of romanized transcription with implications both for nineteenth-century historical linguistics and twentieth-century structural linguistics.

The broader, historical scope of this speculative dialectic provides useful tools for explaining some of the characteristic riddles of romanization. These tools can be applied elsewhere in literary and cultural studies more generally, enabling future comparative readings of literary form within a multilingual and multiscript perspective. Such readings promise to illuminate the striking paradox that the time-space (chronotope) of print romanization comes into view as the eclipse of the space of print itself and its transformation into diverse media. Just as oral forms of recitation are inscribed in the very origins of world literature (as told by the Sanskrit epics), and just as the rise of print media depends on older hierarchies of prestige scripts (of scriptworlds and worldscripts), the space of digitized reading, writing, and coding produced by the conversion of letters into alphanumerical code continues to be haunted by the effect of the printed roman letter.

1
The English Case of Romanization: From Conrad's "blank space" to Joyce's "iSpace"

In this first chapter, I consider the role of English in mediating, defining, and standardizing forms of romanization that emerged over the turn of the twentieth century. English is by no means the only language with a claim to predominance in the accelerating drive to romanize the world's languages. Nonetheless, it is difficult to ignore the hegemonic influence of English over debates about romanization throughout the world. The global reach of the English language, linked to the global reach of the roman alphabet, leads (all too easily) to its conflation with roman alphabetic forms of script. This might be explained as an effect of what sociolinguist İlker Aytürk calls "script charisma":

> If it is permissible to use Max Weber's notion of "charismatic authority" in a field that he did not intend it for, the Roman alphabet had in effect become a charismatic script by the 1920s and 1930s. It owed its charisma less to its Roman or Catholic background, and more to a rather secular association with the advent of modernity, Westernization, and, later, the ascendancy of English as the global lingua franca.[1]

The prestige of English itself contributes to, and reinforces, the prestige of the roman alphabet as a "charismatic script," presumed destined to become the one universal writing system for all languages.

What makes the case of English romanization exemplary is the highly ambiguous effect produced in the attempt to make English a worldscript, heir to Rome's imposition of Latin in antiquity. As with Romanization in antiquity, English romanization imposes on the world standard forms of writing and language that assimilate, but displace, many other languages and scripts. In the process, however, romanization transforms the space of English print literacy, resituating English between multiple European and non-European languages and multiple forms of roman alphabetic and non-roman alphabetic writing systems. The linguistic act of romanized transliteration reveals how Standard English emerges from a double process of standardization and destabilization, as the English alphabet comes to mediate between a wide variety of non-English languages and scripts. The implications are both far-reaching and complicated. These involve philosophical challenges to the basic phonetic assumption behind the conflation of English with the alphabet. They also point to profound transformations in print media. The twenty-six letters of *the* (English) alphabet, initially defined by the uniquely phonetic function of its letters, come to serve an ideographic function in the alphanumerical recoding of roman letters with digital computing.

I first examine the definition of romanization as it appears in the *Oxford English Dictionary* (OED), and how it is problematized by the dictionary's own acts of romanized transliteration. With close attention to the way that the OED cites from Conrad's work, I then consider how Conrad's fiction organizes these linguistic questions of romanized transliteration into literary form. Specifically, I examine the literary form of the chronotope of romanization that emerges from micro-lexical effects of his own use of English, from the narrative themes of individual novels, and from the changing contours of his entire *oeuvre*. I conclude with a comparative consideration of the case of English romanization, underlying English literary modernism, from Conrad to James Joyce, with a special focus on two characteristic examples of the chronotope of romanization: the Conradian "blank space" on the map of Africa that has since been filled in with place names; and the Joycean "iSpace" of typographical play with the temporal and spatial arrangement of letters in *Finnegans Wake*.

Defining Romanization: The *Oxford English Dictionary* and Joseph Conrad

The prestige of English, amidst the international proliferation of attempts to adopt romanization systems from the late nineteenth century through the first part of the twentieth century, is something that deserves fuller attention for its complex global impact on questions of language, literature, and culture in the most general of senses. Yet in many respects, a focus on English can hardly do justice to grasping the international scope of language reforms, involving as it does (among other things) attempts to romanize Chinese and Japanese (beginning in the late 1880s and extending into the 1930s and beyond); debates over converting from Arabic to either Cyrillic or roman script in Central Asia in the early years of the Soviet Union; and including two contrasting examples from 1928: the state-mandated conversion in Turkey from Perso-Arabic to roman letters enacted by Atatürk; and the adoption of *bahasa Indonesia* as the language of anti-colonial nationalism in the Dutch East Indies, disseminated in the form of romanized print Malay used in the so-called "Oath of Youth" (*Sembah Sumpah*).[2] These reforms may appear distant from debates about the English language, but my claim is that they are crucial for understanding the case of English romanization as a sociolinguistic phenomenon, as well as a question of linguistic-literary form and the changing nature of print media worldwide.

According to the OED, "romanization" means "Transliteration into Roman characters" or the "adoption of a system for such transliteration with regard to a particular language."[3] This definition calls attention to two rather different sides of the phenomenon of romanization. There is, on the one hand, the act of transliteration itself (as when one transliterates the capital city of Japan "Tokyo," say, rather than "Tokio"). There is, on the other hand, the "system" used to enact such a transliteration. The OED offers an example of this second sense, drawn from debates about the proposed Hepburn romanization system (*Hebon-shiki Rōmaji*) for the Japanese language. Citing a *Times* article from 1885: "Mr. Dillon . . . presents certain objections to the proposed Romanization of Japanese." Whereas the first part of the definition foregrounds a process at work since the very beginnings of the roman alphabet, the second part calls attention to a proliferating set of proposed systems, over the turn from the nineteenth to the twentieth century, to romanize languages (like Japanese), historically not written using roman letters. There is a complex and ongoing interaction between these two different sides of "romanization": the basic problem of transliteration underlying any use of roman letters, and the historically recent proliferation of multiple systems of transliteration into roman letters.

The case of English as a language that mediates between these multiple systems of transliteration, emerges in the difference between the two sides of the OED's definition of "romanization." The first part of the definition looks back to the long history of the relation between English and the Latin alphabet, while the second part concerns the English use of roman letters to transliterate other languages and scripts. In shifting from the first to the second sense of "romanization," however, the OED tends to blur a range of different things implied by the roman alphabet. The linguist Florian Coulmas brings more precision to these differences when he points out that, "Latin and English writing should not be treated as writing systems of the same type": the "Latin alphabet," he argues, ambiguously expresses both "the writing system of the Latin language" and "a set of 26 letters serving the writing systems of a great number of different languages."[4] Noting that the second sense "is also referred to as 'Roman' and 'roman,'" he goes on to argue that "The spelling with a small initial r is indicative of the general significance of this script which is no longer associated with a particular language or culture."[5] In making this contrast, Coulmas suggests a way to supplement the OED's definition by distinguishing between "Romanization" with an uppercase "R" (the imposition of the Latin alphabet associated with the Latin language) and "romanization" with a lowercase "r" ("the use of 26 letters to serve the writing systems of a great number of different languages"). This is the distinction that I briefly discussed in the Introduction and will continue to use throughout this book. From a sociolinguistic perspective, it disentangles the function of the alphabet as related to the historical phenomenon of Romanization in classical times from the function of the alphabet as related to the late nineteenth- and early twentieth-century proliferation of romanization systems. The case of English romanization, in this sense, is a matter of lowercase romanization.

With (uppercase) Romanization the scriptworld of Latin coincides with the worldscript of roman letters: language and script are closely bound together. By contrast, with (lowercase) romanization, the worldscript is no longer associated with a particular language. The hierarchy of relations between script and language gets mediated through the interaction of multiple scriptworlds in relation to the worldscript of romanized lettering. English may play a dominant role in this mediation of language and script, scriptworld, and worldscript; but English is by no means the only language to lay claim to identification with the roman alphabet. Nonetheless, it is important to note how difficult it is to keep these distinctions from blurring, especially in the case of English romanization. The OED's own definitions of "romanize" and "romanization" have changed to emphasize the historical and qualitative distinctions. But even its most recent entries suggest a link between the very different historical sense of Romanization as related to ancient Rome and romanization in the technical sense of "transliteration into Roman characters."[6] To an important degree, the prestige of English depends on maintaining the historical connection between the two very different senses, and the shift from one to the other continues to shape the way (lowercase) romanization is practiced and performed. The case of English romanization, then, is actually a matter of (lowercase) romanization emulating the imperial designs of (uppercase) Romanization, with English substituting for Latin as the global lingua franca.

The blurring of historical perspective, built into the English definition of the word "romanization," evokes the prestige of English as a global language, but conceals the role that English plays in mediating between other languages and scripts. The mediating function of English in (lowercase) romanization tends to get subsumed as a more technical question (the question of transliteration) within that broader horizon of the history of language, writing, and script, projected by (uppercase) Romanization. The conflation of (uppercase) Romanization and (lowercase) romanization makes the twenty-six letters of the English alphabet appear, not only heir to the Latin alphabet, but also an embodiment of the *one and only* alphabet. This conflation of ancient and modern alphabets may be found even in established sociolinguistic studies. As Coulmas notes, it shapes I. J. Gelb's pioneering study of writing systems (or "grammatology" as Gelb termed it), whose "teleological evolutionism" made him view "the history of writing" as culminating in "the twenty-six letters of the alphabet."[7] This "common Latin alphabet fetishism"[8] reduces the complexity of romanized transliteration across scripts to a singular history of "the alphabet."

The persistence of this "Latin alphabet fetishism" is epitomized by Walter Ong when he insists, in *Orality and Literacy*, that there are "many scripts, but only one alphabet."[9] As Yurou Zhong succinctly notes, this reads as "an unequivocal statement of the hierarchy within the world's writing systems, catapulting the Roman-Latin alphabet to the top while downgrading other non-Roman-Latin writings altogether."[10] Zhong's point is useful, not only in showing how Ong (like Gelb) exhibits a "Latin alphabet fetishism." It also draws attention to the hierarchy of writing systems underlying Ong's juxtaposition of a single alphabet alongside multiple scripts. Ong's insistence on the singularity of the "one alphabet" asserts a hierarchy but leaves an unexplained riddle regarding the role of romanized transliteration (lowercase romanization) in mediating that hierarchy of writing systems. Ong's assertion might be reformulated slightly in this way: there may be many scripts in the world, but only one worldscript is dominant (the roman alphabetic worldscript). English, moreover, tends to dominate the way that worldscript mediates between different scriptworlds.

The riddle of Ong's "one alphabet" points to the hidden significance of (lowercase) romanization for his account of the relation between orality and literacy. It is a riddle, above all, of print culture and print literacy. The distinctive features of literacy, according to Ong, emerge from an important break in the implied continuity of that evolutionary model whereby a series of different alphabets—Semitic, Greek, roman—gives shape to the singularity of a history of the "one alphabet." The unique invention of "alphabetic letterpress print in fifteenth-century Europe," repeats for modern print literacy what the unique invention of the "phonetic alphabet" did for writing in antiquity: "like the alphabet, alphabetic letterpress print was a nonce invention."[11] If Ong's argument strongly implies a continuity between alphabetic writing in antiquity and "alphabetic letterpress printing," blurring the distinction between (uppercase) Romanization and (lowercase) romanization, the way that he turns from the one to the other also ties the shift in historical and geographical perspectives to the changing conditions of typography and print. Ong himself elides the effects of romanized transliteration between scripts, but the emphasis he places on this repetition of the historical uniqueness of the "one alphabet" suggests how the temporal and spatial features of (lowercase) romanization are intricately related to the advent of print literacy, when the typographical letter determines the spatialization of time characteristic of modern literate consciousness. As Ong puts it: "Print situates words in space more relentlessly than writing ever did. Writing moves words from the sound world to a world of visual space, but print locks words into position in this space."[12]

Ong's argument harks back to the work of media theorist Marshall McLuhan, who repeatedly enacts a confusion between (uppercase) Romanization and (lowercase) romanization, each time he refers to "the phonetic alphabet" in discussing the transformation from the medium of print to new electric media and technologies. The riddle of Ong's assertion about the "one alphabet" derives, indeed, from McLuhan: "The phonetic alphabet is a unique technology. There have been many kinds of writing, pictographic and syllabic, but there is only one alphabet in which semantically meaningless letters correspond to semantically meaningless sounds."[13] Especially revealing is the way in which McLuhan characterizes this singular "phonetic alphabet" as marking the break between "tribal and individualist man."[14] Offering an example, adapted from the opening to Conrad's *Heart of Darkness*, he writes, "a single generation of alphabetic literacy suffices in Africa today, as in Gaul two thousand years ago, to release the individual initially, at least, from the tribal web."[15] Here, the comparison between ancient Rome's conquest of Gaul and modern Europe's presence in Africa conflates the different historical, social, and linguistic features of Romanization and romanization to produce a shorthand formulation—"alphabetic literacy"—that grants "the phonetic alphabet" an agency, a cultural consistency, and a durability in both space and time that makes even more evident the kind of ethnocentrism Zhong critiques in Ong's statement that there are "many scripts, but only one alphabet." To be sure, in both cases, language is an instrument of imperial ambitions; but in the first case, the Latin alphabet imposes a particular writing system (Latin) to the exclusion of others, whereas in the second, what is imposed is a phonetic system presumed to be the universal measure for mediating between any and all other languages. McLuhan conflates a range of different

European languages (all using variants of the roman alphabet) in relation to an enormous variety of different languages and writing systems throughout Africa. He also overlooks the significance of Arabic as a worldscript mediating various forms of oral and literate traditions, long before the European partition of Africa. Fetishizing the phonetic alphabet, as imposed with (uppercase) Romanization, McLuhan ignores the work of (lowercase) romanized transliteration across languages and scripts. The complexity of linguistic relations is reduced to the "Latin alphabet fetishism" of a "phonetic" ideal, projected as regulating a hugely varied historical process, involving multiple languages and scripts (including multiple alphabets), across a varied geographical range (especially across the entire continent of Africa).

Drawing on McLuhan for his vision of print literacy, Ong also enlists Derrida's critique of "phonocentrism" to show that an overemphasis on "the sounded word as primary" ("debasing writing by comparison with oral speech") belongs to a culture of writing (even more so, typography) and print literacy. Derrida's critique of phonocentrism foregrounds, for Ong, the limiting medium of typographic space in relation to orality. Ong indeed connects Derrida and McLuhan: "In breaking up what he calls phonocentrism and logocentrism, Derrida is performing a welcome service, in the same territory that Marshall McLuhan swept through with his famous dictum, 'The medium is the message.'"[16] There are important differences between these three theorists, but all three tend to rely on a singular focus on "alphabetic writing." McLuhan's is the most sweeping conflation of Romanization and romanization. Ong gives more historical and geographical specificity to the ascendancy of roman alphabetic writing, turning to a historical moment midway between the early imposition of the Latin alphabet and the recent spike in script conversion to roman letters, emphasizing the advent of print culture. Derrida repeatedly returns to the formulation "alphabetic writing," in effect conflating the roman alphabet with *the* alphabet, although he does this precisely to draw attention to the historical and philosophical limitations in any attempt to account for a history of writing and *the* alphabet.[17]

What all three theorists overlook is the transliterating function of roman letters in the process of print romanization. All three complicate assumptions about the "medium" of print culture—its historical and geographical spread (McLuhan); the way it "locks words into position in [typographic] space" (Ong); or the fundamental problems of verbal spacing (*espacement*) and the deferral of meaning (*différance*) it entails (Derrida). At the heart of each of those distinct challenges to the way that we perceive the timing and spacing of print culture, lies the technical question of romanized transliteration. What Ong's claim, that "there are many scripts, but only one alphabet," evokes in the form of a riddle is the regulating function of that "one alphabet" used by multiple languages in transliterating across multiple scripts.

Sociolinguists may, rightly, want to emphasize the historical phenomenon marked by the second part of the OED's definition of "romanization." This is what İlker Aytürk does, going on to provide an even narrower definition: "Sociolinguists coined the term 'romanisation' to describe a peculiar form of change in writing systems, the first examples of which were observed from the mid-nineteenth century onward. To be precise, romanisation is a reform process, initiated by the ruling authorities and supervised oft-times by language experts, whereby the Roman-based alphabet is prepared and then enforced to replace the former writing system of a speech community."[18] The precision of Aytürk's definition, in one sense, helps clear up an ambiguity in the OED definition, emphasizing that the "system" is one proposed to replace a former writing system. The majority of debates about romanization over the turn of the century fit Aytürk's definition and so, from a sociolinguistic and historical perspective, it is surely an important way to define romanization as an object of social and political study.[19] At the same time, Aytürk's more precise definition misses a quite revealing ambiguity in the OED definition. The OED definition never specifies 1) what language the "system" of romanization in question is meant to serve (whether the "particular language" being transliterated, or some other language or languages); or 2) whether the "system" is intended to *replace* an existing writing system or stand *alongside* that writing system.

Some of the consequences of this ambiguity may be glimpsed from the OED's example of the Hepburn romanization system, proposed in 1885 for transliterating Japanese. Historically, this is precisely the kind of example Aytürk has in mind.[20] Yet while the Japanese Romanization Club that proposed the system wanted it to replace the existing (and relatively recently standardized) Japanese writing system, this effort failed. Instead, the Hepburn system has come (like other romanization systems) to serve as an ancillary writing system, one that is used in Japanese alongside the existing writing system, and also (more consistently) as a system of transcription used by other languages. The OED's example, then, magnifies the semantic ambiguity of its definition to encompass the historical fate of the Hepburn system itself: originally intended as a system meant to replace the complex writing system of Japanese kanji, katakana, and hiragana, it continues to serve as one among a range of systems used both internationally and in Japan (albeit officially subordinated to the *Kunrei-shiki* system). Perhaps the most striking analogous example of the use of roman letters as an ancillary writing system is the widespread use of *pinyin* to access Chinese characters from smartphones with QWERTY keyboards.

What the OED definition registers, in its ambiguity, is the multilinguistic, multiscript environment within which debates about romanization necessarily occur. Whether or not a romanization system is successfully adopted (as in the contrasting cases of the state-mandated Turkish reform of 1928 and the anti-colonial nationalist adoption of *bahasa Indonesia* in the "Oath of Youth" that same year), the proliferating forms of romanization, characteristic of the turn of the century, affect more than the "particular language" for which such systems were being proposed. As the first part of the OED definition already indicates, individual instances of romanization create effects that cross over languages and scripts. Whether focusing on the micro-lexical effects of romanization suggested by the first part of the definition (the difference between "Tokyo" and "Tokio") or on the macro-historical questions raised by attempts to exchange one writing system for another (roman letters in place of Japanese kanji, katakana, and hiragana), romanization necessarily involves acts of transcription, transliteration, and translation across multiple languages and multiple scripts.

The OED registers this from the particular perspective of the English language, whose history and evolution it is designed authoritatively and definitively to record. It is precisely this bias toward English—indeed, the assumption of the hegemony of English over the hierarchy of languages and scripts involved in language reforms—that makes the OED an especially instructive archive: not only as evidence of the presumed superiority of English over other languages but also as evidence of the blind spots raised by the hegemony of English and the way English itself has been and continues to be transformed by the process of romanization.

The OED also suggests a significant link between such assumptions and the assumption that roman letters provide a superior writing system. There is, indeed, a particular prestige placed on the English form of the roman alphabet that belongs to international debates over romanization across languages. Yet the English use of roman letters is itself a special case of romanization, all at once presenting a language with a long history of having used roman letters (giving it what linguists call a "deep orthography"[21]) and situating its modern standardization alongside those more recent instances of language reform noted above. Although English is one of those languages that has long used the roman alphabet, efforts to standardize its orthography (of which the OED itself is a significant instance) coincide with the linguistic reforms that fit Aytürk's narrower definition of "romanisation." The OED, begun in the 1880s, was completed in 1928, the same year that Turkey instituted its conversion from Arabic to romanized script, and the same year that the Indonesian "Oath of Youth" codified the conversion to roman script in writing the form of Malay, declared as the anti-colonial language of *bahasa Indonesia*. This is also the year in which the Chinese *Gwoyeu Romatzyh* received official recognition by the ruling Guomindang government of the Chinese Republic, the "first and hitherto strongest official endorsement of Romanization [in China]."[22] These are all instances of the proliferating forms of romanization, characteristic of this historical moment of global linguistic standardization.

The case of English romanization, from one perspective, is a sociolinguistic story of standardization: the emergence of the basic English alphabet from a long historical process of codifying the way roman letters are used in the scripting of English. This is not only what the OED exemplifies as an authoritative account of the English language. It is also the story the OED seeks to tell in each of its entries—for example, in each entry for each letter of the alphabet. As already discussed in the Introduction, its entry for the letter K traces the etymology of the "eleventh letter of the alphabet in English and other modern languages" back to the "original letter of the Roman alphabet" (noting also the roman letter's Greek, Phoenician, and Semitic roots). First explaining the changing use of the letter K in Latin orthography (its gradual disappearance from all but a few words and its association with transliterations from the Greek), the etymology then turns to a discussion of the history of words beginning with the letter K in "the Romano-British alphabet" (where it was rare, as in Latin usage), Old English (sometimes alternating with C), Norman English (which introduced a few more words beginning with K), and "Standard English." The use of the term "Standard English" itself attests to the OED's investment in standardizing English usage and orthography.[23]

Here, the OED complicates its account of the standardization of English by shifting from the etymology's historical perspective (governed by the letter's evolution from Latin) to consideration of the use of K to mark the first letter of words from foreign languages. The OED distinguishes between "the native K words" and "foreign words of recent adoption, many of them very imperfectly naturalized." In shifting from "native" words, considered part of the legacy of the long evolution of English, to "foreign words of recent adoption," the OED turns from the legacy of (uppercase) Romanization to the question of (lowercase) romanization, and the specific way in which the letter K has more recently been used to characterize "the uncouth or barbarous character" of those "words of recent adoption . . . with which this letter is crowded." As noted earlier, this K-effect marks the foreign origin of transliterated words and calls attention to the double-effect of romanization. It bears repeating that this K-effect is produced through the blurring of perspectives as one moves from viewing English in historical relation to (uppercase) Romanization, to viewing English in light of the effects of (lowercase) romanization.

The prestige of English, then, is not only a story of standardization. The emergence of the basic English alphabet also tells a more complicated story of the prestige of English within a changing heteroglot, multiscript, transcriptural environment. In attempting to account for the place of English in the hidden hierarchy of translinguistic, transcriptural, and translational effects of (lower-case) romanization, the OED provides a glimpse of this rather different story: the way that the prestige of the basic English alphabet mediates other languages and scripts, potentially destabilizing its own prestige. Sarah Ogilvie discusses, in detail, the story of a significant shift in the way the OED used to mark words of "foreign" adoption with a vertical double line (a so-called "tramline"). As Ogilvie explains, with the publication of the OED Supplement in 1933, these marks disappeared, offering a case study in disputes among editors over how to register the significance of such words for the story of English as a global language.[24] The case of the "vanishing tramlines," as she discusses it in *Words of the World* belongs to the complex story of the OED's attempts to track the prestige of English in relation to other global languages.

This more complex case of the changing prestige of English surfaces in the appearance of Joseph Conrad in the OED, as a point of reference for English usage of the Malay word "Tuan," which first appeared in the 1933 Supplement (see Figure 2). The entry is revealing, both for what it shows about the OED's role in standardizing romanized print form, and what it shows about the role of romanization in Conrad's entire *oeuvre*. The word itself, as the OED defines it, is a matter of English prestige: "Tuan," the original entry claims is "a title of respect given by Malays to an Englishman or other European." The entry cites three passages from Conrad's work, one from *Almayer's Folly*, one from *An Outcast of the Islands*, and the one that later editions of the OED will retain, from *Lord Jim*, a passage that shapes the title-phrase of that novel: "They called him Tuan Jim: as one might say—Lord Jim."

Tuan² (tu*ā*·n). [Malay *tuan, tuwan* lord, master.] A title of respect given by Malays to an Englishman or other European.
   1895 CONRAD *Almayer's Folly* i. (1920) 20 Tuan Almayer is speaking to a friend. *Ibid.* iv. 70 Tuan will be angry. **1896** — *Outcast of Islands* I. iv. (1919) 43 Take that to this white Tuan's house. **1900** — *Lord Jim* i. (1926) 3 They called him Tuan Jim: as one might say—Lord Jim. **1927** H. M. TOMLINSON *Gallions Reach* xxxi. § 3 The Malays .. went down on their hams .. while watching the tuans preparing to disappear.

Figure 2. *Oxford English Dictionary* entry for "Tuan."

The entry on "Tuan" presents an interesting sociolinguistic case study of English romanization. It appears as one of those cases of "foreign words of recent adoption."[25] The choice of Conrad as a point of reference for its citations may be related to this "class" of words, since most of the other references to Conrad in the 1933 Supplement focus on similarly "foreign words" (such as "cargador," "mozo," "pulperia," and "rattan"). The way that the OED presents this Malay word, as adopted, and transcribed into English, reveals a number of fundamental problems of romanization that surface in these kinds of words, but that ultimately attend all classes of English words, not just those of "recent adoption." As with other entries, it begins with a condensed etymological explanation put in parentheses: "Malay *tuan, tuwan*, lord, master." This abbreviates what is, in fact, a quite complicated process of transcription, transliteration, and translation from Malay into English. There is the act of transcribing the spoken Malay word into the spelling of its adopted English form. There is also an act of transliteration from whatever written form of Malay may be involved. The difference between transcription and transliteration is implied in the italicized variant spellings (*tuan, tuwan*), but it is impossible to tell whether these variants reflect alternative spoken or alternative written versions of the Malay word. As part of the phonetic ideal on which the dictionary is premised, the spoken word is given priority, although that same phonetic ideal relies on the written evidence to establish authority for the spoken word (and notably here, in the spacing and timing, the phonetic spelling out of the roman letters).[26] Whatever exchange has occurred in the transcription between scripts remains hidden, elided in the etymological spelling out of the italicized roman letters "*tuan, tuwan*."

The etymology's translation (into "lord, master") complicates this hidden question of transliteration between scripts even further. It is almost inevitable that things will get lost in the complex interrelation between the transcription of speech, the transliteration of script, and the translation of meaning.[27] In the case of "tuan"—a word whose English meaning hinges on acknowledgment, recognition, or attribution of "respect" within a translinguistic context—quite a lot indeed goes missing. It is, after all, impossible (here) to disentangle the act of translation from the acts of transcription and transliteration. The OED's abbreviated etymological description—"Malay *tuan, tuwan*, lord, master"—folds together all three procedures in a condensed and highly charged case of the English romanization of Malay. Even before claiming (for the English meaning of the word) that it is "a title of respect given by Malays to an Englishman or other European," its etymological description raises questions about the hidden hierarchies of language and script informing this cross-linguistic exchange. Whereas the OED seeks to standardize and stabilize those hierarchies in its etymology and in its definition, the citations it quotes from Conrad deliberately work to question and ironize those hierarchies: "They called him Tuan Jim: *as one might say*—Lord Jim" (my emphasis). Even as spelled out in this one sentence, the way that "Tuan Jim" translates into "Lord Jim" turns on a deliberately questionable transcription, transliteration, and translation of a Malay word that comes to stand for an irony of English entitlement. That irony, written into the famous title of Conrad's novel, gets embedded in turn in the OED.

The OED's etymology notably fails to explain what written form of Malay may be implied. The etymological distinction between the two versions of the Malay word suggests a likely allusion to the written versions of what might better be classified as two different Malay words: "tuan" as a form of address and "Tuhan" as a word for God. An established precedent for this is William Marsden's *Dictionary of the Malayan Language* (1812), which gives both of these forms, suggesting that "tūan" (master, lord, sir) might be derived from "tūhan" ("the Lord, the almighty ruler"). Marsden's example is notable for its emphasis on the Arabic script that is the basis for his own transliterations into roman letters (see Figure 3). The OED itself provides ample examples to suggest that this word's etymology is derived through transliteration from the form of Arabic script (known as *jawi*) traditionally used for written Malay. The word

توٗن *tūan* master, lord, sir. Mistress, madam. Owner. (Vid. توهٗن *tūhan*.) It is commonly used as a pronoun of the second person in addressing a superiour. *Tūan amba* my master. توانکو *tūan-kū* my lord; his highness. *Iyā tūan* yes, sir. *Tīada tūan* no, sir. *Tūan putrī* the princess. *Tūan-lah istrī-kū iang tantu* thou (madam) art my undoubted wife. *Kambali-kan-lah gādei ka-pada tūan-nia* return the pledge to its owner. *Apa tūan-pūnia sūka* what is your pleasure? *Ka-māna tūan andak pergi* whither do you mean to go? *Jekalau ada ang-kau ber-tūan* if you have a master. *Iäng de per-tūan* he who ruleth (an usual title of the person exercising sovereign power in the Malayan governments). *Iäng de per-tūan mūda* (equivalent to *rāja mūda*) the heir apparent. *Iäng de per-tūan dan iang de per-amba* royal master and (his) subject. *Iya ada de per-tūan atas kāmī* they are rulers over us. فرتوانن *per-*

Figure 3. William Marsden, *Dictionary of the Malayan Language*, entry for "Tuan."

> **Malay** (mălē¹·), *sb.* and *a.* Also 6 **Malayo,**
> **Melayo,** 8 **Malaya.** [repr. the native name,
> Malay ملايو *malāyu.*] **A.** *sb.*

Figure 4. *Oxford English Dictionary* entry for "Malay."

> **Rattan, ratan** (rătæ·n), *sb.*¹ Also 7 rat(t)oon,
> 8 rat-tan. [var. ROTANG, a. Malay روتن *rōtan,*
> app. for *rautan,* f. *rāut* to pare, trim, strip.]

Figure 5. *Oxford English Dictionary* entry for "Rattan."

"Malay" itself is one example (see Figure 4), but there are numerous other examples, including the word "rattan" (see Figure 5). In these entries the Arabic (*jawi*) script is shown in the opening parenthesis where the Malay etymology is given, so the English word is visibly presented as a romanized version of a form originally written in the Arabic script. Yet in the case of "Tuan," the OED is silent on the question of what—if any—script informs its etymology.

This silence stands in testimony to a process of romanization that continues to frame the historical archive of the OED. Put simply, it exemplifies the way that Arabic script disappears from the OED's record of the English language. By extension, it raises questions about the whole range of other scripts within which English words might be placed. There is nothing simple about this sociolinguistic fact, but in the case of the relation between roman and Arabic script, it provides evidence of the changing relation between two worldscripts, in which the one (in its romanized English print form) displaces the other (in all the variant forms of Arabic script that were featured from the 1880s through 1928 in the *New English Dictionary,* as the OED was then called). The disappearance of Arabic script from the OED stands as a graphic example of Aytürk's argument about the "charisma" that roman script acquires with "the ascendancy of English as the global lingua franca."

The disappearance of Arabic script from the OED also registers a shift from one kind of hierarchical organization of language and script to another. In the original OED entries, Arabic was visibly accorded a status alongside roman. English words, adopted or adapted from various languages, were framed by a visual parallel between two different worldscripts (Arabic and roman). To be sure, the recognition given to various forms of Arabic script—ranging from Perso-Arabic, Turkish, to the *jawi* script used for Malay—subordinated those forms to an Orientalist philological understanding of the comparative relation between the world's scripts. The fundamental premise of those Orientalist assumptions, moreover, remains the same as Arabic script disappears from its entries. Yet something important happens to the hierarchy of language and script when that visible contrast between worldscripts is taken away. Above all, as emerges in the case of "tuan," henceforth, the English word's relation to the Malay language can only be measured in roman letters.

This might be explained by reference to the distinction between "worldscript" (referring to scripts that have been used for a variety of languages—roman, Arabic, Chinese) and "scriptworld" (the term developed by David Damrosch for comparative global literary study, but adapted here to describe the way a language comes to be identified with its written form). In the earlier OED entries, the use of Arabic as a recognized worldscript signaled the sense in which this or that English word was adopted or adapted from a Malay (or Turkish, Persian, Arabic) scriptworld. The Malay scriptworld is marked as Arabic. In the case of "tuan," however, only roman letters can serve to signal the relation between language and script. A Malay scriptworld may be implied (e.g., by the use of italics or capital letters), but there is nothing to mark the role of the Arabic worldscript in measuring the timing and spacing, or phonetic spelling out, of that romanized print form. One way to understand the significance of the OED for the phenomenon of romanization, then, is to note how it reflects a shift in the perspectival relation between worldscripts and scriptworlds: from representing English as a language situated between a range of different contrasting, rival worldscripts, to representing English as the single hegemonic worldscript (romanized print form) used to represent the relation between a variety of different scriptworlds. The OED registers this changing interaction between worldscripts and scriptworlds as part of its own changing historical archive.

The displacement of Arabic script offers a particular historical—and geopolitical—example of the emerging combination of the hegemony of English and the prestige of romanized print form. That particular case is important to consider further, but it also underscores a more general point that applies to the way in which English is positioned in relation to a range of other worldscripts and scriptworlds. The changing relation between English and Arabic as worldscript, also reflects what happens in the OED's account of the letter K as it moves from positioning English words, first in relation to the (uppercase) Roman alphabet and then later in relation to the (lowercase) romanization of "foreign" words. In this sense there is an analogous K-effect at work in each entry of the OED. Often condensed into the abbreviated space of the etymology, each entry enacts a turn from projecting English in relation to worldscripts (like Latin, Arabic, etc.) to projecting English as itself the worldscript, by which to measure a range and hierarchy of scriptworlds.

The entry for "tuan" in the OED's 1933 Supplement registers the linguistic hegemony of English through a process of romanization that displaces Arabic as a worldscript and makes the single worldscript of English romanized print form the measure for transcribing, transliterating, and translating between different scriptworlds. At the same time, however, the disappearance of Arabic script generates an ambiguity about the Malay scriptworld from which the word "tuan" is derived. This ambiguity points toward another register of romanization that is equally as important for understanding the mediating role of English in a changing hierarchy of language and script. The OED's shift away from using Arabic script for Malay words coincides historically with that significant shift taking place in the Malay scriptworld which will lead to the 1928 declaration of anti-colonial allegiance to the form of romanized print Malay that becomes *bahasa Indonesia*. This is the culmination of a gradual change in the way in which Malay texts of all kinds were written, from the traditional form of Arabic (*jawi*) used in the circulation of manuscripts throughout the Malay-speaking world from roughly the year 1600 until the middle of the nineteenth century, when a modern form of romanized print came to dominate the circulation of Malay texts; first (primarily) in the Dutch East Indies, but then in British-controlled Malaysia as well. This gradual shift presents a case of what Aytürk calls the "script conversion," from one writing system (the *jawi* Arabic script) to another (romanized print form). By contrast to the script reform enacted in 1928 by Atatürk in Turkey, this conversion to romanized print form took place outside the main centers of power, with the rise of print media, and then through the formation of anti-colonial political organizing.[28] The archive of the OED does not directly represent this complex and important historical case of romanization, in part because the main actors involved (printers, journalists, writers, colonial settlers, and anti-colonial activists) are situated in peripheral relation to the anglophone world (the Dutch and Chinese were more important than the English in mediating this shift to romanized forms of print). Rather than reflecting a hegemonic, colonial imposition of one script form (roman) over another (Arabic), this story of script conversion involves a decolonizing rearrangement of a variety of different hierarchies of language and script. Far from simply reinforcing European colonial hierarchies, romanization in this case points toward an anti-colonial linguistic, literary, and political phenomenon.

The OED's entry on "tuan," then, registers two contrasting, contradictory features of the shift from Arabic script to romanized print. On the one hand, it reflects the subordination of Arabic as worldscript to the romanized print form of English as preeminent worldscript. On the other hand, it registers the emergence of a form of "revolutionary Malay,"[29] or "pre-Indonesian"[30] that positions the prestige of English within a space of romanized print form, engaged in a contest over colonial linguistic hierarchy. This ambiguity—romanization as colonization *and* decolonization—is what underpins the significance of Conrad's appearance in the OED. The OED cites Conrad in order to provide a standard authority for those "foreign" words recently adopted into English. Yet with the word "tuan," the citation from *Lord Jim* explicitly presents a problem of English colonial entitlement, opened up by the questionable translation of the word. If the OED's entries seek to stabilize the status of its English words (whether "native" or "foreign"), standardizing the authority of English, Conrad's appearance in the OED points toward those destabilizing effects that are part of the hidden work of romanized transliteration mediating the interrelation of worldscripts and scriptworlds.

This is not to say that Conrad's work is the anti-colonial counterpart to the OED. Both are bound to the colonial moment that produced them, and both are bound to reproduce its colonial biases. Yet, whereas the OED seeks to standardize, codify, and stabilize the English meaning of words as part of its lexicographical imperative, Conrad's fiction exploits the ambiguities and ironies of English. The OED wants to give the authoritative account of the derivation and meaning of a word like "tuan." Conrad's fiction, by contrast, gives artistic form to the questions of entitlement it poses, the gaps it opens up between the Malay and English languages. The technical linguistic questions posed by the transliterations of the OED's etymology (*tuan, tuwan*, lord, master), for Conrad, open up to rich ironies in measuring English entitlement to colonial "lord"ship and "mastery."

The very first words of Conrad's first novel—"Kaspar! Makan!"—inaugurate Conrad's career by turning these linguistic questions into literary ironies, organizing a timing and spacing of English novel form (in Bakhtin's terminology, a "chronotope") around the transcription, transliteration, and translation of Malay into romanized print form. The spoken utterance (Almayer's wife calling him to dinner) may not seem to directly raise the question of Malay script posed by the OED as a whole. Indeed, the OED's citations from *Almayer's Folly* and *An Outcast of the Islands* might initially appear to resolve any question of script by emphasizing the spoken, rather than the written word. Nonetheless, the spoken Malay evokes a scriptworld that ties together the novel's imagined community and the English print space of the novel itself. Hidden in the novel's opening form of Malay address, is a question of "respect" between characters whose interrelation unfolds the plot around a set of social and linguistic hierarchies (evoked each time the word "tuan" appears). From early on, the novel frames these hierarchies around a rivalry between the Englishman Lingard and his competitor, the Arab trader Abdulla, a rivalry between different cultures and different languages that unfolds also as a rivalry of different scriptworlds.

The name of "Lingard and Co."—the trading concern Almayer represents—foreshadows this ironic plotting of rival scriptworlds in the decaying roman letters of the unfinished house that will later sarcastically be named "Almayer's Folly": "Half obliterated words—"Office: Lingard and Co."—were still legible on the dusty door . . ." (*Almayer's*, 15). This chronotope of decaying, romanized, English lettering focalizes the way the narrative of Conrad's first novel, as a whole, is framed. While the novel begins with a mundane form of everyday address (a wife calling her husband to dinner), it ends with the invocation of Arabic scripture, as Abdulla, the Arab trader and rival to Almayer's benefactor, the English Lingard, invokes the bismillah at Almayer's deathbed: "in a solemn whisper he breathed out piously the name of Allah! The Merciful! The Compassionate!" (*Almayer's*, 208). The English print of the novel is reframed within a typographic spelling out of the formulaic Arabic scripture and script.

What Conrad's novelistic plotting captures ironically, the OED registers in its later revisions, and in its changing historical archive, as a silencing, an erasure in its writing out of Arabic script in the act of romanized transcription, transliteration, and translation. There is of course a difference between the OED's definition of "tuan" as a title of "respect" and the unfolding of Conrad's ironic plotting of that question of "respect" and entitlement. That difference opens up even more with the later revisions to the OED entry. These later revisions shed light on the changing historical archive of the OED, revealing gaps and silences that the phenomenon of romanization embeds in all its entries. From "A title of respect given by Malays to an Englishman or other European," the OED changes the definition to: "A master, a lord, formerly esp. a European as spoken to or of by Malays; freq. used as a title of respect or form of address, = 'sir', 'mister.'"[31] The revised version appears to be more objective in giving the Malay meaning "a master, a lord," and qualifying the earlier version's "title of respect" as a "former" colonial usage. And yet the revision cannot easily cordon off the "former" sense from the present. In what actual sense the term "tuan" would have applied to a European either as a "master" or "lord" is even less clear than in the original entry. What the revised entry has done is to shift the etymological meaning up front, subordinating the earlier entry's main sense of "title of respect" to a denotative meaning, which the previous entry referenced as the Malay origin of the English word. Relegating the colonial meaning to the past (with the word "formerly"), the revised entry seeks to give a neutral denotative meaning to apply to the present. This erases the original entry's emphasis on the term as an English word adopted, adapted, and transformed from Malay. What was already a silence in the original entry's transcription or transliteration from Malay (*tuan, tuwan*, lord, master) is compounded as the act of transcription, transliteration, and translation gets converted into the main English definition for the word. In the process, the OED's revised entry erases the linguistic act of romanization registered in the first version.

This erasure of the original entry's act of romanization leaves a blank in the space where the etymology gave the alternate spellings *tuan, tuwan*. The question of Malay script raised by those alternate spellings is now folded silently into the simple designation of derivation "Malay." Attempting to seal off the problem of the original entry's claim of "respect," the revised entry's main definition ("master, lord") strangely reproduces, without apparent irony, the questions of respect that Conrad will organize into the unfolding narratives of his Malay fiction around chronotopes of romanization. The gap between this revised entry and its citations from Conrad is also increased by the disappearance of the "Englishman" of the original entry. Where the OED entry once defined "tuan" as "A title of respect given by Malays to *an Englishman* or other European," the revised entry reads "A master, a lord, formerly esp. a European . . ."

The OED's vanishing Englishman bears an uncanny resemblance to the role of Conrad's Englishman, Lingard, in the plotting of Conrad's Malay trilogy. In the chronological setting of *Almayer's Folly*, Lingard has disappeared, reappearing only in flashbacks or in the "half obliterated" roman letters of "Office: Lingard and Co." The shadow of this absent Englishman may still haunt the revised OED entry in the form of its citation from *Lord Jim*; but it stands mute witness to the way that the dictionary's revisions cover up the tracks of its own act of romanization.[32] The OED's vanishing Englishman aptly represents the vanishing mediation of English in that changing hierarchy of language and script that characterizes the shift from the status of Arabic as worldscript to the prestige of romanized print form in the Malay scriptworld.

In attempting to historicize the colonial sense of "tuan," the revised versions of the OED call attention to multiple gaps and silences in the changing nature of its own historical archive. These gaps and silences—the places where the act of romanized transliteration was once marked (e.g., by Arabic script)—are what Conrad's fiction exaggerates as ironic effects (e.g., of exaggerated "respect"), reshaping them into chronotopes of romanization. In the OED's dictionary entries, wherever the term "formerly" appears, it is quite likely that some similar act of transliteration has been erased in the editing, creating a corresponding blank space in the changing hierarchy of worldscript to scriptworld. "Tuan" provides a rather special case study, but it reveals a process at work in each and every OED entry, formed as they all are by an ongoing process of romanization—and the ongoing erasure of that process—that continues to shape the OED.

It is this ongoing process of (lowercase) romanization that is revealed by the retrospective erasure of all the forms of Arabic script that used to appear in the etymologies of Malay words in the first edition of the OED. This is not to say that those specific Arabic script forms anchored the romanized print form of the English words more correctly, more properly, or with more cultural sensitivity. One might indeed doubt that, given how "formerly" the writing of those entries coincided with the heyday of Orientalist philology. Yet, with the later twentieth-century digitization of the whole of the OED, the gaps and silences of each entry open up to multiple—ongoing—questions about the role of English in mediating those hierarchies of language and script registered as part of its changing historical archive.

"Tuan" is a word recently adopted into English. This is, in part, what makes it an exemplary case study of English romanization, one of a number of cases the OED itself identifies as instances of words "adopted" into English. The status of words not considered "natural" or "denizens" is itself a matter of considerable and changing significance for evaluating the archive of the OED.[33] The dictionary's attempt to classify certain words as "aliens" or "casuals"—along with the attempt to define the process of "naturalization"—already points to the historical conjuncture of the OED with the proliferation of forms of romanization worldwide. Here, too, the first appearance of Conrad in the OED (in its 1933 Supplement) is revealing. As with "tuan," most of the words for which his authority is invoked might be considered "aliens": "cargador," "mozo," "pulperia," and "rattan." In attempting to make the distinction between these classifications ("naturals," "denizens," "aliens," and "casuals"), the OED also shows that the implications of the kind of romanized transliteration from one worldscript (like Arabic) found with "adopted" "alien" or "casual" words, also attends just about every English word there is.

What each OED entry does, indeed, is reproduce the effect found in its long etymological account of the letter K, positioning English as a language in a shifting hierarchy of languages and scripts. The way in which K indexes the past (uppercase) Romanization and ongoing (lowercase) romanization of English, builds into each and every entry of the OED a kind of dizzying, perspectival shift of historical perspective in the phonetic spelling out of, or (to borrow McLuhan's phrase) "typographic spell," of its roman letters. The example of English as a case of (lowercase) romanization aspiring to take the hegemonic place of Latin in (uppercase) Romanization leads to this constant shifting of linguistic perspectives. I turn now to consider how Conrad's fiction gives aesthetic form to that constant switching of perspectives between English as hegemonic worldscript and the scriptworlds it mediates through romanized print transliteration.

Conrad's Accusative Case: *Lord Jim* and *Nostromo*

Those moments when Conrad's fiction gives artistic form to the phenomenon of transliteration into roman letters, defined and documented by the OED, I have called chronotopes of romanization. These are places where the narrative foregrounds some particular effect in the timing and spacing of roman letters: the "half obliterated" letters "Lingard and Co."; and the questionable transcription, transliteration, and translation of "Tuan Jim." Later I will consider one of Conrad's most condensed, and important chronotopes, the example of the "blank space" on the map of Africa "filled since . . . with rivers and lakes and names" from *Heart of Darkness* (*Youth*, 52). These chronotopes give aesthetic form to the sociolinguistic phenomenon of romanization that frames Conrad's entire *oeuvre*, beginning with the first words of Conrad's first novel, the Malay utterance "Kaspar! Makan!" rendered in the romanized print form of Conrad's English.

Some of the places where the lexical effects of romanization are most powerfully felt are moments of address: naming of just about any kind, but perhaps especially pejorative, racialized, or downright racist naming. Besides the ambiguity of the opening to *Almayer's Folly* ("Kaspar! Makan!") one might consider the title and naming of *The Nigger of the 'Narcissus'* (orchestrated around reading out the "smudge" of the last name "Wait!" [*The Narcissus*, 17] in the roll call that introduces the title-character); reading Marlow's name: "Marlow, at least I think that's how he spelled his name" (*Youth*, 3); "Mistah Kurtz—he dead" (*Youth*, 150); in the spelling out of the title that conceals Jim's last name "They call him . . . Tuan Jim here. As you may say Lord Jim" (*Lord Jim*, 367); and in the naming of characters in *Nostromo*: "'Our excellent Señor Mitchell'"; or "he whom the English called Nostromo" (*Nostromo*, 10, 29). This sort of naming (always a kind of misnaming and very often with an implicit, oblique accusative charge) reveals an elementary principle of Conradian narrative, tied to effects of romanization at the micro-narrative level of *lexis*. This elementary principle, shaping the phenomenon of romanization into the chronotopes of Conradian narrative, might be classified according to the *accusative* case.

In a purely grammatical sense, the accusative case simply marks the way in which a word is inflected when positioned as a direct object in relation to the verb. This oblique, accusative charge found in Conrad's work reveals a grammar of naming produced in the crossing over from one script to another. The English term "accusative case" suggests the twinning of grammatical principle and accusatory gesture, based on a mistake in transcription that is itself an effect of romanization. As the OED helpfully notes:

> The formation of classical Latin *accūsātīvus* rests upon a misinterpretation of Hellenistic Greek αἰτιατικός 'of or relating to that which is caused or effected (ancient Greek τὸ αἰτιατόν)', designating the case of the effect, or thing directly affected by verbal agency, but misinterpreted by the Latin grammarians as '(the case) of accusing' (< ancient Greek αἰτιᾶσθαι to accuse).

English, as an "uninflected" language, has few examples of the "accusative" case except in the sense of referring (generally) to the object of a transitive verb. Yet, beside the fact that English still has vestiges of inflected forms, the lexical effects involved in Conradian chronotopes of romanization bear the mark of grammatical inflections from other languages. The accusative case, then, might be applied to that break in the transcription, transliteration, and translation effected in the process of romanization. What better term to use than a technical term, a grammatical term, which itself betrays the mark of this break in the transliteration from Greek to Latin? Both the Greek sense of *effect* and the Latin sense of *accusation* seem applicable to that micro-narrative lexical effect which, seeming to follow elementary grammatical rules of language, in fact betrays a fundamental distortion of grammar, language, and form that occurs in the crossing over between different linguistic, literary, and cultural systems. In this sense, then, the elementary grammar of Conrad's chronotopes of romanization revolve around the accusative case: the performative act of naming which, through a crossing over of worldscripts and scriptworlds, generates a profoundly unstable switching of loyalties across languages and scripts.

As noted earlier, Conrad's first novel is framed by an open question about the rivalry between Arabic and roman as worldscripts for the scriptworlds of Conrad's imagined Malay communities. This rivalry inaugurates the grammar of Conrad's poetics in a way analogous to the role of Arabic script in the changing historical archive of the OED. By contrast to the OED, Conrad never attempted to use Arabic script. Nonetheless, the romance of his Malay world does, in certain important respects, hinge on a romance of Malay titles, strongly suggesting a scriptworld marked by Arab titles and Islamic honorifics. The so-called Lingard trilogy, with which he began his career, may be read as an inquest into the failed romance of English investment in such titles and honorifics—notably, in Lingard's title "Rajah Laut."[34] To the extent that this Malay romance depended on a romantic investment in the religious, political, and cultural prestige of a scriptworld marked by the Arabic worldscript, one might say that Conrad's Malay fiction shared, with the OED, an Orientalist vision of the Malay language as embodied by an ethos aligned religiously, politically, and linguistically with Arabic script and scripture.

Yet the changing hierarchy of prestige, in the relation between Arabic script and romanized print form, is more complicated than this. The broader significance of this framing shift in linguistic hierarchies of language and script becomes clearer considering what happens to the accusative case of naming as Conrad turns from the Malay scriptworld of the Lingard trilogy to the Latin American scriptworld of *Nostromo*. This turn in Conrad's overall career is anticipated by a letter written in 1898 to the Scottish writer, traveler, and socialist R. B. Cunninghame Graham. Addressing his friend, first using Islamic honorifics—"Istaghfir Allah! O! Sheik Mohammed! I take refuge with the One the Invincible"—he then shifts to Spanish: "By all means Viva l'España!!!!" Conrad's comment comes in a letter famously revealing for the views that he expresses on the Spanish-American war.[35] In this same letter he performs his own revealing lexical shifting of scriptworlds. The shift from one scriptworld to another registers Conrad's turn from the Malay world of *Almayer's Folly* and *Lord Jim* to that of *Nostromo*, a turn in Conrad's overall career that presents two different sides to the case of English romanization. Incidentally, the OED's first selections of quotations from Conrad, all in the 1933 Supplement, and most concerning examples of "foreign" words recently adopted into English, seem to be drawn mostly from these works. I choose them, not only as different examples of the accusative case, but also because each illuminates how Conrad's narrative projects, as a whole, are generated by the effects of such lexical switching. Both, together, stage an imaginative turn *away* from the Malay trilogy, registered already in the letter from 1898—a switching from the Malay scene of *The Rescue* (the last in the trilogy projected with *Almayer's Folly*) to the Latin American scene of *Nostromo*.

(Lowercase) romanization effects a switching of loyalties and switching of scripts, less at the level of plot (*mythos*) or character (*ethos*), than at the level of *lexis*, as Aristotle puts it in *The Poetics* (at the level of the letter, the word, or the phrase ["diction" is sometimes how Aristotle's "lexis" gets translated]).[36] In turning to this micro-narrative level of the text, it may never be possible to separate those other parts of narrative—plot and character—along with the even larger, macro-narrative elements (genre, ideology, history).[37] What Conrad calls (in the same letter cited above) the "peripeties and accidents"[38] of life pivot on minute turns of phrasing and wording that link the smallest of lexical effects to transformative shifts in global political and historical perspective.

In its first appearance in *Lord Jim*, the phrase "They called him Tuan Jim" may not appear to carry the accusative charge of betrayal. Although the conditional clause that follows —"as one might say"—already insinuates an ironic gap between the transliteration "Tuan Jim" and the translation that follows ("Lord Jim"), it seems accusative only in the grammatical sense. Yet the fact that this covers up for the name he was "anxious... should not be pronounced," already attaches an accusative charge to the questionably translated title. The whole first part of the novel, with its inquest into Jim's "jump" from the *Patna*, reenforces the accusative charge that dogs Jim's name (the meeting with Marlow occurring over Jim's mistaken belief that he has been called a "wretched cur"). The court trial concerning the crew's abandonment of the ship carrying pilgrims back from Mecca, stages an example of the use of "tuan," more as accusation than respect when one of the Malay helmsmen addresses the official assessor, Captain Brierly, as "*that* white Tuan," insinuating that the white skippers may have had their own "secret reasons" for abandoning ship: "He was a man of great experience, and he wanted *that* white Tuan to know—he turned towards Brierly, who didn't raise his head—that he had acquired a knowledge of many things by serving white men on the sea for a great number of years . . ." (*Lord Jim*, 98–99). In the hierarchy of "respect" that Malays accord to Europeans, there is quite a range of potential interpretive possibilities, and *Lord Jim* opens up this range of possibilities to the fullest extent.

"Tuan," as a form of address in the accusative case, has deep roots in the lexical formation of Conrad's texts, going back to the first appearance of the word "Tuan" in *Almayer's Folly* (cited, incidentally, in the OED's entry on "Tuan"). There, it marks a complicated case of cross-cultural exchange, highlighting the hierarchy of languages and scripts with which that novel unfolds. "Tuan Almayer is speaking as a friend"—this is the Balinese prince, Dain Maroola, correcting Almayer who has mistaken him for the Arab trader Abdulla. "There is no Arab here" (*Almayer's*, 13)[39] he adds, a correction that is one of the earliest, if also one of the more cryptic, indications of the rivalry between "Lingard and Co." and Abdulla. A friendly accusation of mistaken identity, it poses a question of alliances amongst Europeans, Arabs, Malays, and Chinese (among others) that Almayer, in his "folly," will never fully be able to read correctly. It also harks back to the first dialogic exchange of the novel—"Kaspar! Makan!" The delayed decoding of what the Malay word "makan" means is accompanied by a reader's dawning awareness—spaced out over the narrative timing of the whole novel (which in turn frames the projected Malay trilogy to come, and indeed Conrad's entire literary career)—that this, too, has an accusatory charge. It is marked by the fact that she is *not* using the honorific title of respect, "Tuan," for her European husband.

When Conrad wrote *Lord Jim*, he was still trying to complete the Malay trilogy with which he began his career. The use of Malay titles is, then, in some senses still related to the romance of that so-called Lingard trilogy. The trilogy is called this after the name of the Englishman who vanishes in the first novel, to which the other two novels form prequels. Lingard is the vanishing Englishman who, as I suggested above, haunts the OED citations from the first two novels in the sequence. His absent presence is also marked by the trope of decaying letters on the house that Almayer is building: "Office: Lingard and Co." That trilogy invests its romance in a Malay scriptworld of honorific titles that the last novel, *The Rescue*, stages around Lingard's political alliance with the Malay Bugis prince and princess, Hassim and Immada. In some important respects, the translation of "Tuan" into "Lord Jim" echoes the way in which Lingard's title—"Rajah Laut"—evokes the historical era of British, white Rajahs (Sir James Brooke is the most memorable such figure) on whom Lingard was modeled. This romance is an important part of the contrast that Conrad sets up between the romanized scriptworld of European imperialism ("Lingard and Co.") and the Malay scriptworld of honorific titles on which the fable of Lingard's prestige precariously depends (the "Rajah Laut").

Yet "Tuan" is not precisely a title like "Rajah." It is, indeed, precisely *not* a title like Rajah. Late in the novel, when Cornelius is egging on Gentleman Brown, the first seemingly neutral grammatical case of Jim's title comes to be fully charged with insinuation and accusation—"They call him," said Cornelius scornfully, 'Tuan Jim here. As you may say Lord Jim'" (*Lord Jim*, 367). The way "Tuan" works, as a lexical switch word in this moment of *Lord Jim*, is not so much to effect a switching of loyalties between two different worldscripts, the way Lingard's title ("Rajah Laut") works in evoking the prestige of a Malay scriptworld transcribed from a worldscript of Arabic political and religious honorifics. Neither Cornelius nor Gentleman Brown, whom he is addressing (nor for that matter Marlow, who is narrating the dialogic exchange), has any kind of loyalty, solidarity, or affiliation with the Malay sovereignty and power that Lingard attempts to rescue, or himself embody, in relation to his title "Rajah Laut." Cornelius's explanation of Jim's "title" still rehearses that romanized transcription, transliteration, and translation of the Malay word "Tuan" given at the beginning of the novel, but here the accusative charge in Cornelius's "scornful" explanation discounts the significance of Jim's being called "Tuan," turning the term into an exaggerated title of prestige (Lord, king) that clearly has no sort of connection to the kind of formal respect marked by Lingard's title.

The lexical effect of "Tuan," here, has less to do with a rivalry between different worldscripts and more to do with a contest among scriptworlds occupying a shared spacing and timing of roman letters. It is less about the prestige of English titles as opposed to Malay titles, and more about the deflation of all hierarchical claims to entitlement across multiple languages and scripts.

Accentuating the difficulty raised by the OED's handling of the etymology of "tuan," as an adopted English word, it fully ironizes, in the process of romanized transliteration, what was once a term for respect. The effect is closer to what happens with Conrad's Latin American forms of address: "Our excellent Señor Mitchell"—or, indeed, "he whom the English called Nostromo." Cornelius's accusative address to Gentleman Brown and his motley creole crew, signaling the final tragic unraveling of Jim's prestige as leader amongst the Bugis, also signals that radical switching of global perspectives (of loyalties and scripts) that occurs when Conrad abandons the Malay worldscript of the Lingard trilogy and turns to the "Latin" scriptworld of *Nostromo*. In the letter of May 1898, this is registered in Conrad's switching from addressing Cunninghame Graham with the Arabic invocations "Istaghfir Allah! Sheik Mohammed!" to—"Viva l'España!"

In terms of plot, Cornelius's accusations and insinuations deflate the aura of English entitlement to lordship overseas. The lexical effect of "tuan," as ultimately revealed in Cornelius's accusative utterance, is to break the illusion of any kind of faithful, reliable, or trustworthy fit between identity and script, *ethos* and character, lexicon and script. If the Lingard trilogy is premised on the attempt to measure Lingard's English character against the Malay *ethos* of his title "Rajah Laut," *Lord Jim* considerably widens the gap between title and character as between language and scriptworld. In this respect, it reveals what happens when Conrad switches from his Malay-speaking to his Spanish American-speaking fictions. The first (especially in *The Rescue*) opposes Malay-Arabic and English-roman worldscripts and scriptworlds as opposing *ethos*, religion, culture, and identity. With *Nostromo*, a subtler, more unsettling switching takes place between two different, but overlapping roman scripts. In the modern Penguin edition of the novel, on the very first page, the word *estancias* is italicized, marking a break from the roman font of the page, and suggesting a marked difference between the English medium of roman print and the Spanish lexicon of the novel's imagined Latin American community. Although not, in fact, marked by a shift between italicized and roman script in the original print editions, the fictive register of this difference is (arguably) even more unsettling without such graphic marks—all the languages and scripts of the novel's characters are rendered in the same romanized print form. "Tuan Jim" looks toward the lexical effects of this kind of English romanization of romanization. This romanization intensifies and unsettles the gap between lexicon and scriptworld required to sustain the fiction of any Conradian, English framing of a non-English-speaking world.

Put another way, English romanization reveals how this gap between English as worldscript, and all the other languages underwriting that script, has been, all along, generative of the Conradian narrative. It helps pinpoint that small hinge, or break between *lexis* and *ethos*, between speech-pattern (as captured in writing) and character or temperament that plots the fable of identity whose betrayal generates those sudden twists and turns ("peripeties and accidents," as Conrad puts it) in the Conradian text. At the micro-narrative level, this is what always threatens to erupt in the accusative cases of Conradian naming. It is, for example, just below the surface of the way Almayer's wife addresses her husband at the beginning of *Almayer's Folly*, "Kaspar! Makan!" It is the moment when—potentially, at least in fiction—the power of English (its power to represent all the other languages and scripts) is used to write back in a language that is not only English and a script that is not only its romanized print form.

Nostromo, as a name, involves more than any seemingly simple alternation between the spelling out of English and Spanish. Captain Mitchell's English "mispronunciation" translates the Italian term for "bos'n" into a heroic epithet adopted by various linguistic communities—a crossing of at least English, Italian, and Spanish, entirely characteristic of the novel's romanization of Latin American titles. Giorgio Viola's formulation—"he whom the English called Nostromo" (*Nostromo*, 29)—suggests that the sense in which the hybrid Anglo-Italian carries an accusative charge, something made even clearer in his wife's implication that the name of "our Nostromo" encodes a constitutive betrayal of his own people: "He would take a name that is properly no word from them" (*Nostromo*, 23). The name knits solidarity and conflict together into a trope of Conradian betrayal, legible at all levels—plot, character, and diction. Its own peculiar problem of transcription, transliteration, and translation (none of these are easily explained) reveals how the craft of Conrad's English has always depended on an ongoing romanization—here a global *latinization*, or Latin Americanization—that opens English romanized print form to a range of shifting national, political, racial, historical, and geopolitical loyalties.

The scriptworlds of Conrad's fiction are always premised on a switching within, as well as between, worldscripts. The Oceanic Steam Navigation Company's imposition of Roman names and Roman gods offers an almost classical instance: "Their names, the names of all mythology, became the household words of a coast that had never been ruled by the gods of Olympus. The *Juno* ... the *Saturn* ... the *Ganymede* ... the *Cerberus*" (*Nostromo*, 9–10). These "gods of Olympus" have already undergone a transformation from Greek to Latin scripts, a classical switching of worldscripts so deeply engrained within the English invocation of "all mythology." The names evoke a long historical displacement and forgetting—multiple conflicts, solidarities, and betrayals—involved in the break between Greek and Latin worldscripts (and consolidated by the hegemony of English). The names of these steamships reveal a constitutive doubling and tripling of scriptworlds and worldscripts. And as with the evocation of the names of Conrad's ships—especially steamships like the *Judea* of "Youth: A Narrative" and the *Patna* of *Lord Jim*—their roman lettering betrays perspectival shifts in global cultural and political loyalties. As with ship names, so with titles. In a gesture reminiscent of Conrad's May 1898 letter to Cunninghame Graham, Giorgio Viola's political solidarities are signaled (twice) by invoking an Arabic scriptworld: "'the Garibaldino' (as Mohammedans are called after their prophet)" (*Nostromo*, 16); and "He, Giorgio, had reached the rank of ensign—alferez." The word "alferez" provides a sort of algorithm for this English global latinization of romanization, where the switching between two scriptworlds will almost always involve a third: here, the Arabic underwriting the Spanish title of the English text. What all these cases of the accusative have in common, is a process of English romanization that implicates multiple scriptworlds and worldscripts in an unpredictable switching of loyalties and historical perspectives.

The accusative case reveals a grammatical principle of sorts, underlying the various chronotopes of romanization found throughout Conrad. This micronarrative lexical effect depends, first, on romanization in the sense of switching from one worldscript to another. This is what is on display in the romanization of Malay titles and the plot of the Lingard trilogy's displacement, abandonment, and betrayal of an Arabic scriptworld of sovereignty, power, and identity. However, it also depends on a shifting hierarchy of relations between scriptworlds and the worldscripts used to measure those scriptworlds: not just a rivalry between Arabic and roman worldscripts, for example, but a shift in the way those worldscripts relate to the various different languages they have historically, or traditionally scripted. The case of English romanization reveals a complex, even contradictory process, simultaneously standardizing the prestige of English as worldscript, but one that is premised on its own displacement, abandonment, and betrayal. All the accusative cases of naming (beginning with Mrs. Almayer's opening call to dinner and extending to the long list of titles and names of Conrad's ships and men) point to a much more complex switching of scripts (and loyalties) than any switching between two supposedly self-contained scriptworlds or rivalry between two mutually exclusive worldscripts. So, for example, the romanized Malay that inaugurates Conrad's literary career is premised on a switching between many more scriptworlds than just the Arabic and the roman worldscripts. Behind the opening address of *Almayer's Folly*, and behind each of that novel's uses of the word "Tuan," there is also a switching between (at least) Buginese, Javanese, and Chinese scriptworlds (to be explored more fully in Chapter 3). All these Conradian examples of the accusative case reveal a constant process of transcription, transliteration, and translation, opening Conrad's English to a perspectival switching of loyalties and switching of scripts, the ceaseless work of the worldscript of global latinized or romanized print form betraying all its own other scriptworlds.

Joycean "iSpace" and the Conradian "blank space"

Chronotopes of romanization in Conrad's fiction illuminate how English functions as a hegemonic worldscript mediating between multiple different scriptworlds. All the accusative cases of naming that I have highlighted, turn on the contradictory and ambiguous effect with which English assumes a privileged position in the hierarchy of relations between languages and scripts. Acting as if English were heir to the global worldscript that Romanization created out of its own Latin scriptworld in antiquity, the work of modern, romanized transliteration, in effect, makes English the site of a profoundly destabilizing encounter between worldscripts and scriptworlds. Now, I want to compare what Conrad does with English to the example of James Joyce, in order to consider how both situate the case of English romanization within a broader transformation of global print media.

The sociolinguistic case of conversion from Arabic script to romanized print already provides one important example of how the global turn toward romanization reforms entails a broader transformation in print media. In this case, the change involves a shift from manuscript to print culture: from the Arabic, or *jawi* script used in traditional Malay forms of circulating manuscripts from around the year 1600 until the nineteenth century, to the *rumi* script that began to dominate in the later part of the nineteenth century with the spread of print newspapers and books. The implications of this transformation are far-reaching. It provided the conditions, for example, for the emergence of the new anti-colonial, nationalist language, forged through the romanized print form of newspapers, circulated among readers from a wide variety of different linguistic backgrounds throughout the Dutch-controlled East Indies. The shift makes the medium of romanized print Malay the site of a historical and geographical unfolding of simultaneously colonial and anti-colonial imaginings.

Intersecting with this shift from manuscript to print culture in the Malay scriptworld, is the rise of new global forms of telecommunication, accompanied by the use of the telegraph, the telephone, the typewriter, and other related technologies. It is this network of new media that prompts Marshall McLuhan, Walter Ong, and Jacques Derrida to reconceptualize the older medium of print. Each theorist, as noted above, characterizes the transformation somewhat differently. McLuhan's is perhaps the most hyperbolic, with its emphasis on the "implosion" of print culture with the onset of electric telecommunications ("our electric extensions of ourselves simply by-pass space and time").[40] For Ong, the new media transform the old medium of print literacy, but without substantially altering the significance of the way alphabetic print culture spatializes oral temporality: "sequential processing and spatialising of the word, initiated by writing and raised to a new order of intensity by print, is further intensified by the computer."[41] For Derrida, print culture is something that cannot be historicized (either hyperbolically as with McLuhan or in the more positivist historicizing of Ong), because the phonetic timing and spacing of letters is an inherently unstable textual movement of difference (*différance*) and spacing (*espacement*).[42] Each offers insights into the various different levels at which romanization constitutes the timing and spacing of print culture. Implicit in all these theoretical considerations of the changing medium of print—but elided, too, in each case—is the transliterating function of roman letters. To explore that implicit (but elided) question of (lowercase) romanization, I compare the way in which Conrad and Joyce each give it artistic form in the chronotopes of, respectively, the "blank space" on the map of Africa in *Heart of Darkness* and the "iSpace" of *Finnegans Wake*.

Finnegans Wake (a touchstone for McLuhan, Ong, and Derrida) is perhaps the most famous, most notorious, most extreme example of English modernist experimentation with the phonetic and typographic spacing and timing of roman letters. More exuberant than the examples of the accusative case I have just explored at the root of Conrad's work, what Joyce does with the effects of romanization can also more easily be connected to the development of computer coding, cybernetic theory, and digital technologies that would transform print culture in the middle of the twentieth century. The chronotope of romanization in Conrad may seem quite traditional compared with what Lydia Liu describes as the *"mise en abîme* of graphic spacing, punctuation marks, irregular types, and letter sequences" in *Finnegans Wake*.[43] She is referring specifically to the passage at the end of the so-called "mamafesta" section (*Wake*, Book 1, Chapter 5) in which Joyce coins the term "iSpace." The passage illustrates her argument about the "ideographic turn" in which "the phonetic alphabet" becomes "a system of actual or potential ideograms." "iSpace" felicitously captures the way that *Finnegans Wake* anticipated, indeed inspired, theorists involved in the development of cybernetic theory. "Joyce's literary experiment," Liu argues, "suggests that the ideographic view of alphabetical writing did not originate with [Claude] Shannon or [Norbert] Wiener but rather asserted itself through an extraordinary period of intellectual fermentation in the early decades of the twentieth century marked by a fascination with technical inscription, psychic energy, and prosthetic machines."[44]

Conrad's chronotopes of romanization belong to this moment in media history as well. By comparison to Joyce's experiments, explicitly taken up by Shannon and Wiener, Conrad's experiments may appear to look more to older communication technologies. Joyce's "iSpace" sounds like it already inhabits the electronic world of iMacs and iPhones. By contrast, the trope of the "blank space" on the map of Africa, from the opening to *Heart of Darkness*, harks back to an older technology of cartography and print. Print technology is crucial for the way in which that famous trope grounds the symbolism of the novella's title, an essential part of Conrad's critique of European representations of Africa as the "dark continent" and, simultaneously, as Achebe points out, a repetition of that racist "image of Africa." The "blank space," as Marlow points out in explaining his childhood "passion for maps," "was not a blank space any more." This critique of the colonial fantasy of adventure, turns into a highly condensed chronotope of romanization—"It had got filled since my boyhood with rivers and lakes and names" (*Youth*, 52). Although none of those "rivers" and "lakes" are actually named (reinforcing Achebe's point about the negation of African languages in the novella), it is the imposition of those names on the cartographic space of the map that leads to the critical reversal in the trope: "It had become a place of darkness." That reversal encapsulates the colonial nightmare, the "horror" that Marlow's narrative will go on to unfold around the story of Kurtz (as the "darkness" imposed on Africa, even if that "darkness" will also repeatedly get reinscribed as the racist "image of Africa" of Achebe's critique). The highly condensed, temporal, and historical displacement of this iconic trope of colonial fantasy is also (as has less often been observed) a highly condensed reflection on the function of naming places on the map. Whether in the colonial imposition of "European-bestowed names,"[45] or in the transliteration from African names, the romanized print form of cartographic displacement makes this one of the most condensed examples of the chronotope of romanization in Conrad's *oeuvre*.[46]

At the generative heart of both Joyce's "iSpace" and Conrad's "blank space," romanized transliteration mediates the transformation from older technologies of typography and print to the new media networks of telecommunications, computer coding, and digital electronics. N. Katherine Hayles offers a useful overview of the broadest horizon of media history within which to situate the sociolinguistic phenomenon of (lowercase) romanization, condensed into the aesthetic form of Conrad's and Joyce's chronotopes of romanization. She presents this in the heuristic distinction between the three "worldviews" of "speech," "writing," and "computer code." Characterizing the shift from the worldview of "speech" to that of "print" in terms of Derrida's concept of "*différance*" (where the spacing of print results in an indefinite "deferral" of signification), Hayles argues that the advent of digital media enacts a radical transformation from a worldview premised on the "durably imprinted" text, to a worldview premised on the "flickering signification underwritten by binary digits."[47] Faced with the destabilizing effects of digital processing on any definition of the "text," Hayles uses the terms "intermediation" and "media translation" (also adapting the term "remediation") to consider what happens when print culture gets displaced by digital media. Although none of these terms directly addresses the question of (lowercase) romanization that I am considering here, they all point toward the function of romanized transliteration in the "intermediation," "media translation," or "remediation" of print and electronic media.[48]

Consider the passage from *Finnegans Wake* where Joyce formulates the term "iSpace":

> These paper wounds, four in type, were gradually and correctly understood to mean stop, please stop, do please stop, and O do please stop respectively, and following up their one true clue, the circumflexuous wall of a singleminded men's asylum, accentuated by bi tso fb rok engl a ssan dspl itch ina, — Yard inquiries pointed out → that they ad bîn "provoked" ay ˄ fork, of à grave Brofèsor; àth é's Brèak — fast — table; ; acùtely profèššionally *piquéd*, to introdùce a notion of time [ùpon à plane (?) sù ' ' fàç'e'] by pùnct! ingh oles (sic) in iSpace?! (*Wake*, 124)

This whole passage helpfully illustrates Lydia Liu's argument (discussed earlier). Yet in order to highlight the technical (and technological) importance of romanized transliteration, I want to dwell on one aspect that Liu overlooks: its exaggerated emphasis on diacritical marks.

As Tekla Mecsnóber notes, the passage is somewhat "puzzling"—and also rather unique in the *Wake*—for what it shows about Joyce's long-standing "preoccupation with diacritics."[49] Although clearly showcasing a rich variety of diacritical marks (and, as Mecsnóber also notes, many more than elsewhere in the *Wake*), "the diacritics that Joyce uses here (the circumflex, acute and grave accents, the cedilla, and the caron) do not suggest any particular language and are difficult to interpret in any systematic way."[50] Mecsnóber points to two different (but related) ways of viewing the function of diacritical marks: in the first case, diacritical marks are added to adapt the basic letters of the alphabet to a "particular language" (as with French, German, Hungarian, or Turkish); in the second case, diacritical marks are used to turn the basic letters of the alphabet into a universal phonetic system, disconnected from any particular language. On the evidence of an earlier draft (with many more diacritical marks, and where "iSpace" appears with an over-ring above the letter "a"— "iSpåce") Mecsnóber argues that "what Joyce meant to evoke here were not national alphabets but, primarily, phonetic notations." She goes on to provide an illuminating paraphrase of the passage in question: "the grave professor tries to introduce a notion of time upon a plane surface by making marks that indicate the precise pronunciation (in time) of the letters written on the surface of the sheet of paper."[51]

Mecsnóber emphasizes Joyce's changing interest in diacritical marks as developed from *Ulysses* through the composition of *Finnegans Wake*, and I will return to this argument in a moment. Her reading also provides a helpful reminder of the importance of Joyce's concern, overall, for a variety of languages, scripts, and the history of writing systems (one of the things that makes Joyce such an important touchstone for McLuhan, Ong, Derrida, Liu, and other media theorists). The particular section in which "iSpace" appears, might itself be read as a kind of virtuoso rehearsal of the history of print media. Such a reading should give pause before characterizing the trope of "iSpace" as a sign of the shift from print to digital media. Following Hayles's distinction between the "durably imprinted" form of the pre-digital forms of writing and the "flickering signification" of computer code, it would seem that Joyce's "iSpace" passage is ineluctably bound to the "durably imprinted" form of print. The "*mise en abîme*" into graphic and phonemic play that Liu emphasizes is premised on the conceit of a document printed in a particular script ("Hanno O'Nonhanno's unbrookable script") that appears to have "no signs of punctuation of any sort" (*Wake*, 123). Only once held in a certain way ("holding the verso against a lit rush"), the punctuation marks appear as "paper wounds." What Joyce is doing here depends on the conception of the "durably imprinted" text, pushing (to an extreme) the sense in which that space is made readable through the material marks of punctuation and diacritical notations that enable the eye to see in the graphemic sign what the ear can then phonetically hear. Beginning with the "unbrookable" script, it improvises a miniature version of that chronotope of English romanization with which the whole of the *Wake* unfolds, continually rehearsing versions of the same old story of letters (the way the alphabet arose, the emergence of writing, and the consolidation of a variety of different, standardized print forms using diacritical marks). In the process, this passage serves as a reminder that Joyce's experiment is still bound by, even as it pushes the limits of, that space of print culture Hayles describes as the worldview of "writing."[52]

Yet it is precisely that "durably imprinted" form that stages the "ideographic turn" Liu is describing. Here is where the narrower focus on diacritical marks may illuminate the role of (lowercase) romanization in the mediation of that transformation, whereby the older medium of print anticipates the newer interface of computer coding. Although Mecsnóber argues that Joyce originally intended to have the diacritics evoke a phonetic system rather than a distinct alphabet, the "puzzle" of the passage may be more revealing for evoking *neither* a distinct alphabet *nor* a phonetic system, but rather the impasse (for readers, writers, printers, and characters) of being caught between the two.

The "puzzle" of diacritics is related to the riddle of Ong's insistence that there are "many scripts, but only one alphabet." The function of diacritical marks at first seems to confirm Ong's point, since the marks are added to the "one alphabet" to serve the phonetic needs of different languages. This results, however, in many rival alphabetic systems, as illuminated by Mecsnóber's discussion of the way that diacritics produce the appearance of proliferating forms of distinct and different national alphabets (Hungarian, Gaelic, German). Joyce's fascination with the politics of national alphabets and scripts is evident in certain key passages of *Ulysses*.[53] In Mecsnóber's reading, Joyce's experimentation with diacritics mark these many contested alphabets, with a turn, in the *Wake*, toward one single, international phonetic worldscript. Her reading of the "iSpace" passage sees a shift in Joyce's turn from "national" to "international diacritics": "By the time he was preparing the first complete edition of the *Wake*, he had clearly lost the eagerness with which he had explored national diacritics in his late 1921 additions to *Ulysses* and added international diacritics to the Wakean mamafesta in 1925."[54]

Considering this shift in relation to the chronotope of romanization in Joyce's work, the diacritical marks of "iSpace" may be read as the impasse of roman letters that are neither a national alphabet nor an international phonetic system. This, indeed, is the space ("iSpace") of Joyce's English. All those diacritical marks—circumflex, acute and grave accents, cedilla, caron—might, at first, appear to signal a distinct alphabet adapted to a language other than English. If, parodically, such an alphabet is evoked, it is done so by using the spacing and timing of the English alphabet—where, at least initially and by presumption, the space of English is the unmarked roman letters as they appear (without accents) on the page. Yet, that supposedly neutral, unmarked space is what is, after all, marked by diacritical accents, turning reading in space ("iSpace") into a parody of what needs to be added to the alphabet in order to pronounce the sequence of letters on the printed page. In this sense, Joyce's "iSpace" epitomizes the case of English romanization as the attempt to use the unmarked letters of the (English) alphabet to mediate between all the world's languages and scripts.[55]

Already in *Ulysses*, Joyce developed chronotopes of romanization that anticipate the moment that Lydia Liu calls the "ideographic turn" when the English phonetic alphabet ("basically English")[56] as developed by C. K. Ogden and Claude Shannon, in conjunction with the experiments of the *Wake*, is transformed into the alphanumeric code for computational systems. The title of *Ulysses*, with the Romanized form of its allusion to Homer's *Odyssey*, entails a perspectival and historical shift from (uppercase) Romanization to (lowercase) romanization, from the role of Latin letters in the Roman Empire to the role of English letters in modern Ireland. In the so-called "Ithaca" chapter, which refracts the interaction between Stephen Dedalus and Leopold Bloom, through a catechism of questions, comparing and contrasting their respective worldviews, Joyce presents a revealing counterpointing of each character's sense of the development of the alphabet:

> In what common study did their mutual reflections merge?
>
> The increasing simplification traceable from the Egyptian epigraphic hieroglyphs to the Greek and Roman alphabets and the anticipation of modern stenography and telegraphic code in the cuneiform inscriptions (Semitic) and the virgular quinquecostate ogham writing (Celtic). (*Ulysses*, 689)

If the first part of the response would appear to have both Bloom and Stephen recount the linear history of the development of what Ong, following McLuhan, calls the "one alphabet," the second part of the response looks to the new order of information systems already supplanting alphabetic writing. In its condensed account of the world's writing systems, it describes a process of "simplification" (alphabetic writing) and then information coding that implicitly situates romanization between the two.

This example foregrounds the difference between the way *Ulysses* and *Finnegans Wake* each develops the chronotope of romanization. While *Ulysses* tracks the shift outlined in the OED's different definitions from Romanization (the imposition of Roman culture in ancient times) through Romanize (associated with the Catholic church), to English romanization (the role of English letters in contemporary Ireland), *Finnegans Wake* is almost entirely devoted to turning "basically English" into the worldscript that might access (almost) all scripts. One characteristic formulation for *Wake*'s worldscript is evoked at the beginning of Book II as "celtelleneteutoslavzendlatinsoundscript" (*Wake*, 219). Here, all the languages are merged together into a single line of roman letters that stands in contrast to the way diacritics mark either a universal phonetic sound or the sound of a particular language. The chronotope of romanization in Joyce presents the case of English (lowercase) romanization caught on the cusp between alphabet and code.

By contrast to the print-bound "iSpace" anticipating a world to come of computer coding, the "blank space" of Conrad's *Heart of Darkness*, quintessential trope and topos of cartographic print technology, in some ways more directly evokes the worldview of computer code. In its formalist abstraction of the romanized print form of those "rivers, lakes, and names" that have turned Central Africa into "a place of darkness," the "blank space" condenses the work of romanized transliteration even more radically than the examples of the accusative case discussed above. The cartographic formalism of the trope echoes the mathematical formalism with which Claude Shannon (in 1948) will draw from the dots and dashes of Morse code to invent the twenty-seventh letter of the English alphabet—the "space"—to complete what Liu calls the "ideographic" turn, transforming the English alphabet into the alphanumerical code for computational systems.

The chronotope of romanization, condensed in the trope of the "blank space" on the map of Africa, is framed in advance by that sudden switching of historical and geographical coordinates, precipitated by Marlow's first entrance: "And this also . . . has been one of the dark places of the earth" (*Youth*, 48). In this famous opening to *Heart of Darkness*, there is something analogous to the perspectival shifting of worldscript and scriptworld that accompanies Conrad's turn from a scriptworld of Malay titles and entitlement to the worldscript of romanized print form. Like the effect of Joyce's title *Ulysses*, this offers a paradigmatic, literary, modernist instantiation of the shift from (uppercase) Romanization to (lowercase) romanization. When Marlow reframes the primary narrator's nationalist evocation of the "great spirit" of "the ships and the men" of the British Empire, he creates a perspectival switching back and forth between (uppercase) Romanization and (lowercase) romanization. Reaching back before the period of the frame narrator's national-historical perspective, which extols "the great knights-errant of the sea," Marlow compares the present to "very old times": "I was thinking of very old times, when the Romans first came here, nineteen hundred years ago—the other day . . . . Light came out of this river since—you say Knights? Yes, but it is like a running blaze on a plain, like a flash of lightning in the clouds. We live in the flicker" (*Youth*, 49).

"We live in the flicker": it may only be coincidence that this phrase anticipates Hayles's notion of "flickering signification underwritten by binary digits."[57] Consider, though, how the timing and spacing of this silent K-effect in Marlow's "you say Knights?" reveals the interrelation between each of Hayles's three "worldviews." First, it marks the way in which roman letters are used to transcribe the "speech" of Marlow as oral storyteller. Whether or not the reader is conscious of the effect of this graphic mark, it reinforces the framing fiction of an oral story that has been then (second) transcribed into written form. Yet the typographic emphasis on the capital K foregrounds the fact that the speaking Marlow occupies the same space and time of the printed page as the frame narrator, calling attention to uneven effects of phonetic and orthographic variations involved in the standardization of romanized English print. The combination of both of these reading-effects turns the roman letter K, in a third sense, into a sort of switch-code, alternating back and forth between phonemic and graphemic effects meant to be read together without having to choose between the two.[58] This K-effect condenses and displaces into a single sign, the "**knights**-errant of the sea" and the "**night** of time," in the primary narrator's earlier phrase, signaling Marlow's sudden foreshortening of the temporal and spatial perspectives characterized in the shift from (uppercase) Romanization to (lowercase) romanization. The capitalized roman letter K momentarily reveals a semiotic code at work in the roman letters of Conrad's text. It recalls the operation of computer code that Hayles calls "flickering signification." The coding of this K-effect reveals, moreover, how Marlow's entrance reorganizes narrative sequence, not only for *Heart of Darkness* (in the shift from Romanization to romanization), but also for all three of the Marlow tales Conrad originally conceived as a sequence ("Youth: A Narrative," *Heart of Darkness*, and the story that became *Lord Jim*), and then, by extension, for Conrad's work as a whole, underwriting all of Conrad's narratives with the binary alternation of C and K in the K-effect of his authorial signature.

When the first narrator writes that the Thames "had borne all the ships whose names are like jewels flashing in the night of time," the imagery suggests the development of an international system of naval codes, including the adoption of Morse code, which served, as Lydia Liu argues, as a "prototype for information theory,"[59] underpinning, too, the use of the terms "code," "sign," and "signal" by Charles Sanders Peirce and Ferdinand de Saussure. These are the new forms of coding and information systems evoked in the second part of Bloom's and Stephen's mutual reflections on writing systems in *Ulysses*. Marlow's "you say Knights?" reformulates this link between the technology of communication systems, Morse code, and the spacing and timing of romanized print. Read in sequence, it tends to conceal the semiotic code, even as it enacts that concealment as forgetting in the spacing and timing of the narrative shift from frame narrator to Marlow. The compressed phonemic and graphemic play on "nights" and "knights" elides the linguistic artifice of the narrator's imagery, which simultaneously suggests semaphore, and foregrounds the romanized letters in the writing of ships' names. Instead, Marlow provides a natural image, a flash of lightning; and moreover, one that then appears to be replacing another natural image, the daily rolling of the earth and the rising and setting sun.

Marlow's rhetorical rescripting of the earlier passage seems to have suggestively influenced what McLuhan does when he blurs the difference between (uppercase) Romanization and (lowercase) romanization in his account of "the phonetic alphabet":

> The phonetic alphabet is a unique technology. There have been many kinds of writing, pictographic and syllabic, but there is only one phonetic alphabet in which semantically meaningless letters are used to correspond to semantically meaningless sounds. . . . The phonetically written word sacrifices worlds of meaning and perception that were secured by forms like the hieroglyph and the Chinese ideogram. These culturally richer forms of writing, however, offered men no means of sudden transfer from the magically discontinuous and traditional world of the tribal word into the cool and uniform visual medium. Many centuries of ideogrammic use have not threatened the seamless web of family and tribal subtleties of Chinese society. On the other hand, a single generation of alphabetic literacy suffices in Africa today, as in Gaul two thousand years ago, to release the individual initially, at least, from the tribal web.[60]

McLuhan makes explicit the sense of (uppercase) Romanization (the imposition of the roman alphabet) implied in Marlow's reference to the Roman conquest. As noted earlier, what McLuhan misses is the transliterating function of romanization in mediating between a much broader variety of languages and scripts throughout "Africa today." That mediating function is at work as well in the problem of (lowercase) romanization that Conrad's passage foregrounds as a problem of sequential reading: the multiple effects of phonetic, grammatological, and (also) ideogrammatic marks at work in the K-effect of Marlow's "you say Knights?" All of this is what gets condensed and displaced into the trope of the "blank space."

McLuhan's implicit reference to *Heart of Darkness* is made explicit later, when he suggestively quotes Conrad (he is in fact misquoting Conrad): "The implosive (compressional) character of the electric technology plays the disk or film of Western man backward, into the heart of tribal darkness, or into what Joseph Conrad called 'the Africa within.'"[61] McLuhan's suggestive misreading of Conrad may be anachronistic, but it also captures an important truth about the multimedia effects of the Conradian trope of the "blank space" of Africa. It bears repeating that what is elided in this suggestive evocation is the mediating effect of romanized transliteration. McLuhan's insistence that "there is only one phonetic alphabet" not only simplifies the multiplicity of European alphabets at work in the late nineteenth-century mapping of Africa; it also displaces other forms of script, and above all Arabic script, the dominant writing system in Central and Eastern Africa prior to the European imposition of romanized print forms.

The silent elision of Arabic worldscript plays as important a role in the Conradian chronotope of the "blank space" as it does in the changing archive of the OED. McLuhan is, arguably, simply repeating the elision of Conrad's trope, compounding that distorted image of Africa—as so many of us always do with every variation of Conrad's title *Heart of Darkness* (as with McLuhan's "heart of tribal darkness")—that imposes, again and again, the displacement of prior mappings of Africa. Chinua Achebe's critique remains as relevant as ever: *Heart of Darkness* negates African languages. To which we might add— languages *and* scripts, including the form of Arabic (*ajami*) used for a range of African languages. This negation lies at the heart of the media transformation which concerns McLuhan here, although, ironically, he confuses it with the message. The "blank space" is precisely an abstraction—a negation— of the forms of writing involved in mapping Africa. As important as the shift from (uppercase) Romanization to (lowercase) romanization, the displacement of Arabic script is inseparable from the idealized instrumentality of that alphabet which McLuhan universalizes as the one and only, "unique" "phonetic alphabet."

The way in which Conrad's "blank space" turns the Victorian topos and trope of the "dark continent" into a chronotope of romanization, has a revealing counterpoint in the recurring motif of the Nile in *Finnegans Wake*. For Joyce, the Victorian obsession with the search for the Central African source of the Nile enables a series of rich puns on the name of the river (such as "Nihil" [*Wake*, 202] and "Nil" [*Wake*, 598]). Joyce himself glossed the coded significance of this loaded pun, explaining as "the source of the Nile" the first reference in the phrase "Livia Noanswa?" and the last reference in the phrase "Victorias neanzas." As Laurent Milesi explains, "Out of nil(e) comes nothing ... or paradoxically too much: the question put to the source, deemed to be lost and silent, presupposes a unique origin in Victoria Nyanza (i.e. Lake), the source of the White Nile only (through the Albert Nyanza), and thus fails to obtain an answer."[62] The historical references are to Victorian British attempts to find the Nile's source—what Conrad, rewriting Marlow's map-pointing memory as his own, described as "the news of the existence of Tanganyika and of Victoria Nyanza."[63] As historian Adrian S. Wisnicki explains, the record of this notorious moment of Victorian British exploration created "Africa's discursive darkness" around a failure to read the Arab and local documentation of the very thing—the source of the River Nile—that was then figured as the "Dark Unknown."⁶⁴

There is considerably more cryptic symbolism and wordplay in Joyce's version of the Conradian "blank space" of Central Africa, but Joyce's motif also presents an embedded chronotope of romanization. Stephen Heath's explication of the recurrent Nile motif draws attention to its links with the all-important *Wakean* motif of the alphabet: "The question of origins, getting back. Suppose we try finding the unknown source of a great river. ALP carries with her the Alpheus, the sacred river of Arcadia, described by Plutarch as deriving from the sun, and no doubt all rivers too but most especially the Nile, supremely invested with religion and myth, beginnings."⁶⁵ Laurent Milesis, citing Heath, notes "ALP, long for Δ and short for Alph . . . bears the root involved in the process of linguistic derivation and as such, its bed is also the "allaphbed" (18.18) or riverbed bearing the first letter (aleph) of the Biblical language, whose alphabet lies at the origin of all Western alphabets."⁶⁶ Joyce's own gloss, again, offers a kind of algorithm for this more cryptic version of the Conradian "blank space" on the map of Africa: "the source of the Nile, later supposed to represent ⊔ + Δ."⁶⁷

The same "ideographic" turn, then, is at work in Joycean "iSpace" and the Conradian "blank space" on the map of Africa. Both anticipate the mathematical formalism of Shannon's invention of the "space" as twenty-seventh letter of the English alphabet, completing Liu's "ideographic" turn.⁶⁸ This media transformation, moreover, is anticipated already in the K-effect of the OED's attempt to track the historical roots of "naturalized" and "unnaturalized" English words in relation, simultaneously, to their origins in the roman alphabet and to the foreign languages and scripts from which they come. In short, each passage of English text (from Conrad, from Joyce, from the OED) is the result of a complex, multilayered, and ongoing effect of romanization. English becomes the site of an ongoing romanized transliteration of multiple languages, scripts, and cultures. For both Conrad and Joyce, the sociolinguistic phenomenon of romanization is reconstituted in chronotopes of romanized English print form (heard, seen, in the silence and darkness of print: "blank space"; "iSpace"). The case of English romanization enacts a transformation in the space-time of print culture: simultaneously anticipating the passage of romanized print into digital text (Joycean "iSpace") and showing how the digital passage of text reenacts (even after digitization) the problem of print romanization (the Conradian "blank space").

The blank space that is introduced into the OED by the displacement of Arabic script makes the phonetic spelling out of English letters (e.g., *tuan, tuwan*—"tuan") the measure for an ambiguous relation between worldscript and scriptworld. James Joyce famously submits this ambiguous relation to the extended paronomasia of *Finnegans Wake*. The *Wake* deliberately opens up those gaps and silences at work in the OED's process of romanization, turning the "allforabit" (*Wake*, 19) into "bits of broken glass and split china"—spelled out, however, "bi tso fb rok engl a ssan dspl itch ina"—turning the timing and spacing of roman letters into what the *Wake* improvises as "iSpace" (*Wake*, 124). In another telling example, Joyce uses the Malay word "Tuan" as an invitation to see the word for "Lord" in "Tuan" but to spell out the letters as if they sounded like "turn"—"Tuan about whattinghim!" punning on the lines of the English song "Turn again Whittington . . . Lord Mayor of London" (*Wake*, 346). What the Conradian "blank space" reveals about these contrasting instances of the sounding and spacing out of roman letters is the extent to which both turn on a hidden hierarchy of language and script, of worldscripts and scriptworlds. Where the OED makes standardized English the privileged space, mediating between language and script, and between the worldscript of its romanized print form and the scriptworld of other languages, and where Joyce opens English to the "iSpace" of an exuberant polysemic play on all languages and all scripts, the Conradian "blank space" turns English into a place of constant switching between languages and scripts.

Both the Conradian "blank space" and the Joycean "iSpace" are chronotopes of English modernist experimentation with the typographic spelling of roman letters. Both may be understood as artistic ways of reshaping the same sociolinguistic historical phenomenon. Each calls attention in different ways to the prestige of English in orchestrating a multilingual, multiscript use of roman letters. Both together stage English as a multimedia transformation in forms of print worldwide, each anticipating the use of the basic English alphabet as a template for the digital conversion of letters into alphanumeric computer coding.

2
The Russian Face of Romanization: The K in Conrad and Kafka

In this chapter, I explore how Conrad's mid-career turn to the subject of Russia reveals a sociolinguistic feature of romanization characteristic of the changing face of Central Europe at the beginning of the twentieth century. The Russian face of the phenomenon of romanization surfaces in the way that Conrad makes thematic use of Cyrillic script, especially in *Under Western Eyes*; but its implications extend beyond the particular features of Cyrillic, involving questions of writing, script, and identity across European languages and scripts. These questions are condensed in the way that the letter K functions as an index of the relation between language, identity, and script in the work of both Conrad and Kafka.

Although Conrad's Polish childhood was spent "under the oppressive shadow of the great Russian Empire" (as he puts it in his autobiographical reminiscences, *A Personal Record* [24]), Conrad repeatedly claimed not to know Russian. In a 1922 letter to George T. Keating, attempting to correct H. L. Mencken's "harping on my Sclavonism," he wrote: "If he means that I have been influenced by so-called Slavonic literature then he is utterly wrong. I suppose he means Russian; but as a matter of fact I never knew Russian. The few novels I have read I have read in translation."[1] In 1917, he wrote to Edward Garnett: "The trouble is that I too don't know Russian; I don't even know the alphabet."[2] It may, perhaps, be that Conrad never formally learned Russian, or forgot whatever Russian he learned as a child, but these disavowals of any firsthand knowledge of Russian are also part of a long-standing attempt to repudiate any affiliation of Russian with his Polish background.

A vexed relation to Russia informs all of Conrad's work, but it was not until midway through his writing career that he sought to correct the way critics characterized his Polish background as "Slav," "Slavonic," or with the label "Sclavonism." The accusation that he was "a man without country and language" (Conrad's paraphrase of a 1908 review by Robert Lynd that also compared his work to Russian writers) provoked Conrad's rage in letters to Garnett and Jack Galsworthy ("any answer would involve too many feelings of one's inner life, stir too much secret bitterness and complex loyalty to be even attempted with any hope of being understood").[3] In the midst of writing his Russian novel *Under Western Eyes* (begun in December 1907 and published in book form in 1911), Conrad began *A Personal Record* (published between 1908 and 1909), in which, for the first time, he addressed the question of his Polish past, offering something like an "answer," both to hostile critics like Lynd and also to friendly critics like Garnett, to whom, in October 1907, Conrad had complained, "You remember always that I am a Slav (it's your *idée fixe*) but you seem to forget that I am a Pole."[4] In his signature for the 1911 "Familiar Preface" to *A Personal Record*—"JCK"—the unique addition of the letter K appears to mark the success with which he has affirmed a Polish identity, separate from Russian associations.[5] Yet that additional letter K serves only to highlight, all the more, the problem of cultural identification encoded in the switch from K to C in the adoption of his authorial name. The "trouble" of Conrad's own personal relation to the Russian language belongs to a much more extensive troubling of language, script, and national identity, characteristic of European modernism. The trouble that Conrad faces with the almost slanderous label "Sclavonism" or "so-called Slavonic literature" registers a linguistic, literary, and political trouble abbreviated in the K-effect of his own authorial signature. This trouble registers a revealing feature of the phenomenon of romanization throughout Central Europe, surfacing both in Conrad's work and, as I explore at the end of this chapter, the work of Franz Kafka.

What this chapter explores as the Russian face of romanization turns on a seemingly contradictory linguistic fact highlighted by Conrad's own disavowal of Russian. Cyrillic and roman script appear to be foreign scriptworlds and rival worldscripts. So, for example, in *Heart of Darkness*, Conrad makes use of this contrast as a key plot device when Marlow encounters a note with an "illegible" signature and what appears at first to be "cipher" in the margins of an English book on seamanship (*Youth*, 98, 99). Yet Cyrillic as a script itself belongs to the history and development of the roman alphabet.[6] At an especially interesting moment, almost exactly halfway through *Under Western Eyes*, the protagonist, Razumov, confronts the English narrator with a claim that seems to contradict Conrad's own disavowal of knowledge of "the alphabet": "In Russia, and in general everywhere—in a newspaper, for instance. The colour of the ink and the shapes of the letters are the same" (*Western*, 188). The way that Conrad makes use of this seemingly contradictory linguistic fact plays an important role in the unfolding of the novel's plot (as I explore later). As with the appearance of Cyrillic in the margins of the English book Marlow discovers on his journey up the river Congo, the contrast between scripts presents an initial riddle. While in *Heart of Darkness* the riddle is solved when the "cipher" is explained as Russian script, in *Under Western Eyes* it is further complicated, as part of the title-conceit of Razumov's written document now being read "under Western eyes." Clear examples of what Bakhtin calls "chronotopes" ("the place where the knots of narrative are tied and untied")[7], these chronotopes of romanization are especially revealing for showing the importance of Cyrillic script in the delayed decoding of Conrad's narratives. In the texts that characterize what might be called Conrad's Russian turn—*Under Western Eyes*, *A Personal Record*, and also the reminiscence "Prince Roman," originally intended for inclusion in the *Record*—these chronotopes reveal the Russian face of romanization that had always been at work in Conrad's *oeuvre*. The addition of K to his authorial signature in 1911, even as it acknowledges the Polish last name Korzeniowski, points to a personal problem of affiliation everywhere that the letter K appears in Conrad's work, as it often does both in the margins in his own handwriting and typescripts, and in the names of his fictional characters.[8]

This Russian face of romanization turns on the contradictory linguistic fact that roman and Cyrillic letters are both different and the same. The letter K, for instance, is the same for both (by contrast to the letter Ж [zhe] found only in Cyrillic). A historical account of the origins, development, and reform of Cyrillic script helps explain this seeming contradiction as an effect of the separate paths of development in European and Russian adaptations of the roman alphabet. One important feature of this divergence in the adaptation of roman letters, is the early eighteenth-century reform of the script to make "civil script" conform more fully to the roman alphabet as used in Western Europe. This makes the history of Cyrillic an early model for the kinds of language reform that shaped the phenomenon of romanization in the late nineteenth and early twentieth centuries. In this sense, the Russian face of romanization may be taken to refer, historically, to this early example of linguistic standardization in script and typography. Yet within the sociolinguistic context of language reforms in the later nineteenth century, the standardization of Russian script also comes to represent a rather different kind of model, in which script becomes the expression of an ethno-nationalist identity, imposed to the exclusion of other languages and scripts as the driving force of Russification. In this later sense, the Russian face of romanization reveals the political use of a standardized national script to impose an ethno-nationalist identity through language edicts and reforms.

The linguistic manifestation of this policy of Russification casts its "shadow" over all of Conrad's writing from this period, explaining what links the treatment of Russia in his novels with the attempt to record his Polish past in the reminiscences. The K added to his authorial signature reflects this personal struggle to correct the record of his own national identity and answer the charge of being "a man without country and language." *A Personal Record*, in particular, may be read as testament to the traumatic effects of Russian language policies. What Conrad describes as "the oppressive shadow of the great Russian Empire" in the first section of *A Personal Record*, directly refers to the "Russification" policies that took root in the reaction against Polish nationalism, especially the rebellion of 1863. The immediate context of Conrad's childhood is especially relevant for understanding the rise of Russian nationalism and the consolidation of those ethno-nationalist language policies that characterize Russification. As historian Faith Hillis notes, the "unique, multilingual hybrid culture" of the southwestern frontier of the Russian Empire (the region of Conrad's childhood) became a crucible for the formation of Russian imperial nationalism.[9] It is precisely this particular social, historical, and linguistic conjuncture that makes Conrad's vexed relation to Russification relevant for the experience of Central Europe in general. Within the wider orbit of all three of the Central European Empires—Prussia, Austro-Hungary, and Russia— Conrad's childhood coincides with an extended period of transformation in debates over language, orthography, and script. The Europe of Conrad's childhood was a Europe of multiple scripts, a place where multiple worldscripts converged, and a place where worldscripts and scriptworlds often—and increasingly—collided.[10] What makes the Russian face of romanization relevant for this wider sociolinguistic context is the explicit attempt to impose a single language and a single script on a multilingual and multiscript world. If Central Europe (generally at this time) was a place characterized by multiple languages and multiple scripts, all its Empires were increasingly governed by a monolingual, single worldscript imperative.

Yasemin Yildiz has described this imperative in terms of the "monolingual paradigm" that emerged in late eighteenth-century Europe and, especially in Germany, through the presumptions of a "mother tongue": "According to this paradigm, individuals and social formations are imagined to possess one 'true' language only, their 'mother tongue,' and through this possession to be organically linked to an exclusive, clearly demarcated ethnicity, culture, and nation."[11] Although this paradigm comes to dominate all of Europe, a primary example for Yildiz is the Austro-Hungarian Empire—by contrast to Russia, an explicitly multilingual political structure. As she notes, despite the multilingual makeup of the Habsburg Empire, "the multilingualism of empire increasingly shifted from being constituted by subjects with diverse multilingual competences to a multilingualism constituted by the side-by-side existence of a series of monolingual communities. . . .Thus what looks like a multilingual context . . . [is] governed by a monolingual paradigm."[12] This argument illuminates the linguistic consequences of that model of "official nationalism" adopted, according to Benedict Anderson, by all the large Empires of Europe in the later nineteenth century. Yildiz's argument is especially interesting for the emphasis it places on the significance of Kafka's writing. As a Jewish writer, writing in German in a Czech-speaking country, Kafka exemplifies the dilemmas of the "monolingual paradigm" in ways that may fruitfully be compared to Conrad: "Kafka's writing itself explores the modern problem of a putative homology between native language and ethno-cultural identity—that is, the monolingual paradigm—in a concentrated manner as part of his very aesthetics."[13]

Kafka's K is perhaps the most concentrated effect of this problem of script and ethno-cultural identity. A mark, not only of the monolingual, German paradigm of writing in Kafka, the letter K also underscores the way that this monolingual paradigm expresses itself as a matter of writing and script. For Kafka, the letter K is the minimal mark of his most memorable characters' names. Walter Benjamin calls it the "mumbled initial" letter of the author's own name.[14] Deleuze and Guattari call it "an assemblage that becomes all the more machine-like, an agent that becomes all the more collective because an individual is locked into it."[15] It presents the most concentrated form of that "impossible" situation that Kafka himself described as facing the Jewish writer writing in German. Initially this K-effect in Kafka might be set in contrast to the K-effect in Conrad, since for Conrad, the addition of K to his signature seems to mark the success in having added the sign of his Polish identity to his standing as an English writer. Yet, after all, Conrad can never right the record of the "Sclavonism" attributed, even by sympathetic critics like Mencken or Garnett, to his Polish background. The letter K serves as a reminder of the impossible act of making writing naturalize the "putative homology between native language and ethno-cultural identity." For both Conrad and Kafka, albeit in different ways, writing is an impossible act of ethno-national identification. In both cases, the characteristically Conradian and Kafkaesque features of this impossible situation are premised on the "monolingual paradigm" governing Kafka's Prague and Conrad's Ukraine. Kafka's Prague "became one of the frontlines in the language wars of the Austro-Hungarian Empire."[16] This is not unlike Conrad's Ukraine, the southwestern frontier of the Russian

Empire and, according to Hillis, crucible for Russification policies. In both cases, the sociolinguistic context of language debates is reshaped into those concentrated aesthetic articulations of the impossibility of writing that constitute—around the K-effects of the chronotopes of romanization—what is distinctly Conradian and Kafkaesque about their writing.

Language, Script, and Reform in the Russian Empire

When Conrad's Razumov tells the English narrator of *Under Western Eyes* that, "In Russia, and in general everywhere . . . the shapes of the letters are the same," he is, in part, pointing out a sociolinguistic fact about Cyrillic script's relation to the history of the roman alphabet. Within the longer history of Cyrillic script and its modern standardization, from the Petrine reforms of the early eighteenth century up until the orthographic reforms put in place following the Russian revolution of 1917, modern Cyrillic emerges from a process of increasing romanization. This is the argument made by Vladimir Yefimov, reviewing the historical forms of Cyrillic from the perspective of typeface design. During the reign of Peter the Great (1689–1725) a new Civil Type (later called *"grazhdanskiy shrift"* and modeled on "the shapes of Western (Latin) letters") replaced the old *"poluustav"* type that was retained only for the printing of liturgical, Old Church Slavonic. As Yefimov puts it, "Cyrillic took on the form of roman serif type, in much the same way that Muscovy was dressed up in European clothes."[17] Focusing on the "shapes of the letters" in a typographic sense, Yefimov describes the emergence and development of Cyrillic typescript as a history of romanization: "Since the Petrine type reform, the latinized form of Cyrillic has been traditional in Russia for nearly 300 years, and Cyrillic type has developed in parallel to Latin, repeating virtually all the stages of its development and changes of style: Classical, Romantic, Art Nouveau, Constructivist, Post-Modernist, etc."[18]

Various typographic reforms throughout the eighteenth and nineteenth centuries—not necessarily linked to language reforms in the broader sense—led to a standardization of modern Cyrillic, aligned with the typographic questions that Yefimov characterizes as parallel to the standardization of the Latin alphabet in modern European print types. Even as Cyrillic typeface came to shape the distinctive forms of a Russian scriptworld over the European scriptworld of roman letters, and even as that modern print standard came to be associated culturally, politically, and linguistically with the "official nationalism" of an expanding Russian Empire, the modernization of a distinctive Cyrillic script should nonetheless be viewed as part of a broader process of romanization alongside the standardization of European forms of print.

Conrad's Razumov is not wrong then, in saying that "In Russia, and in general everywhere . . . the shapes of the letters are the same."

Indeed, as one of its earliest, original models, the romanizing reform of Cyrillic script reveals an important fact about the widespread development of romanizing schemes throughout the world in the late nineteenth and early twentieth centuries. Based on the same Latin alphabet, they all aspire to a standard, universally applicable form, nonetheless tailored to suit the phonetic needs of the particular language that they serve. The result is not, then, *one* alphabet (as Walter Ong, following Marshall McLuhan, claimed), but a multiplicity of different ways of applying Latin letters; or different faces (and typefaces) in the application of the Latin alphabet. This is recognized even by those linguists afflicted by the "Latin alphabet fetishism" that privileges "the alphabet" as telos of the history of the world's writing systems—most notably, I. J. Gelb, who qualifies his most insistent emphasis on the universal adoption of the Latin alphabet with the following comment:

> However, the wide acceptance of the Latin alphabet in modern times has led to no unity. In many cases the signs of the Latin alphabet received widely variant phonetic values in different countries. The Turks, for instance, use the Latin sign *c* for the sound *j* as in our 'jig', a correspondence which is without parallel in any Western writing. The limitless homophony of signs is best illustrated by the spelling of the name of the famous Russian writer Chekhov, in which the initial sound can be written as *Ch, Tch, C, Tsch, Tsj, Tj, Cz, Cs,* or *Ci,* the medial consonant as *kh, ch, k, h,* or *x,* and the final one as *v, f,* or *ff* in various systems of the world, all using Latin signs.[19]

Following Gelb's suggestive illustration, the romanized spelling of Chekhov provides a good example of the Russian face of romanization, and the way it illustrates a "limitless homophony of [Latin] signs," revealing the wide variety of romanization systems proliferating throughout the world. Sociolinguistically, the Russian face of romanization reveals the multiple other alternative ways to transliterate script into roman letters: English, French, German, Czech, Polish, and so on.

If this begins to illuminate how the standardization of romanization throughout Central Europe is premised on multilingual, multiscript social formations, the other side to this face of Russian romanization is the imposition of what Yildiz calls the "monolingual paradigm" and a corresponding monoscript, or single script imperative. It is the later nineteenth-century Russian language policies that draw attention to this side of the Russian face of romanization and help explain what makes Razumov's claim appear counterfactual, based on that seemingly contradictory fact that Cyrillic both *is* and *is not* roman script.

The Russian language policies that were being enacted and introduced during Conrad's childhood, and in the region of Ukraine where he spent the first decade of his life, are instructive. Guided by the general program of Russification, Russian language policies of the mid-nineteenth century became the vehicle for imposing a vernacular Russian (language and script) on a heterogeneous population of German, Polish, Yiddish, and Ukrainian speakers. As Hillis notes, the "unique, multilingual hybrid culture" of Russia's southwestern frontier was critical in the formation of Russian imperial nationalism.[20] Some of the specific historical details of this formative moment in the development of Russification emerge as part of the very structure of Conrad's famously evasive autobiographical *Record*. Toward the end of the first reminiscence, writing for the first time about his Polish past, Conrad recalls, "Over all this hung the oppressive shadow of the great Russian Empire—the shadow lowering with the darkness of a new-born national hatred fostered by the Moscow school of journalists against the Poles after the ill-omened rising of 1863" (*Record*, 24). Referring to the role of journalism in consolidating the Russification policies that took root in the reaction against Polish nationalism, especially the rebellion of 1863, the reference to the "Moscow school of journalists" includes, above all, the figure of Mikhail Nikiforovich Katkov, editor of the *Moskovskie Vedomosti* (and also publisher of Dostoevsky). According to Andreas Renner, "it was Katkov who, in the 1860s, set the course for a new period in the history of Russian nationalism, defending the integrity of Russia foremostly against the Polish insurrection of 1863."[21] And according to Hillis, "the political crisis connected to the second Polish revolt stimulated a conversation about how to manage ethnic and national difference within the empire—one that ultimately transcended the confines of government offices and engaged the imperial educated public. Perhaps the most influential, nonbureaucratic interlocutor in this dialogue, the journalist M. N. Katkov, professed his devotion to the "Russian cause" and his determination to save the empire from dangerous external threats as well as its internal enemies."[22] Hillis later details Katkov's role in establishing the political discourse that would be enforced by government language decrees against Ukrainian variants of Cyrillic.[23]

In one of the final Polish reminiscences of the *Record*, Conrad goes out of his way to name one of the official figures, notoriously known for enforcing the strict laws against Polish, Ukrainian, and other ethnic minorities on the southwestern frontier. In this case, the order concerned the eviction of his mother, who was then close to death. Although not explicitly articulated in terms of the language policies enforcing standard Russian as language and script, the anecdote emphasizes the role of edicts, letters, and writing which characterizes all the anecdotes that Conrad tells in the *Record* (and stands in counterpoint to the role of writing and the chronotope of Cyrillic script developed in *Under Western Eyes*):

> ... I am in a position to state the name of the Governor-General who signed the order with the marginal note 'to be carried out to the letter' in his own handwriting. The gentleman's name was Bezak. A high dignitary, an energetic official, the idol for a time of the Russian Patriotic Press. (*Record*, 67)

This anecdote, referring back to the earlier reference to the "Moscow school of journalists," captures the general spirit of the reaction against Poles. It implicitly registers the logic of a set of language policies directed against German, Polish, Yiddish, Hebrew, and, above all, Ukrainian languages and scripts.

Language policies are intimately intertwined with the Polish rising of 1863, and so, are inseparable from what Conrad describes as "the oppressive shadow of the great Russian Empire." A series of official (secret) decrees (*ukase*) marks the increasing significance of these language debates and policies in shaping the ethno-nationalist definition of language and script underlying the policies of Russification. The Lithuanian press ban (put in place in 1865 and not lifted until 1904) sought to diminish Polish influence by limiting publications using Latin script, while encouraging the use of Cyrillic. This press ban underscores the difference between Russian use of Cyrillic and Polish use of Latin letters. More significant, though related, were the decrees that sought to curtail the use of Ukrainian script, a variant of Cyrillic. First, the Valuev Circular (1863) and then, still more important, the Ems decree (1876), banned the use of Ukrainian publications. As Johannes Remy notes, in his study of the variety of attempts to standardize the Ukrainian alphabet in the years leading up to 1876, the Ems decree stipulated that all Ukrainian publications had to use the "general Russian orthography."[24] This clause, banning the so-called *kulishivka* Ukrainian alphabet that had come to be associated with Ukrainian nationalism (and by extension Polish nationalism), indicates the consolidation of an official national policy aligning language, script, and a (greater) Russian national identity. As Remy explores, however, before that time, relatively little official attention was paid to the efforts to standardize orthography for Ukrainian publications. More attention was paid to efforts at using the Polish Latin alphabet. It was the perceived link between Ukrainian nationalism and Polish nationalism that fueled these restrictions. These attempts to regulate the Ukrainian orthography shaped the official consolidation of a standardized Greater Russian Cyrillic script. The enforcement, by decree, of this standardized scriptworld, calls attention to a dynamic rivalry of scripts equally as important, if not more so, than the rivalry between the different scriptworlds of Latin and Cyrillic. It calls attention to a politicization of scripts that cuts across a much wider variety of different worldscripts (Latin, Cyrillic, Arabic, Hebrew, Chinese) and, in seeking to align the dominant language with one official, national, and standardized scriptworld, calls attention to the troubling presence of many other minor (and sometimes not quite so minor) languages and scripts claiming identity and identification within that same scriptworld.[25]

Russification, in this political sense, informs the standardization of a Cyrillic script that reinforces, through script reform and the regulation of print, what Yildiz calls the "monolingual paradigm." The role of the Ukrainian alphabet illuminates the extent to which standardized script forms produce a compulsively enforced alignment of script and national identity. This Russian face of romanization underscores a contradiction that informs the notion of a "scriptworld" that Damrosch has so helpfully developed for a broad, global, and comparative study of world literatures.[26] On the one hand, it presumes a fit between language, identity, and writing system, driven by an ideological ethno-nationalist imperative. This is a key feature of what is so vexed in the accusation that Conrad is "a man without country and language." Script is destiny; one inhabits a scriptworld the way one inhabits a national identity. On the other hand, a scriptworld projects its script as a standardized form of the world's universal script. A scriptworld stands in relation to other scriptworlds as one (albeit specially privileged) version for transliterating all the world's scripts. This is the contradictory, political imperative accompanying the double-face of Russian romanization: identifying nationality with a single script while projecting that scriptworld as the universal horizon for all the world's scripts.

This contradictory imperative to align scriptworld and worldscript is the trouble spot marked by the function of the letter K in the work of both Conrad and Kafka. As an index of all the Cyrillic and Latin scripts used across the linguistic borders of Central Europe (and perhaps most especially, as embodied in the variety of Slavic languages using some variation of either Cyrillic, roman scripts, or both), the letter K signals the convergence of a single-script imperative with the multiplicity of languages and scripts on which that imperative depends. The K-effect is an especially concentrated, abbreviated example of the chronotope of romanization for both Kafka and Conrad, a recurring knot in the timing and spacing of that ensemble of texts, shaping language into the aesthetic forms of Kafkaesque and Conradian narratives. In both cases, this K-effect is intimately bound to the authorial signature and the names of characters, signaling an often-nightmarish relation to writing and script. Kafka's most grotesque version of this is the juridical-writing torture machine in "The

Penal Colony" that imposes the sentence of the law directly onto the body of the prisoner. This nightmare judgment of a writing to come is an aesthetic articulation of the imperative to impose a fit between scriptworld and worldscript. A counterpart in *Under Western Eyes* is Razumov's vision, in the moment of "conversion" when he decides to betray Haldin, of the landscape before him appearing as "a monstrous blank page awaiting the record of an inconceivable history" (*Western*, 33).

Razumov's rejection of the difference between Cyrillic and roman script belongs to this aesthetic articulation of an impossible alignment of scriptworld and worldscript. Indeed, it represents an especially important twist in the narrative timing and spacing of the novel's contrast between Cyrillic and roman script. As I turn to consider, more closely, the aesthetic effect of the way that Conrad uses the chronotope of Cyrillic romanization in *Under Western Eyes*, I want to emphasize that this novel belongs to the wider ensemble of texts in which Conrad sought to disentangle his Polish past from the "shadow" of Russia (the autobiographical reminiscences published as *A Personal Record*, and including "Prince Roman" published separately). *A Personal Record* and *Under Western Eyes* both use this same metaphor of the "shadow." In *Under Western Eyes*, early in the face-off between the English narrator and Razumov, the narrator describes the moment that he turns to face Razumov: "I did not wish to indispose him still further by an appearance of marked curiosity. It might have been distasteful to such a young and secret refugee from under the pestilential shadow hiding the true, kindly face of his land. And the shadow, the attendant of his countrymen, stretching across the middle of Europe, was lying on him too, darkening his figure to my mental vision" (*Western*, 184). Later, I will consider more closely how the metaphors of "shadow" and "face" work in this ensemble of Conradian texts. They reveal the Russian face of that timing and spacing of narrative throughout Conrad's *oeuvre*, including the role of Cyrillic script in *Heart of Darkness*, and going back to the K-effect of Conrad's characters' names and his own authorial signature. The turning point in Conrad's *oeuvre* toward Russian—more generally Slavic—topics can also be considered in relation to the ensemble of texts that Kafka was producing at much the same time. Very different though Conrad and Kafka certainly are, there are some striking points of convergence. For each writer, the letter K reflects a contradictory, "monolingual" imperative of alignment between scriptworld and worldscript, especially characteristic of the Slavic countries of Central and Eastern Europe. The Russian face of romanization reveals the multiple other, alternative ways to transliterate script into roman letters.

Under Western Eyes, *A Personal Record*, and "Prince Roman"

Under Western Eyes

In *Under Western Eyes*, more so than elsewhere in Conrad, script and ethos, writing and identity, language and character, seem fatefully entangled. The narrative conceit of a Russian document, translated for an English readership, is perhaps the clearest example in Conrad of the chronotope of romanization, organizing the overall temporal and spatial arrangement of the novel's plot, character, dialogue, and other narrative devices. This conceit is established at the very beginning of the narrative with the narrator's comment that "the readers of these pages will be able to detect in the story the marks of documentary evidence" (*Western*, 3). It is the different layers of "documentary evidence," presented by the "record" of Razumov's confession as transcribed and translated by the narrator, that determine the timing and pacing of the story: of Razumov's relation to Haldin after the assassination of Mr. de P___; his betrayal of Haldin to the police; and the circumstances under which he becomes a part of the inner circle of Russian revolutionaries in Geneva. There are many more "marks" of "documentary evidence" than the narrator admits to, and many of the most important revelations in the plotting of the story turn on the multiplicity of different texts, records, letters, and documents circulating throughout the narrative. All these "marks of documentary evidence" are structured in advance by the chronotope of a Russian document partially transcribed, transliterated, and translated into the text that we are currently reading. Already encoded in the title-metaphor "under Western eyes," this chronotope of Russian script is reinforced by the narrator's exaggerated emphasis, in describing Haldin's letter to his sister, on the "cabalistic, incomprehensible" look of Cyrillic letters (*Western*, 99). It structures, both overtly and covertly, the unfolding plot of the novel. As the narrator puts it, in the final pages, describing Sophia Antonovna's account of Mikulin's meeting with Peter Ivanovitch, "And this story, too, I received without comment in my character of a mute witness of things Russian, unrolling their Eastern logic under my Western eyes" (*Western*, 381).

The implied opposition between Cyrillic script and the printed page of the novel orchestrates the unfolding of plot around a contrast between two different scriptworlds. It is this contrast that will make Razumov's comment about "the shapes of the letters" seem contradictory during his dialogue with the English narrator at the end of the novel's second part. That dialogue may be read as a face-off between the Cyrillic and Western European scriptworlds that structures the turning point in the novel's setting, as Razumov moves from St. Petersburg to Geneva. A contrast between different scriptworlds begins in the opening paragraph, with the romanization of Razumov's Russian name. The narrator's explanation of the name of "the man who called himself, after the Russian custom, Cyril son of Isidor—Kirylo Sidorovitch—Razumov" (*Western*, 3). The doubly-romanized, English rendition of Razumov's name "Kirylo" as "Cyril," exaggerates the significance of what it means to transliterate from Cyrillic Russian into romanized English. The etymological speculation on the first two names, invites a reading of Razumov's unfolding story in relation to the symbolic significance of successive parts of the name: those parts ("Cyril son of Isidor—Kirylo Sidorovitch") whose double transliteration and translation evokes the formation of Cyrillic as Russia's identifiable writing system; and the last part (Razumov) that hints at a "reason" or "reasoning," either in accord or at war with that identity (Razumov means "son of reason," although this is not something the narrator draws attention to). Proleptically encoded in this overdetermined romanization of Razumov's full name, are the novel's ideological divisions—between revolution and autocracy, between Westernizing and Slavophile sympathies, between Russia and Europe—all of which give shape to Razumov's dialogue with Haldin and the account of his decision to betray Haldin in the first part of the novel.[27]

The English narrator's repeated recourse to the conceit of a Russian document as the source for his narrative, frames the presentation of Razumov's own interior, narrative voice around a dense network of interrelated metaphors of writing and script. There is the prize essay that Razumov is planning to write before Haldin appears in his room. On the long walk during which Razumov decides to betray Haldin, he has a vision of the Russian landscape as "a monstrous blank page awaiting the record of an inconceivable history" (*Western*, 33). Following his betrayal of Haldin, instead of composing the essay, he writes out a series of lines that seem to epitomize the crystallization of his reactionary, counter-revolutionary consciousness—in "long scrawly letters" that contrast with "his neat minute handwriting," prompting the further comment that, "When he wrote a large hand his neat writing lost its character altogether—became unsteady, almost childish" (*Western*, 66). Metaphors of writing (repeatedly) frame the presentation of Razumov's consciousness, itself divided between kinds of script, contending ideological positions, and different voices—as in the lengthy dialogue with Haldin which sets the stage for what might be called (borrowing Bakhtin's term for one of Dostoevsky's characteristic narrative techniques), the "dialogized interior monologue" of Razumov's journal account.[28]

Bakhtin's analysis of Dostoevsky is especially relevant, since so much of Razumov's narrative reads like a Dostoevsky novel. What Conrad does to create the effect of that "never-ending struggle with others' words"[29] that Bakhtin finds so characteristic of Dostoevsky's narratives, is to contain the "speaking person" through a network of metaphors of writing and script, organized by the exaggerated contrast between Cyrillic and roman script. The conceit of a Russian document translated for an English readership, succeeds in highlighting the effects of this "dialogized interior monologue," framing Razumov's voice through the narrator's commentary on that voice. So, for example, at the beginning of Chapter 2 of the novel's first part, the narrator comments on what the reader has just read in Chapter 1: "The words and events of that evening must have been graven as if with a steel tool on Mr. Razumov's brain since he was able to write his relation with such fullness and precision a good many months afterwards" (*Western*, 24). Simultaneously enhancing, and yet also distancing Razumov's consciousness, the narrator's commentary reinforces the contrast between Cyrillic and Western European scriptworlds embodied in the contrasting, narrative "speaking persons" of Razumov and the English narrator. The conceit of a narrative consciousness relayed through an English rendering of a Russian document, refracts the reader's understanding of Razumov's character through metaphors of writing and script. All too often this organizing chronotope follows a contradictory logic, as when (in the example just cited) Razumov is characterized as both a writer writing and a brain written upon ("graven as with a steel tool").

The complexity of this chronotope of Cyrillic romanization emerges from the different layers of "documentary evidence" presented by the "record" of Razumov's confession, as transcribed and translated by the narrator.[30] As many critics have noted, *Under Western Eyes* presents a bewildering number of different levels of narrative, based on multiple forms of "documentary evidence." Besides Razumov's diary, the narrator refers to various letters, newspaper reports, published books, revolutionary pamphlets, spy reports, and more. Wisely noting that the "sheer complexity" of the novel makes readers and critics "unavoidably" limit their attention "to only a selection of its constitutive elements," Jakob Lothe nonetheless provides a useful overview of this complexity, by referring to the four types of text proposed by Avrom Fleishman as organizing the narrative: the "A-text," referring to the fiction authored by Joseph Conrad; the "B-text," referring to "the document prepared" by the narrator; the "C-text," referring to the documents on which the narrator's report is based; and the "D-text," "consisting of Haldin's letters to his sister and his spoken words to Razumov."[31] The interaction between all four levels—orchestrating each twist in the telling of the story—turns on the conceit of a Russian document translated into English, that is set up in the opening page of the novel and abbreviated in the novel's riddling, title-metaphor.

The key turning point in the plotting of this conceit of the Russian script, transcribed for "Western" eyes, is the moment when Razumov first encounters the English narrator, face-to-face toward the end of the second part of the novel. Here, almost exactly midway through the novel, the different levels of documentation are superimposed to produce an uncanny doubling of diegetic levels. Razumov, the "speaking person" of the Russian text, directly faces and talks back to the English editor and translator of that Russian text. This creates a cognitive dissonance in the reader's sense of narrative time and space. Razumov's rejection of the narrator's dichotomy between Cyrillic and roman script is only one among a number of peculiar effects produced in this rearrangement of the narrative's layering of "documentary evidence," but it is integrally related to the range of those effects, large and small, that make this moment (Chapter V of Part Second) a turning point in the overall arc of the plot, as the narrative turns from Razumov's Petersburg to his Geneva experience; and as the narrative pivots toward the revelation (still to come in Part Third) that Razumov has been enlisted as a police spy to infiltrate the revolutionaries.

In its cumulative effects, this turning point in the plot reinforces a contrast between Cyrillic and Western European scriptworlds by positioning Razumov in an impossible, contradictory relation to both. It splits the character and consciousness of Razumov between the "dialogized interior monologue" of the written document presented in the first part of the novel, and the physical appearance of Razumov in Geneva in dialogue with the English narrator in the second part of the novel. Repeatedly, the narrator marks the difference between the two by referencing "the document which is the main source of this narrative" (*Western*, 192), superimposing different temporal and spatial coordinates of the story—St. Petersburg and Geneva—around an opposing logic of languages and script.[32]

Razumov's physical appearance also presents a riddle, highlighted at this turning point in the plot, as the reader is presented with a very different description of the protagonist's face from the one offered at the beginning of the novel. The novel's very first description of Razumov's face reads:

> Mr. Razumov was a tall, well-proportioned young man, quite unusually dark for a Russian from the Central Provinces. His good looks would have been unquestionable if it had not been for a peculiar lack of fineness in the features. It was as if a face modelled vigorously in wax (with some approach even to a classical correctness of type) had been held close to the fire till all sharpness of line had been lost in the softening of the material. (*Western*, 5)

Yet, in the novel's Part Second, at the very end of Chapter IV, the narrator describes his first impression of Razumov:

> I was upon the whole favourably impressed. He had an air of intelligence and even some distinction quite above the average of the students and other inhabitants of the *Petite Russie*. His features were more decided than in the generality of Russian faces; he had a line of the jaw, a clean-shaven, sallow cheek; his nose was a ridge, and not a mere protuberance. (*Western*, 179)

There is no easy way to explain these two very different descriptions of Razumov's face. The first emphasizes a "peculiar lack of fineness in the features," while the latter seems to flatly contradict that account: "His features were more decided than in the generality of Russian faces; he had a line of the jaw, a clean-shaven, sallow cheek; his nose was a ridge, and not a mere protuberance." If the second description carries the authority of the English narrator's eyewitness account, the first description, presumably based on the "documentary evidence" of Razumov's journal (since we now know this is not the face as the English narrator saw it), poses an interesting riddle: is it likely Razumov would describe *himself* this way? These two different faces defy any obvious narrative logic. In a suggestive metonymy of face and script, the first face may evoke Cyrillic script (in its departure from "a classical correctness of type") while the second face ("more decided than in the generality of Russian faces") may evoke Western European roman script. These two physical descriptions of Razumov's face, then, may embody the contradictory logic around which the whole novel turns, the logic—a sociolinguistic logic—that the novel invites us to consider in terms of the double-face of Russian romanization.

References to faces throughout *Under Western Eyes* are almost always implicated in the novel's dense network of metaphors of writing and script. So, for example, the Minister of State, Mr. de P__, whose assassination constitutes the novel's *mise-en-scène*, is described as having "a face of crumpled parchment" (*Western*, 7).[33] The metaphor of the face itself is foregrounded, repeatedly, at the midway turning point in the novel. It is prefigured in the chapter before, in the narrator's description of Razumov's first meeting with Nathalie, where their mutual recognition is narrated through a combination of Nathalie's account to the narrator and the narrator's account based on Razumov's document—the relation between the two suggestively captured in the simplest of narrative cues: "He faced about" (*Western*, 167), a merely physical movement heightened—like all Razumov's physical gestures in these face-to-face meetings—by the different "marks of documentary evidence," demonstrably presented by the narrator's turning back and forth between Nathalie's account of her first "face to face" meeting, and Razumov's account as it "stands recorded in the pages of his self-confession."

The increasing number of references to faces in Chapter V, Part Second, is surely (in part) related to the fact that, here, the narrator is giving a firsthand description of his first meeting with Razumov, marking that shift from the character of Razumov emerging from the written document to the physical presence of the character with whom the narrator speaks. In the convergence of different levels of "documentary evidence," these references to faces accrue a double connotation, reinforcing a sense of the physical presence of the "face to face" encounter in this moment in the plot, but combining that with the metonymy, linking faces and script, that has already produced the extended metaphor of a document being read "under Western eyes." Both come together in the narrator's evocation of the "pestilential shadow . . . stretching across the middle of Europe" (which, incidentally, echoes Conrad's description of "the oppressive shadow of the great Russian Empire" in A *Personal Record*). The whole passage is worth citing again, to emphasize the combination of gesture, physical description, metaphor, and metonymy, with which the narrative brings together the different layers of textual documentation framing Razumov's experience, as a nightmare logic of writing, script, and identity:

> He shrugged his shoulders so violently that he tottered again. I saw it out of the corner of my eye as I moved on, with him at my elbow. He had fallen back a little and was practically out of my sight, unless I turned my head to look at him. I did not wish to indispose him still further by an appearance of marked curiosity. It might have been distasteful to such a young and secret refugee from under the pestilential shadow hiding the true, kindly face of his land. And the shadow, the attendant of his countrymen, stretching across the middle of Europe, was lying on him too, darkening his figure to my mental vision. (*Western*, 184)

The narrator's figuration of the "true, kindly face of his land" seems incongruous, fitting neither a physical description of Razumov's face (in either of its two different descriptions), nor anything but the most benign and misplaced assessment of Russia. Shifting away from a description of Razumov and toward the narrator's anxious efforts not to "indispose" him, the passage projects a benevolent, liberal, Western European misunderstanding of Russian society, enacting that misunderstanding through the metonymic slippage that takes us from Razumov's face to the narrator's, before elaborating the complex figurative comparison between a "kindly face" and the Russian "land" overshadowed by autocracy. The figure of the face here, emerges from a confusing doubling of the two, rather different, diegetic premises of the narrative: on the one hand, the face-to-face encounter between Razumov and the English narrator; and, on the other, the English narrator's transcription and translation of Razumov's private journal. All these figurative faces are fused together in the title's conceit of a document being read "under Western eyes." The chronotope of romanized Cyrillic script emerges in the figure of a face which is, at one moment, reading and, in another moment, being read.

The metaphors and metonymies of face and script throughout the novel complicate any simple reading (for example, of the two different physical features of Razumov's face as articulating the double Cyrillic and roman features of Russian script). In the figurative slippage of the narrator's description of "the kindly face of his land," the network of associations defies any stable metaphorical logic. The multiplication of different associations of face and script works, over the course of the narrative, to increase—not to solve—the riddle of contrasting Cyrillic and Western European scriptworlds. In this, *Under Western Eyes* does something rather different with the chronotope of Cyrillic romanization than *Heart of Darkness*. In *Heart of Darkness* the "extravagant mystery" of the English book is solved by the discovery that the "cipher" is Russian script, written in the margins of the English text. The timing and spacing of this riddle of script serves to foreground the prestige of English as a hegemonic language, mediating a whole range of European and African languages and scripts. The riddle of Cyrillic script still plays an important role in the novel's plotting. It heightens that work's complex, aesthetic condensation and displacement of language and script; but it is the problem of "Englishness," and the problem of English as worldscript that it presents.[34] Like a false clue in a detective story, though, once the riddle of the harlequin's "illegible" signature and marginal notes is solved, the whole question of Cyrillic as script is dropped. It is a fascination for the discovery of an English book in Africa that guides that novel's chronotope of romanization, the timing and spacing of that (lowercase) romanization of modern print form on the "blank space" on the map of Africa.

By contrast, the plot of *Under Western Eyes* depends on insisting that Cyrillic is itself a riddle that cannot be solved. This riddle is embodied in the two very different descriptions of Razumov's face. In the chapter before the first face-to-face meeting with Razumov (Chapter III, Part Second), the narrator reinforces the novel's overall conceit in his description of Haldin's letter to his sister (which will play an important role in the dialogue with Razumov—indeed, one might imagine this letter is where the very first description of Razumov's face comes from): "I glanced down at the flimsy blackened pages whose very handwriting seemed cabalistic, incomprehensible to the experience of Western Europe" (*Western*, 133).

This emphasis on the "cabalistic, incomprehensible" nature of Cyrillic script organizes the metaphors of face and script around an unstable opposition between Russia and Western Europe to produce the enduring riddle of the title's "under Western eyes." The two sides of that opposition—the Cyrillic text being read and the "Western" eyes reading—are more intricately linked than the dichotomy suggests, but the novel constantly works to keep each side facing, as it were, in different directions: on the one hand, to evoke the fictional world of Razumov's Russian experience; and on the other, to construct that "Western" perspective that finds the Russian character and script incomprehensible. One of the remarkable things about *Under Western Eyes* is the way in which the construction of this limited "Western" perspective is generated through the narrator's increasingly uncomprehending and clichéd use of the word "Western" itself. It is worth emphasizing here, the difference between the case of English romanization at work in *Heart of Darkness*—where the term "the West" never appears—and the face of Russian romanization as it generates the term "the West" from the narrative timing and spacing of *Under Western Eyes*. In the early chapters of the second part of the novel, the narrator repeatedly uses this keyword and its cognates ("West," "Occident") in dialogue with Nathalie, adopting her use of the term to describe himself, for example, as a "dense Occidental" (*Western*, 112). The later characterization of Haldin's Cyrillic script as appearing "cabalistic, incomprehensible to the experience of Western Europe" ties together those earlier moments to reinforce that limited perspective in the conceit of the title's "Western eyes." What is striking, however, is the extent to which the word itself comes, not from "Western European" discourses, but from precisely those Russian terms of debate that the narrator keeps insisting are "incomprehensible" when read through "Western" eyes. This is one important facet of the novel's hidden work of Russian romanization—the transliteration and translation of the Russian idea of "the West" as a rhetorical abbreviation for Western Europe's own self-definition. As a key aesthetic device, enabling Conrad to reframe and distance the influence and legacy of Russian novels, this appropriation of a Russian term produces a highly ironic staging of the formation of a "Western" identity, defining itself according to the terms of a debate it cannot comprehend. This irony extends well beyond Conrad, marking a key twist in the ideological formation of the twentieth-century notion of the "West."[35]

Paying more attention to the sociolinguistic features of Cyrillic, or Russian romanization, I want to note that *Under Western Eyes*'s success in coining this ironic cliché of "Western" identity also depends on the other face of the chronotope of Cyrillic script, namely, the Russian text that reveals Razumov's first-person experience. The irony here, points in a somewhat different direction from the ironic, ideological construction of the trope of the "West." For all the narrator's claims to the contrary, the nightmare of Razumov's experience of having betrayed Haldin is vividly present to the English reader. Razumov's experience is all the more vivid, paradoxically, because of the narrator's disavowals, beginning with the comment on the very first page of the novel "Yet I confess that I have no comprehension of the Russian character" (*Western*, 3). Echoing Conrad's own disavowal of Russian literature and language, it underscores the contradictory logic, set in place by the narrative's chronotope of Cyrillic script.

What makes for the uncanny effect of Razumov's encounter with the narrator midway through the novel, is the fact that the English reader, by this time, has such an intimate knowledge of the experiences recounted in Razumov's journal, that Razumov's physical presence creates a ghostly doubling of Razumov's spoken word, and the dialogized interior monologue of the written words of his first-person narrative. The two different narrative levels, presented as if they existed in two entirely different, mutually incomprehensible, scriptworlds, confront each other as the riddling effect of a double narrative converging on the timing and spacing of the same words on the page of the novel we are reading. Like the two different descriptions of Razumov's face, these two narrative levels converge in a logic that is, all at once, tautological and contradictory. Razumov's Russian identity as described in the novel's first part, registered in the written form of his journal, is both the same, and different from, the Russian identity as it appears in the voice and physical features and gestures of Razumov in the novel's second part.

Narratively, this doubling captures the nightmare of Razumov's identification with Russia as the experience of a betrayal of Russia. Thematically, this is because the narrator's role is doubled: as interlocutor, he thinks Razumov is a friend of Haldin's and one of the revolutionaries; as narrator and editor, he is someone who has read the journal and already knows of the betrayal. Linguistically, the ghostly doubling effect hinges, not only on the "monolingual paradigm" enforcing a fit between language and ethno-national identity, but also, more importantly, on the contradictory imperative linking ethno-national identity with a single scriptworld that also lays claim to being a worldscript. Sociolinguistically, this reproduces the fact that Cyrillic both *is* and *is not* roman script. That tautologically contradictory sense of identity, writing, and script which constitutes such a fundamental sense of Razumov's "Russian" experience (as captured in the figure of "a monstrous blank page awaiting the record of an inconceivable history" [*Western*, 33]) is the unfolding logic of a doubling of writing, script, and identity that constitutes the novel that we are reading. This is why it is so easy to overlook the importance of Razumov's, seemingly counterfactual, statement about the "colour of the ink and the shapes of the letters" "in Russia, and in general everywhere." It reproduces the contradictory, ethno-national imperative, but as the double, Russian face of the romanized print form of the English novel.

This offers an aesthetic reframing and narrative unfolding of the linguistic effect that Gelb illustrates with the romanized spelling of Chekhov "in which the initial sound can be written as *Ch, Tch, C, Tsch, Tsj, Tj, Cz, Cs*, or *Ci*, the medial consonant as *kh, ch, k, h*, or *x*, and the final one as *v, f,* or *ff* in various systems of the world, all using Latin signs."[36] Yet, whereas Gelb's example illustrates the "limitless homophony of signs," Conrad's novel selectively reduces this to a doubling of script, beginning, as already noted, with the double romanization of Razumov's patronymic "Cyril son of Isidor—Kirylo Sidorovitch," and extending through the metaphor and metonymy of writing, script, and face. The inaugural shift from C to K registers, at the outset, how the novel's governing conceit of a Russian scriptworld is generated by a simple binary alternation between two letters of the English alphabet. There is nothing simple about the way in which the narrative makes use of this binary to turn the novelistic space of romanized English print into a polyphony of multiple languages and scripts. Above all, the novel's various languages and scripts—and the multiplying metaphors of language and script—are governed by the way a single script is able to render the transcription and transliteration between two scripts, as if the K of "Kirylo" has translated the reader from the roman scriptworld of "Cyril" to the Russian scriptworld of "Kirylo." It is entirely in keeping with the way that this chronotope of Cyrillic romanization works, that the binary opposition assembles a host of contradictions around the basic contradiction that Cyrillic both is and is not roman script.

The unfolding significance of Razumov's name—grounded in this initial binary alternation between C and K—is quickly caught up in the sequence of metaphors of writing, script, and identity that presents the name as itself a complex, vexed, and tormented unfolding of the hidden significance of that redoubled Russian romanization.[37] The singularity of the way that script generates a ghostly doubling is anticipated, indeed, by a doubling of the K-effect of his patronymic—not only in the name "Kirilyo," but also in the insinuation of a possible relation to Prince K (who both does and does not provide a familial lineage). It is Prince K's attorney who insinuates this in a peculiar double emphasis on the slanderous possibilities of such a connection: "You wonder what he could be doing in the hole of a poor legal rat like myself—eh? These awfully great people have their sentimental curiosities like common sinners. But if I were you, Kirylo Sidorovitch," he continued, leering and laying a peculiar emphasis on the patronymic, "I wouldn't boast at large of the introduction. It would not be prudent, Kirylo Sidorovitch" (*Western*, 13). The accusatory warning is reminiscent in certain ways of the accusative case of Cornelius's sneering repetition of the phrase "Tuan Jim. As you may say, Lord Jim" (*Lord Jim*, 267). For Razumov, this potentially imprudent, slanderous mark of the K in his name, can only reinforce the point that "His closest parentage was defined in the statement that he was a Russian": "The word Razumov was the mere label of a solitary individuality. There were no Razumovs belonging to him anywhere. His closest parentage was defined in the statement that he was a Russian" (*Western*, 10).

A Personal Record

What Conrad does with Razumov's name in *Under Western Eyes* stands in revealing contrast to the way he treats his own name in *A Personal Record*. It is almost as if the addition of the letter K to Conrad's patronymic in the *Record* reenacts the slanderous insinuation of Prince K's lawyer as Conrad's own self-accusation—in order to affirm, through the self-accusative case of the supplemental K, a familial and ethno-national identity hidden in the authorial name. The first half of the *Record* turns to the memory not only of parents but also other members of his family, in a series of reminiscences designed to highlight his Polish lineage. Yet nowhere can he simply state that he is (or was) Polish. And, indeed, nowhere in the autobiography is he able to spell out his Polish name. The closest he will come to doing both is in the second half of the *Record*, where he recounts passing the exam, certifying him as Master in the British Merchant Marine service. Describing the experience as feeling "adopted" and comparing the British examiner to "an ancestor," he writes:

> Writing my long name (it has twelve letters) with laborious care on the slip of blue paper, he remarked:
> "You are of Polish extraction."
> "Born there, sir."
> He laid down the pen and leaned back to look at me as it were for the first time. (*Record*, 118)

The examiner's laborious process of writing out Conrad's Polish name is followed by the laborious attempt to pronounce the name of another Polish sailor with a name almost as long as Conrad's ("Shorter by two letters, sir" [*Record*, 120]). This memory enables Conrad to resolve a number of things all at once: describing the success of his certification as a British sailor, he is able to declare his Polish origin even as he claims a metaphorical English ancestry. The writing out of his name immediately unravels the problem of Russian naming found in *Under Western Eyes* and *Heart of Darkness* ("There was a signature, but it was illegible—not Kurtz—a much longer word" [*Youth*, 98]). Although this moment does indeed dwell on the difficulty of writing and pronouncing Korzeniowski in English, it does so without ever having to spell out the name itself. The passage may seem more interesting for the idealized account of passing his Master's certificate (especially since he conveniently elides the fact that he failed the exam the first time around).[38] It may seem more interesting, too, for the shift it marks in the series of reminiscences which begin by addressing the question of when he first came to write ("the writing of my first book"), and then conclude with reflections on the beginning of his seafaring life ("my first contact with the sea"). Yet considering the importance of names and naming (generally) in Conrad, and, above all, their significance for the chronotopes of romanization that I have been exploring here, it is striking that this is the only place in all the autobiographical reminiscences that he mentions his Polish name. It is all the more striking that the gesture of writing his name, and of pronouncing it out loud, takes place without ever naming the name. Does the supplementary K, added to his signature in the 1911 "Familiar Preface," point to Conrad's Polish name, or does it point to Conrad's success in *not* representing that name in romanized print form?

There is an odd vanishing trick in this writing out of Conrad's Polish name that reflects the evasive structure of the autobiography as a whole (to the extent that the fragments of the *Record* constitute a whole narrative). In "A Familiar Preface" Conrad himself comments on this evasive structure. Defending himself against the "crime" and "impropriety" of the *Record*'s chronology and form, he dramatizes his problem in an improvised conversation with a friend—already distancing the autobiographical first person through an embedded set of quotation marks: "'Alas!' I protested, mildly. "Could I begin with the sacramental words, 'I was born on such a date in such a place?' The remoteness of the locality would have robbed the statement of all interest" (*Record*, xx). The displacement of his own, first-person speaking voice replicates the way in which the reminiscences are organized around a sequence of displacements. The *Record* begins by displacing the traditional focus of autobiography from his own life's experience to that of the physical object of his first book, *Almayer's Folly*, which becomes a kind of mock character in itself, "the MS. of 'Almayer's Folly'" whose journey, growth, and development the *Record* traces until that narrative conceit is displaced, in turn, by an account of the beginnings of Conrad's profession as a sailor. He succinctly sums up these two parts of the *Record* in "A Familiar Preface": "the writing of my first book and . . . my first contact with the sea" (xxi). Couched within the first part—and itself appearing as another displacement from the story of "the MS. of 'Almayer's Folly'"—come the Polish memories. The oddly recessed form in which Conrad sets up the only public record of his Polish past, mirrors the embedding of the first person within a series of quotation marks. And that embedded first-person voice in the "Familiar Preface," unable to say, "I was born on such and such a date," mirrors the dramatized first person in dialogue with the English examiner, who is able to write out his Polish name, enacting the vanishing trick whereby Conrad is able to claim Polish nationality and birthright within the spacing and timing of an English language and script, unmarked by the actual lettering of the Polish name itself.

As part of the *Record*'s evasive structure, these problems of writing, spelling, and pronouncing Conrad's Polish name are displaced onto the spelling of other names. The name of Almayer, in particular, provokes an extended reminiscence, and it is this passage that forms a bridge between the two parts of the autobiography. In section IV, immediately following the last Polish reminiscence (of reading his father's Polish translations of English and French works while in exile in Russia), he turns to a discussion of meeting the man whose name he "converted" to his own uses for his first novel. The repeated emphasis on Almayer's name foregrounds certain aspects of what he will later (successfully) elide with his own Polish name: "I heard his name distinctly pronounced several times in a lot of talk in Malay language. Oh yes, I heard it distinctly—Almayer, Almayer—and saw Captain C__ smile while the fat, dingy Rajah laughed audibly" (*Record*, 75). This focus on the different ways Almayer's name is pronounced, frames a long, discursive account of his first meeting that ends with the oddly, classical rhetorical gesture of addressing the "shade" of Almayer: "It is true, Almayer, that in the world below I have converted your name to my own uses. But that is a very small larceny. What's in a name, O Shade?" (*Record*, 87). This send-off serves to dissolve the mock-autobiographical conceit of the first part of the *Record*. Characteristic of the autobiographical reminiscences in its evasiveness and displacement, this long meditation on the sound of Almayer's name might be read as a cryptic displacement of the problem of romanization embedded in Conrad's Polish name. Conrad's "Almayer" is an English transliteration of the name of Charles William Olmeijer, on whom the fictional character is based. Foregrounding the *sound* of the name (in spoken Malay), it reproduces, in the spacing and timing of the printed page, the problem of lettering elided, too, in the writing out of the letters of his Polish name.

This oblique or hidden question of romanized transliteration in the question of how to spell names is itself a displacement of the problem of romanization, encoded in the organizing conceit of a manuscript whose itinerary, growth, and development enables Conrad to narrate "the writing of my first book." The long meditation on the way that Almayer's name was "distinctly pronounced several times" by all sorts of people so that it became "the property of the winds" (*Record*, 75–88) is itself an extension of the *Record*'s reference to the opening words of *Almayer's Folly* "the opening exclamation calling Almayer to his dinner" (*Record*, 13). The reference comes just before the moment when Conrad improvises the conceit of "the MS. of 'Almayer's Folly'" that gets carried with him to the "region of Stanley Falls which in '68 was the blankest of the blank spaces on the earth's figured surface" (*Record*, 13). Anticipating the formation of this mock autobiographical subject, the written object that will displace the autobiographical first person who accompanies it, as if there were only a metonymical relation between author and work, Conrad offers a condensed plot summary of his first novel that is spliced together with a set of diverse journeys that recalls the opening line of the autobiography, "Books may be written in all sorts of places" (*Record*, 3). It is a rather remarkable single sentence whose itinerary replicates the distorted chronology, displacement of narrative, and recessive embedding of the narrative first person, characteristic of the whole *Record*:

> Between its opening exclamation calling Almayer to his dinner in his wife's voice and Abdullah's (his enemy) mental reference to the God of Islam—"The Merciful, the Compassionate"—which closes the book, there were to come several long sea passages, a visit (to use the elevated phraseology suitable to the occasion) to the scenes (some of them) of my childhood and the realization of childhood's vain words, expressing a light-hearted and romantic whim. (*Record*, 13)

Positioning the autobiographical "I" between the opening and closing phrases of his first novel, the sentence splices together two different chronologies and topologies. The "book" within which Conrad embeds the itinerary of the reminiscences to come, both embodies and displaces the first-person, autobiographical narrator. The "vain words, expressing a light-hearted and romantic whim" are, all at once, outside and embedded within the timing and spacing of the opening and closing words of *Almayer's Folly*. Indeed, this disjunctive chronology and topology projects an autobiographical writing self that is both inside and outside the act of writing that constitutes all its various speaking persons. The writer and the writer's work strangely contain each other in the moment just before the act of speech (those "vain words, expressing a light-hearted and romantic whim") comes to write itself into a place where author and work sit side by side: "And the MS. of 'Almayer's Folly,' carried about me as if it were a talisman or a treasure, went *there* too" (*Record*, 13).[39]

The metaphor of the manuscript as object ("talisman" or "treasure") is also a metonymy of authorship that positions all the various speaking persons of the narrative in relation to this disjunct chronology and topology of writing. In its evocation of a set of widely divergent geographical migrations, all embedded within a kind of impossible topology of writing, its chronotope of authorial design is also an especially condensed and complex chronotope of romanized script form. Anieszka Adamowicz-Pośpiech has described Conrad's *Record* as an "auto-bio-atlas," a phrase that captures, especially well, the way in which Conrad coordinates a whole set of real and imaginary geographies of migration into a single narrative pattern.[40] This one key sentence offers, simultaneously, a description of his first book, an account of the travels of his first book to Africa and to Ukraine, and a glimpse of a logic linking disparate experiences of migration and border crossings. The passage is premised on the crossing-over of widely divergent migratory crossings: Conrad's real voyage to Africa and his home "visit" (to Ukraine); and all the various migrations converging on the imaginary Borneo setting of *Almayer's Folly* (Arab, Bugis, Sulu, Malay, Balinese, Dutch, English, and Romanian). Bringing together African, Malay, European, and English perspectives, momentarily at least, into a single sentence, it juxtaposes real and imaginary journeys, combining vastly different experiences of migration into a singular trope of writing, script, and identity-formation.

This "auto-bio-atlas," or chronotope of authorship, positions all its various speaking persons within a series of frames of reference to forms of romanization that are, as it were, hiding in plain sight. I have already discussed the significance in Conrad's book-ending his first novel between two chronotopes of romanization—the romanized print form of Almayer's wife's "calling [him] to his dinner" and the Arabic script form evoked by "Abdullah's ... mental reference to the God of Islam." Conrad's recapitulation of the book's contrast between romanized and Arabic scriptworlds may be implicit, but this makes it all the more striking that Conrad situates that contrast of scriptworlds in relation to the trope of the "blank space" of Africa. Rewriting the famous map-pointing scene from *Heart of Darkness* as his own autobiographical experience, Conrad's "auto-bio-atlas" submits those divergent geographies of experience to an open-ended question of the framing scene of writing. The opening line of the autobiography, implicitly, might be rephrased: "Books may be written in all sorts of *scripts*." In rewriting Marlow's childhood, map-pointing experience as his own, moreover, Conrad (again implicitly) reframes the English scene of romanization (the imposition of English names on the map of Africa) within a Polish childhood time and place. Embedded here—as everywhere in this miniature "auto-bio-atlas"—is the displaced form of that impossible autobiographical statement "I was born on such a date in such a place."

In the recesses of this embedded chronotope of authorship lies the hidden algorithm around which all of Conrad's work hinges. The whole of the autobiography might be read in terms of the spelling out of his own authorial signature: an extended meditation on the switch from K to C in the adoption of his writing persona.[41] Here, the alternation from K to C reverses the binary switch in the Russian romanization of Razumov's full name. Indeed, the underlying movement of the *Record* can be explained as an effort to untie the vexed knot of Russian identity encoded in the Russian romanization of Razumov's name. Nonetheless, the alternation between C and K is what binds the Polish reminiscences and the Russian novel together. With the addition of the supplementary K to Conrad's authorial signature in the 1911 "Familiar Preface," this condensed algorithm, written into his signature, gets reduced to the effect of the single letter K. What is perhaps most striking of all is the fact that the supplementary K marks, not the *difference* between roman and Cyrillic script, but rather a roman letter that they share in common. It is in this sense, then, that I suggest we read the *Record* as a conversion of the accusative case of the K in Razumov's name into the wish-fulfillment of a self-accusative confession of Russian identity that affirms Conrad's Polishness.

"Prince Roman"

What the Polish reminiscences and the Russian novel secretly share is illuminated by the part of Conrad's Polish reminiscences that seems the most distant from what *Under Western Eyes* does with its exaggerated emphasis on Cyrillic script. "Prince Roman" is a piece that was originally intended for inclusion in the autobiographical reminiscences but was published separately. As the title itself felicitously suggests, the name of the Polish character at the center of this reminiscence seems to pose no problem of transliteration, transcription, or translation, such as one finds with Razumov or with Conrad's own name. Prince Roman is rendered, immediately and directly, into the roman print of English letters. Prince Roman is a character whose appearance, story, experience, and lineage seem to be written into the roman print form of his title and name. By contrast to the story of Razumov, whose full name requires redoubled attention to the Cyrillic scriptworld into which he was born as a Russian, and also by contrast to Conrad's autobiographical evasion in spelling out all twelve letters of his Polish name, Prince Roman's story unfolds according to a logic of perfect alignment with the roman scriptworld that he inhabits and embodies as a Pole.

There is, however, an uncanny exaggeration of the noble, Roman genealogy of this "Prince Roman," a redoubling of emphasis on roman script that reads as the inverted mirror image of the Russian novel's emphasis on Cyrillic script. This emerges even before the reader is introduced to Prince Roman, when a speaker, revealing his identity to be Polish, uses a distinctive Latin phrase to sum up his Polish national identity: "the year 1831 is for us an historical date, one of these fatal years when in the presence of the world's passive indignation and eloquent sympathies we had once more to murmur 'Vae Victis' and count the cost in sorrow" (Tales of Hearsay, 29). The Latin saying (meaning "woe to the conquered") aligns Polish national identity with a Roman lineage in ways that foreshadow the role of script in the story of Prince Roman's participation in the 1831 uprising against Russian rule. Refusing to accept the leniency extended by the Russian authorities, he "reached for a pen and wrote on a sheet of paper he found under his hand: 'I joined the national rising from conviction'" (Tales of Hearsay, 52). The Latinate English word "conviction"—echoing the Latin "Victis"—might suggest a hidden argument over Roman models of justice, the law, and standards of civil rights. What makes Prince Roman's "written testimony" all the more powerful, indeed, is the Russian emperor's comment, written "with his own hand in the margin," converting the Latinate echo of Prince Roman's "conviction" into another Latinate English word, "convict": "The authorities are severely warned to take care that this convict walks in chains like any other criminal every step of the way" (Tales of Hearsay, 53).

The gravity lent to the words "conviction" and "convict" both repeats and reformulates the opening motto "*Vae Victis*," establishing the nobility of Prince Roman's lineage of Polish national resistance, according to a doubly romanized linguistic and script form. Not only does it align Polish national identity with a Latin lineage (something echoed in the "old-time habit of larding . . . speech with Latin words" [*Tales of Hearsay*, 42] attributed to Prince Roman's loyal servant). Latin is the language shared by both the vanquished Poles and the Russian victors. Prince Roman's written testimony is translated into an English word ("conviction") that effaces whatever written form might originally have been used. That is, the reader is not told what language—Polish, Russian, French, or Latin—Prince Roman used for his "written testimony." Nor, for that matter, does the reader know what language Emperor Nicholas used to write "convict" in the margin of that "written testimony." It is clear that a variety, indeed a hierarchy, of languages circulates, both in spoken and in written form. All these languages come together, in the story's telling, in the same time and space—in a scriptworld that seems to align as the worldscript for all these speakers of different European languages, for the victors and the vanquished alike. It is a rare moment in Conrad's *oeuvre*, perhaps utterly unique in its idealized alignment of a history of Roman conquest (uppercase Romanization) with the cosmopolitical exchange between modern European languages (the phenomenon of lowercase romanization). Standing in striking contrast to the role of Cyrillic script in *Under Western Eyes* and *Heart of Darkness*, the story makes Prince Roman's genealogy, the genealogy of a shared Polish and Russian scriptworld. It presents an idealized inversion of the tortured experience of betrayal of national identity written into the double-romanized Cyrillic form of Razumov's name. The (doubly) Russian face of romanization in *Under Western Eyes* here becomes the (doubly) roman print form of Polish history.

As one of the reminiscences originally intended for inclusion in *A Personal Record*, "Prince Roman" belongs to Conrad's attempt to explain his own Polish genealogy. Yet, if "Prince Roman" succeeds in offering an idealized Polish, noble genealogy—one that inverts the Russian novel's genealogy of Cyrillic script—it is striking how much it isolates the first-person narrative voice from that of Conrad himself. Although the opening statement unequivocally identifies with the cause of Polish nationalism ("the year 1831 is *for us* an historical date . . ."), Conrad distances this speaker through quotation marks and a comment of explanation in the second paragraph: "The speaker was of Polish nationality" (*Tales of Hearsay*, 29). Echoing the displaced autobiographical first person of the *Record's* "Familiar Preface," albeit without the complex framing of its speaking persons around multiple framing scripts, it is notable that one of the strongest declarations of political, historical, and national affiliation in all these reminiscences must be narratively framed by a "speaker" separate from the autobiographical first person adopted in the *Record*. This suggests how an identification with "Polish nationality" can only be ascribed to the speaking voice of another—in the grammatical object, rather than from the subject position, displaced, as it were, from the nominative to the accusative case. This is, then, the self-accusative case of Conrad's K, adding the effect of Russian romanization to the case of English romanization—or rather, redoubling the English romanization of Konrad to Conrad with the shadow of the Polish face of a Russian romanization. When Conrad adds the letter K to his authorial signature JC in 1911, he reveals his Polish past and, at the same time, betrays his own familiar relation to the Russian Empire that overshadowed that Polish past. If, on the one hand, it marks his own foreign, Polish identity (doubly so, in fact, with the Konrad and the Korzeniowski of his given Polish name), it also marks the shadow of the Russian scriptworld imposed historically, linguistically, and orthographically on that Polish name and identity.

The effect of adding the unique K to his signature is to draw attention to the difference—which is simultaneously a rivalry and a mimicry—between the

English scriptworld of the British Empire and the Cyrillic scriptworld of the Russian Empire. In 1924, writing to the French translator, Charles Chassé, Conrad appears to be looking back to just this moment when he writes of having betrayed his "neutral pseudonym":

> I have asked myself more than once whether if I had preserved the secret of my origins under the neutral pseudonym "Joseph Conrad" that temperamental similitude ["references to my Slavonism"] would have been put forward at all.[42]

Earlier, for the sake of simplicity, I read this letter as a direct reference to the unique K-effect of the 1911 signature. As the grammar of the sentence already suggests, though, it is not so easy to pin down precisely when he imagines having betrayed "the secret of my origins." Now, however, I want to suggest that we read this undecidability in terms of the double-bind of English and Russian scriptworlds. Although one reading might posit a neutral "Joseph Conrad" that gets betrayed at some point—perhaps in 1908 when he writes publicly about his Polish past; or perhaps in 1911 when he adds the letter K to his signature—another reading might emphasize that "Joseph Conrad" never did serve as the "neutral pseudonym" he imagines (conditionally) it might have been. The letter K ambiguously marks this impossible neutrality, either in its absence from the authorial signature, or in its presence.

The neutral space of romanized English print is never neutral, but rather, always marked by the signs of a multiplicity of languages and scripts, imported into English through the process of romanized transliteration. The space of Russian script provides the inverted mirror image of this universalizing, globalizing romanization of any and every language.[43] It does so, however, in ways that complicate the case of English romanization. The K-effect of English (as described by the OED) already hints at this, but the corresponding K-effect within histories of Russian orthography underscores this all the more: there can never be a monolingualism of script; there can never be a single alphabet. What might appear to be the model of top-down, autocratic imposition of a single, official, orthodox writing system, will always share the space of print with the typeface of another script. As Russian does with Ukrainian; as Polish does with Russian; so, too, the roman letters of English share the same space as the Cyrillic letters of Russian, and all the variant versions of lettering across Slavic languages. Neither merely a technical question of the medium of print, nor only a political question of the relation between language and script, this doubling and splitting of alternative, rival, and overlapping histories of "the" alphabet, of the global space of print, and the universalizing model of "print-capitalism"—produces a K-effect registered within and across the scriptworlds of romanized English, Cyrillic romanization, and all the other variants in the use of Latin letters (lowercase romanization) throughout Europe.

Kafka and Conrad: The Character and Function of K in Central Europe

The K-effect of Conrad's unique authorial signature at the end of the "Familiar Preface" does more than mark the success of the *Record* in negotiating the "secret bitterness and complex loyalty" evoked by critical assessments of his Polish background. It marks an important turning point in Conrad's work, when he sought to address the Slavic context of his own childhood experience. As the conversion of an accusation of betrayal into affirmation of a Polish identity, articulated in the wish-fulfillment of a self-accusative mark of Russianness, the letter K has something in common with the distinctive mark of Kafka's K, which Giorgio Agamben has read as a legacy of Roman law, the mark of self-slander, or false accusation—*kalumnia*.[44]

Both as a matter of intellectual and literary history, Conrad's double-writing of his Russian novel and his Polish autobiography coincides with an especially important moment in the crystallization of Western European responses to Russia and Russian literature, and everything condensed in the stereotype of "Sclavonism." Yet this turning point in Conrad's career also reveals an aesthetic turn, implicit from the very beginning, shaping the timing and spacing of all his narratives, and all the elements of his crafting of narrative form, from the smallest lexical effects to the broadest arc of plotting. The letter K reveals a simultaneous marking and effacing of Russian, Polish, and (more broadly) Slavic languages and scripts in shaping chronotopes of romanization throughout Conrad's work. The logic of the Russian face of romanization—which appears both in the exaggerated use of Cyrillic in the plotting of *Heart of Darkness* and *Under Western Eyes*, and in the exaggerated use of roman and Latin letters in "Prince Roman"—turns on a sociolinguistic fact that is, all at once, entirely simple and almost inexplicably problematic. Cyrillic and Western European scripts are both the same and different. The letter K, shared by Cyrillic and Western European alphabets, reveals a worldscript experienced as both the same and different—shared and contested—by a whole range of languages and scripts across Central Europe.

This sociolinguistic phenomenon brings me back to the "monolingual paradigm" Yasmin Yildiz outlines as a feature of nineteenth-century Europe and finds articulated in the work of Franz Kafka, who "explores the modern problem of a putative homology between native language and ethno-cultural identity." For Yildiz, Kafka is exemplary in giving aesthetic form to the contradictory imperatives of the "monolingual paradigm": "Ultimately, Kafka embraced a paradigm that fundamentally excluded him and from this impossible situation developed his characteristic high modernist aesthetics of negativity."[45] Kafka's K and Conrad's K both share the sociolinguistic and aesthetic features of this modernist moment.

A number of interpretations of Kafka's work might be enlisted to show how the letter K produces a signature-effect across Kafka's *oeuvre*, similar to the signature-effect I have been exploring in Conrad. Many critics have noted Kafka's fondness for the letter K ("which he uses almost flamboyantly in his handwriting"[46]), its apparent connection with the first letter of Kafka's own name (which Beasley-Murray links to a range of Slavic linguistic allusions), and the ubiquity of its appearance in the names of his characters and in multiple smaller ways throughout his work.[47] Max Brod's note on *The Castle* gives as evidence of the shift from a first-person short story into novel form, the fact that Kafka altered the use of the first person in the earlier chapters ""K." being inserted everywhere in the place of "I.""[48] There is, in addition, Giorgio Agamben's emphasis on the letter K as a legacy of Roman law, in his elaboration of Stimilli's argument that K does not stand for Kafka, but for slander, *kalumnia*.

Perhaps the most relevant reading of Kafka is Deleuze and Guattari's influential *Kafka: Toward a Minor Literature*. Their characterization of Kafka's *oeuvre* as an "assemblage" (*agencement*) of various texts (including the letters, diary entries, stories, and novels) provides an alternative way to consider the organization of Conrad's work. The laborious struggle to write is something for which both writers are recognized. The different components of Kafka's "writing machine" or "expression machine," as they call it, include the letters and diary entries: "If the letters really are a part of the work, it is because they are an indispensable gear, a motor part for the literary machine as Kafka conceives of it even if this machine is destined to disappear or explode to a degree comparable to the machine of the Penal Colony."[49] Conrad's letters, too, constitute a kind of writer's workshop, especially his letters to the small circle of friends in whom he confided the agony of laboring to produce his texts (Edward Garnett, R. B. Cunninghame Graham, Ford Madox Ford).

The focus on the "assemblage" of Kafka's texts is especially interesting in light of Deleuze and Guattari's emphasis on what—at the very end of their book—they call "the K function"[50] coordinating the "literary machine." Earlier in the study, developing their distinctive use of the term "assemblage" to describe the literary machinery of Kafka's work, they write: "The letter K no longer designates a narrator or a character but an assemblage."[51] This extends analysis to a range of effects: of narrative voice—the significance of the use of

K drawn from Kafka's own name; of the shift from "I" to "K" in *The Castle*—or the function of characters' names, for example, in the convention of giving an initial letter (with or without a dash), as with Josef K.; extending to an analysis of "assemblages of nouns and effects, of heterogeneous orders of signs"[52]—so, for example, the alliterative effect of cumulative nouns beginning with K, and the "flamboyant" writing of K in manuscripts and diary entries (see Figure 6). All of these effects might be compared to the similar range of K-effects in Conrad—beginning with his own name; extending to his characters; a similar set of cumulative, minute lexical effects; and including the insistent repetition of embellished Ks (similarly "flamboyant") in the margins of Conrad's manuscripts and typescripts (see Figure 7). Conrad's own use of the metaphor of writing and script—in "A Familiar Preface," and in the extensive mirroring of such metaphors in *Under Western Eyes* and *A Personal Record*—all contributes to the sense in which the letter K signals a "literary machine," as suggested by Deleuze and Guattari.

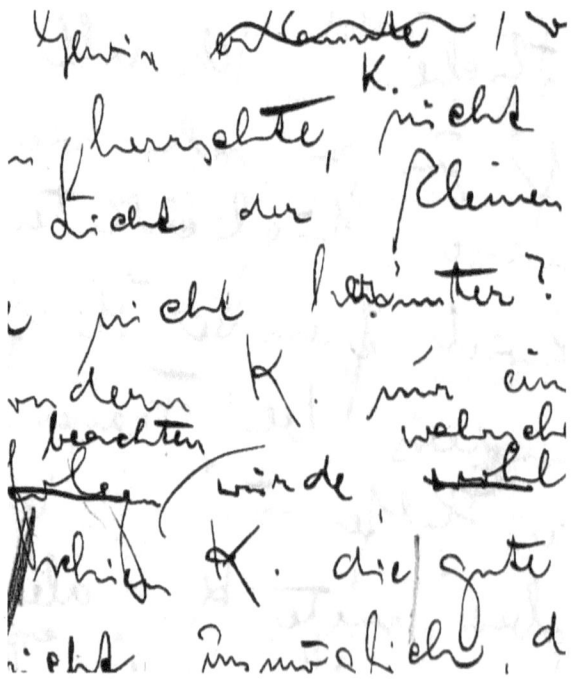

Figure 6. Franz Kafka's handwritten "K" in the manuscript for *Der Prozeß* (*The Trial*). Detail from online manuscript samples in The Kafka Project.

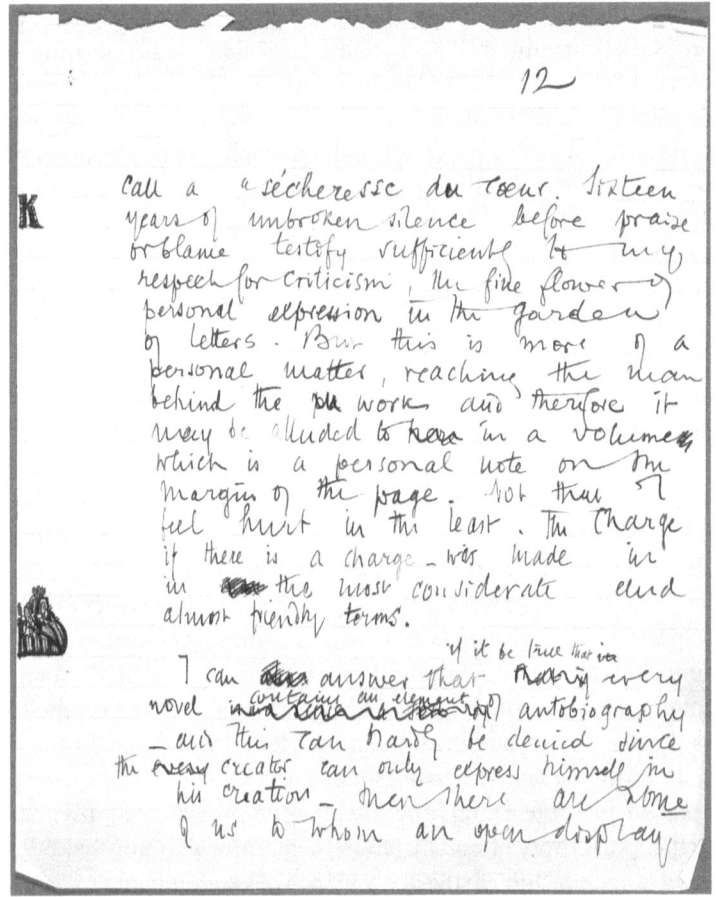

Figure 7. Conrad's marginal "K" doodles. From "A Familiar Preface" to *A Personal Record*. Henry W. and Albert A. Berg Collection of English and American Literature, The New York Public Library.

If Kafka sheds light on the "literary machine" or "assemblage" of Conrad's texts, the chronotope of romanization in Conrad's texts, in turn, sheds light on Kafka. The difficulty presented by Kafka's works (generally) is the temptation to interpret them symbolically, allegorically, or mythically. Theodor Adorno's reading of Kafka follows Walter Benjamin in identifying this difficulty as part of its "parabolic" aesthetic: "Walter Benjamin rightly defined [Kafka's prose] as parable. It expresses itself not through expression but by its repudiation, by breaking off. It is a parabolic system the key to which has been stolen ... Each sentence says 'interpret me,' and none will permit it."[53] Both Benjamin's reading of Kafka, with its focus on the role of "gesture," and Adorno's, with its focus on "Kafka's literalness" ("Kafkasche Buchstäblichkeit")[54] provide suggestive points of reference for a comparison between Kafka and Conrad. The turning point in *Under Western Eyes*, in particular, with its exaggerated emphasis on Razumov's physical gestures, the metaphor and metonymy of face, and the chronotope of Cyrillic script, seems to echo the way that Benjamin formulates the function of gesture in Kafka and the way Adorno articulates the problem of interpretation written into every Kafkaesque sentence. The title-phrase "under Western eyes" itself seems to emerge from a Kafkaesque "parabolic system," implying a set of physical gestures (notably, the face either reading the page or the page itself read as typeface) and posing a riddle of "literalness" that eludes interpretation (the phrase signifies a text that is simultaneously illegible and legible and through an irreducibly metaphorical set of associations that insist on, yet defy, literal sense).[55] Reading these aesthetic effects as effects of what English and Russian scripts secretly share, draws attention to those moments in Kafka's text where the "assemblage" of linguistic signs also turns on the timing and spacing of roman letters.

"The Penal Colony" presents the most striking, if gruesome, example. In some respects, the fullest expression of what Deleuze and Guattari call Kafka's "machine," the torture machine it devises, distills into a single image, the nightmare-version of a timing and spacing of script imposed on the human body as the discipline and punishment of colonial penal law. In the time it takes for the criminal sentence to be tattooed on the body, the convicted person comes to read and understand his crime. It is tempting to read this as an allegory for the long history of romanization (beginning with uppercase Romanization and extending through the phenomenon of lowercase print romanization) as the imposition of European culture in the form of roman letters: a violent history of writing on the body, executed by a juridical writing machinery whose fantasy is the nightmare of European colonization, imposing a technology of script on the body of colonized people.

As with so much in Kafka, however, parable may be a better way to consider this, keeping in mind Adorno's formulation of "a parabolic system the key to which has been stolen." To continue Adorno's argument "any effort to make this fact itself the key is bound to go astray by confounding the abstract thesis of Kafka's work, the obscurity of the existent, with its substance."[56] "The Penal Colony" does indeed offer a parable about technologies of writing, colonial systems of governance, and the discipline and punishment of human bodies. How it positions the phenomenon of romanization, however, deserves closer attention. The story itself emphasizes several features of script that invite further comparison to Conrad's chronotopes of romanization but complicate any simple allegory of the imposition of technologies of romanized print on a colonial body. In the "officer's" early demonstration of the machine, he invites the visiting "explorer" to read the writing used for the programming of the apparatus. For the explorer, however, the writing is illegible, the script unfamiliar: "The explorer would have liked to say something appreciative, but all he could see was a labyrinth of lines crossing and recrossing each other, which covered the paper so thickly that it was difficult to discern the blank spaces between them" ("Penal," 148) ("Der Reisende hätte gerne etwas Anerkennendes gesagt, aber er sah nur labyrinthartige, einander vielfach kreuzende Linien, die so dicht das Papier bedeckten, daß man nur mit Mühe die weißen Zwischenräume erkannte"[57]). The possibility that this is a script not familiar to the explorer/traveler—perhaps like the Cyrillic script Marlow encounters on his journey up the Congo River—is introduced. In response to the traveler's claim that he "can't" read the script, the officer claims that, on the contrary, "it's clear enough" before going on to say "it's no calligraphy for school children. It needs to be studied closely. I'm quite sure that in the end you could understand it too" ("Penal," 149) ("'Es ist doch deutlich,' sagte der Offizier. . . . es ist keine Schönschrift für Schulkinder. Man muß lange darin lesen. Auch Sie würden es schließlich gewiß erkennen"[58]).

A script that is legible and yet illegible: already this is a parable of the Russian face of romanization that I have been exploring in Conrad. In the attention it gives to the script of its grotesque torture machine, "The Penal Colony" suggests a combination of what Conrad does with the "cipher" of Cyrillic script in the plotting of *Heart of Darkness* and what, by contrast, he does with the chronotope of Cyrillic script in *Under Western Eyes*. As in *Heart of Darkness*, there is an explanation for the foreign, "artistic" quality of the script ("I'm quite sure that in the end you would understand it too"). The officer's various explanations of the writing seem (repeatedly) to presume that the apparatus writes a script his interlocuter can read. "This prisoner, for instance," he says of the convict, "will have written on his body: HONOR THY SUPERIORS" ("Penal," 144) ("'Diesem Verurteilten zum Beispiel'—der Offizier zeigte auf den Mann—'wird auf den Leib geschrieben werden: Ehre deinen Vorgesetzten!'"[59]). In the case of the officer's explanation of his own (death) sentence, he reads it out again on the assumption that the "explorer" can read the script, too: "Now the officer began to spell it, letter by letter, and then read out the words. '"BE JUST!' is what is written there," he said, "surely you can read it now" ("Penal," 161) ("Nun begann der Offizier die Aufschrift zu buchstabieren und dann las er sie noch einmal im Zusammenhang. 'Sei gerecht!'—heißt es,' sagte er, 'jetzt können Sie es doch lesen.'"[60]). If the timing and spacing of this script seems to demand that it can be read by all, eventually, the explorer repeatedly contradicts this, insisting, "I told you before that I can't make out these scripts" ("ich sagte schon, ich kann diese Blätter nicht lesen"[61])—and suggesting, more like the logic of *Under Western Eyes*, that they inhabit two different scriptworlds.

The parable of script here is all the more comparable to Conrad's chronotopes of romanization since Kafka poses a fundamental difficulty in determining what kind of script it is that the writing machine imprints on the human body. A script that is simultaneously illegible and legible, it rehearses a similar kind of standoff between the traveler and the officer as between Razumov and the English narrator of *Under Western Eyes*. The grotesque and unique twist Kafka gives to the temporal and spatial arrangement of this script's letters, creates a nightmare fantasy of a script potentially applicable to everyone (a worldscript imposed as part of the design of the penal colony), but whose deciphering is tailored to fit each individual person's crime (with a death sentence written in that person's individual scriptworld, executed on the individual body). There are a number of uncanny echoes of Conrad's work in "The Penal Colony." In part, this may reflect thematic resemblances to *Heart of Darkness* given the "tropical" colonial setting of Kafka's story, although there is a more intimate, if less obvious, connection with *Under Western Eyes* suggested by the bureaucratic imposition of a script as part of the juridical logic of law. The most revealing comparison is to the story "Prince Roman." Both involve a legal punishment written into the form of its own recognition as script: the one, "Prince Roman," a relatively happy resolution of the role of script in adjudicating the relation between victor and vanquished; the other, a nightmare variation of the role of script in executing the machinery of law, writing, script, and identity.

The contrast between "Prince Roman" and "A Penal Colony" may be even more revealing in light of the position that each story occupies in the "assemblage" of texts to which they are related. "Prince Roman," originally intended for inclusion in *A Personal Record*, stands apart from that work in its awkward framing of the relation between its first-person narrator and the "speaker," identified as Polish. A fragment of what is already a fragmentary set of reminiscences, its fantasy resolution draws attention to the unresolved—indeed unresolvable—problem of script and identity in the surrounding texts: namely, how to articulate lineages of Russian and Polish national identity in the timing and spacing of the same worldscript and scriptworld. It amounts to a confession that cannot be made in either the autobiographical record or the Russian novel: the avowal of a narrative "I" who is both Polish and Russian and whose very name is inscribed in the history of Russian romanization that defines their shared and contested scriptworlds and worldscripts. Kafka's "Penal Colony" similarly stands apart from the "assemblage" of texts to which it nonetheless belongs, as an especially revealing example. Although it "makes explicit" the "machine" Deleuze and Guattari find at work in the "assemblage" of all the various Kafka texts (letters, diaries, stories, novels), this machine is "too mechanical."[62] It bears the "seeds" of the "machinic assemblages" of the three novels, but it is still too "transcendental," "too isolated and reified," a "too abstract machine."[63]

"The Penal Colony" plays a similar role in the overall "assemblage" of Kafka's work (the "Kafka-machine") as "Prince Roman" does in the "chronotope" of Conrad's work. Each narrative offers an isolated solution to the problem posed elsewhere in the respective authors' works: the engineering problem of writing in Kafka's work, and, for Conrad, the shared and contested Russian and Polish scriptworlds in the timing and spacing of roman letters. The comparison invites reconsideration of the way in which these terms—"assemblage" and "chronotope"—theorize the function of script (generally) and roman lettering (in particular). "Assemblage," for Deleuze and Guattari, is a term that enables discussion of the aesthetic effects of Kafka's work without falling into the trap of symbolic, allegorical, or mythical readings. As Réda Bensmaïa writes, situating Deleuze and Guattari in the wake of Benjamin:

> Benjamin was one of the first "readers" of Kafka to see and then try to show—to demonstrate—that Kafka's work was, from a certain point of view, to be taken literally: in a word, that it functioned on the surface of its signs and that the issue was not—at least, not *only*—to try to interpret it but, above all, to practice it as an experimental machine or a mass of writing machines that are made of assemblages of nouns and effects, of heterogeneous orders of signs that cannot be reduced to a binary structure, to a dominant or transcendental signifier, or ultimately to some phantasm (originary or not).[64]

To this illuminating account of "assemblage," we might add that the French word *agencement* combines a mechanical, engineering, even computer-programming model with a more formal literary term (the "construction, organization" of a sentence or a novel). In this respect, its literary, theoretical aim has something in common with Bakhtin's term "chronotope," which seeks to explain the artistic organization of time and space, most notably in novel form (where chronotopes form "the organizing centers for the fundamental narrative events of the novel").[65] Both prioritize the literary form of the novel, even as their literary arguments make claims far beyond questions of interpretation, or stylistics, or theories of genre. Both are not so much theorizing novel form as they are theorizing how language is formed in novels.

Most important is the linguistic problem at the heart of each. Both bear on the predicament of what Yasemin Yildiz calls the "monolingual paradigm": Deleuze and Guattari in their formulation of a "minor literature" ("that which a minority constructs within a major language"[66]); Bakhtin in his formulation of the "heteroglossia" or "polyglossia" of the novel (or, more accurately, "novelization"). Although neither seems to focus on the problem of writing and script (its machinery, as evoked in "The Penal Colony," or the genealogy of Latin and roman script in "Prince Roman"), both indirectly illuminate the implications of the other's theory for grasping the linguistic predicament of Yildiz's "monolingual paradigm" as a predicament of romanization.

It is the linguistic condition of Kafka's experience as a Jewish-German writer in Czech-speaking Prague that defines the characteristics of what Deleuze and Guattari call (following Kafka's own writing about "small nations") a "minor literature . . . which a minority constructs within a majority language."[67] With the "breakdown and fall" of the Habsburg Empire, all the various hierarchies of language undergo "movements of deterritorialization" and "all sorts of complex reterritorialization." Leaning on the linguistic model of Henri Gobard, they refer to four levels of language: the vernacular, the vehicular, the referential, and the mythic: "the distribution of these languages varies from one group to the next and, in a single group, from one epoch to the next (for a long time in Europe, Latin was a vehicular language before becoming referential, then mythic; English has become the worldwide vehicular language for today's world)."[68] They go on to explain how these "four language" levels bear on Kafka:

> The vernacular language for these Jews who have come from a rural milieu is Czech, but the Czech language tends to be forgotten and repressed; as for Yiddish, it is often disdained or viewed with suspicion—it *frightens*, as Kafka tells us. German is the vehicular language of the towns, a bureaucratic language of the state, a commercial language of exchange (but English has already started to become indispensable for this purpose). The German language . . . has a cultural and referential function . . . As a mythic language, Hebrew is connected with the start of Zionism and still possesses the quality of an active dream. For each of these languages, we need to evaluate the degrees of territoriality, deterritorialization, and reterritorialization. Kafka's own situation: he is one of the few Jewish writers in Prague to understand and speak Czech . . . German plays precisely the double role of vehicular and cultural language . . . He will not learn Hebrew until later. What is complicated is Kafka's relation to Yiddish; he sees it less as a sort of

linguistic territoriality for the Jews than as a nomadic movement of deterritorialization that reworks German language.⁶⁹

This multilingual context informs the complexity of Kafka's adoption of German under the contradictory imperatives of the "monolingual paradigm"—embracing, as Yildiz puts it, "a paradigm that fundamentally excluded him" and shaping what Deleuze and Guattari call a "minor literature."

This multilingual context is also articulated by a hierarchy of multiple scripts. Despite the importance of the "writing machine" for the "assemblage," they describe Kafka engineering out of the linguistic condition of his situation as a Jewish-German writer in Prague, Deleuze and Guattari do not pay particular attention to the role of different scripts in the relation between Kafka's relation to German, Czech, Yiddish, or Hebrew. It is implicit in the varying differences in oral and written forms between the four different levels of language that they enumerate, most apparent in the "mythic" role of Hebrew as scripture. The status of Hebrew script and scripture, relatively insignificant for Deleuze and Guattari, takes on an outsized importance in interpretations of those moments when writing and script are foregrounded. The model of the commentary on the Torah often emerges as an explanation for those moments of highlighted script. Again, "The Penal Colony" offers an especially vivid example in the officer's explanation of the timing and spacing of the script of the writing machine:

> Of course the script can't be a simple one; it's not supposed to kill a man straight off, but only after an interval of, on an average, twelve hours; the turning point is reckoned to come at the sixth hour. So there have to be lots and lots of flourishes around the actual script; the script itself runs around the body only in a narrow girdle; the rest of the body is reserved for the embellishments. ("Penal," 149)
>
> Es darf natürlich keine einfache Schrift sein; sie soll ja nicht sofort töten, sondern durchschnittlich erst in einem Zeitraum von zwölf Stunden; für die sechste Stunde ist der Wendepunkt berechnet. Es müssen also viele, viele Zieraten die eigentlich Schrift umgeben; die wirkliche Schrift umzieht den Leib nur in einem schmalen Gürtel; der übrige Körper ist für Verzierungen bestimmt.⁷⁰

As Russell Samolsky argues, these "embellishments may well be Kafka's ironic reading of the tradition of Judaic commentary forming a hedge around Torah—the prisoner, after all, will have 'honor thy superiors' inscribed on his body, an inscription that echoes the ten commandments."⁷¹ The distinction between "the script itself," and the "flourishes" that surround it, may certainly suggest a contrast between script and commentary. It may further suggest a difference between two different scripts. In calling attention to a fundamental ambiguity about what constitutes an "actual script"—especially when it has not yet become legible—this particular example emphasizes what will apply to all those moments when Kafka's text foregrounds script. These are precisely the moments when "Kafka's literality" (whether in Benjamin's or Adorno's sense) has something important to say about the "assemblage" of his work—and, by the same token, the timing and spacing of roman letters. Applying to script, what Deleuze and Guattari say about Kafka's "assemblage" of the four different levels of language, there are important differences in the way German, Czech, Yiddish, and Hebrew are all written and printed. Kafka's correspondence and diaries often recur to these differences, so one might reconsider the example from the "Penal Colony" to pause on the possibility of a difference between the way German and Czech are written (noting the flourishes of German *Fraktur* script and the multiple diacritical marks of Czech). Yiddish, as Yildiz notes, might be rendered either in Latin or in its "customary Hebrew script."[72]

The most abbreviated example of the way Kafka's "assemblage" organizes the relation between the hierarchies of language is the letter K. K indexes what remains largely implicit in Deleuze and Guattari's analysis: namely, the multiple combinations and relations between the script forms of German, Czech, Yiddish, and Hebrew. I would suggest adding the function of script to each function of language that (according to Deleuze and Guattari) "divides up in turn and carries with it multiple centers of power." All the languages and scripts that produce the "blur of languages" are momentarily held in place by the K that engineers the assemblage of the three novels ("the three big interminable works"[73]): "In the three novels, K appears in an astonishing mixture: he is an engineer or a mechanic who deals with the gears of the machine; he is a jurist or a legal investigator who follows the statements of the assemblage.... There is no machinic assemblage that is not a social assemblage of desire, no social assemblage of desire that is not a collective assemblage of enunciation."[74] And again: "It is with the novels that Kafka reaches the final and really unlimited solution: K will not be a subject but will be a general function that proliferates and that doesn't cease to segment and to spread over all the segments."[75]

The K-effect in Conrad's work is just such a "general function that proliferates and doesn't cease to segment and to spread over all the segments." From the smallest linguistic elements, to the naming of characters, the letter K in Conrad signifies more than one thing (even in the signature of Conrad's own name, it "segments" into different parts the names Konrad and Korzeniowski, generating a shift in the sequencing and order of first and last, personal and proper, Christian and surname). The analogous moment in the assemblage of

Kafka's texts, when Conrad reaches the "final and really unlimited solution," is when he affixes the letter K to his already established authorial signature, JC, in the "Familiar Preface" to A *Personal Record*. This "solves" the problem of his always being identified as Slavic or Russian by revealing the Polish name (Konrad or Korzeniowski) hidden in the shift from K to C in the name Conrad. But this supplement leads to an "unlimited" play on the ways in which that letter marks a difference that Polish also shares with Russian—based on the "limitless homophony of signs" (to return to the citation from the linguist Gelb) opened up by the romanized transliteration of Russian names. The Conradian K-effect, then, is especially revealing for that assemblage of texts Conrad wrote from around 1908 to 1911—the period of his Russian (or Slavic) turn, with the double-writing of the autobiographical Polish reminiscences and the Russian novel *Under Western Eyes*. But the term "assemblage" provides a way to connect these texts to the whole *oeuvre*. The simultaneously literary and engineering (and computer coding) sense of this term indicates how the supplementary K affixed to the 1911 signature identifies, not a subject (author, character), and certainly not a fixed ethno-national identity. Instead, the letter K becomes an elementary piece of assembly language; an algorithm for the writing machine that knits readers in and out of the characteristically Conradian textual apparatus.

The term "assemblage," then, can designate the letter K in both Kafka and Conrad as a "function" of the shifting hierarchies of language around the fault lines of multiple scripts across Central Europe. Bakhtin's notion of the "chronotope" names a rather similar effect through a slightly different perspective. Implied in his elaboration of the "forms of time and chronotope in the novel" (in the essay from 1937–38) is also an argument about the way that the novel organizes linguistic diversity, as developed more fully and famously in "Discourse in the Novel" (1934–35). Seeking to overcome the impasse of separating linguistic analysis from stylistic analysis—the first, concerned with everyday language to the exclusion of literary form; the second, concerned with literary form to the exclusion of everyday language—Bakhtin focused on the internal stratification of discourses in the novel, what he famously called "heteroglossia" (*raznorecie*; разноречие). This argument theorizes the development of novel form as itself the result of a combination of stylistic and linguistic forces, what he elsewhere describes as the "centripetal" and "centrifugal" forces of literary and linguistic centralization and decentralization: "alongside the centripetal forces, the centrifugal forces of language carry on their uninterrupted work; alongside verbal-ideological centralization and unification, the uninterrupted processes of decentralization and disunification go forward."[76]

Theorizing novel form as the result of these contending centralizing and decentralizing linguistic forces, recalls the way that Deleuze and Guattari characterize the movements of territorialization, deterritorialization, and reterritorialization in relation to the four levels (or hierarchies) of language at work in Kafka's Prague (and, more generally, the collapsing Habsburg Empire). Both perspectives are helpful for considering the convergence of linguistic and aesthetic concerns marked by the letter K in Conrad's and Kafka's work. Implicit in the linguistic diversity is also the multiscript condition underlying both writers' engagement with what Yildiz calls the "monolingual paradigm." The letter K is an index of both those centralizing forces of language and script and the decentralizing forces of multiple languages and multiple scripts that leads Bakhtin to explore the stratification and heteroglossia of discourse as an essential feature of novel form. These reciprocal and countervailing linguistic forces reproduce the double-face of Russian romanization: the simultaneous reality of a multilingual, multiscript social formation and the imperative to impose a single script as the expression of an ethno-nationalist identity. Indeed, Bakhtin's formulation of these centripetal and centrifugal forces, though focused on the entire history of European linguistic and literary forms, refracts them through Russian literary examples that are themselves intimately linked to the history of language and script reform that I reviewed in this chapter's first section. Dostoevsky, in particular, occupies "an extraordinary and unique place"[77] in his argument. If Bakhtin's argument generally (as well as the special emphasis on Dostoevsky) focuses on the importance of the "speaking person," as opposed to written form, that focus itself emerges from the contest between a unified single Russian script and the variety of languages and scripts it sought to centralize and unify.

Bakhtin's own famously neologistic creation of terms enacts just such a contest. As translators Caryl Emerson and Michael Holquist note at the beginning of their extensive "Glossary" appended to *The Dialogic Imagination*, "Bakhtin's technical vocabulary presents certain difficulties; while he does not use jargon, he does invest everyday words with special content . . ."[78] As noted before, the term "chronotope"—an arrangement of Cyrillic letters transliterating a romanized transcription from the Greek—is itself an example of a chronotope of romanization. In its romanization of the Greek it reenacts the historical arc of Bakhtin's own account of the development of novel form from Greek to Latin and then European variations on the timing and spacing of novelistic form. By and large, though, the term "chronotope" in this essay focuses more on what the "Discourse in the Novel" essay characterizes as the centripetal forces of language: a focus more on those places in the novel where the narrative gets formed or knotted, rather than those places where the narrative unravels, or where its knots get untied. That is to say, it theorizes a largely chronological, linear, and progressive sequence from Greek romance, through the Latin novels and ancient forms of biography and autobiography in early antiquity, through the European chivalric forms, and up to Rabelais and the shaping of modern and contemporary novel forms. It would be a mistake to insist that this history of novel form is simply chronological or teleological. Indeed, it challenges traditional literary histories precisely through its emphasis on the way that literary form articulates the temporal and spatial coordinates of human history. If the romanized Greek form of the term Bakhtin uses, seems to emphasize a centralizing, Europeanizing account of novel form, the term itself may also face in another direction. It is, after all, a Russian romanization of a Greek term, in addition to a borrowing from Einstein's theory of relativity. Implicit in the overall argument Bakhtin is developing, moreover, is something more like the argument he had extended in "Discourse in the Novel," with its emphasis on the "heteroglossia" and decentralizing forces of language. In that work, Bakhtin uses another neologism—another example of "investing" an ordinary word with "special content"—when he writes of "novelization" to describe that active force of decentralization, of dialogism, and destabilizing the hierarchies of languages (and I would add scripts) that takes place in novels.

The term "novelization"—in Russian **романизация** (romanizacija)—might alternatively be translated as "romanization." In its more usual connotation, it would evoke (uppercase) Romanization by contrast to (lowercase) romanization. Bakhtin's deliberate attempt to invest the Russian word for novel ("roman") with a special meaning, may also be calling attention to the simultaneously centralizing and decentralizing linguistic work of the novel in transliterating, transcribing, and translating across roman letters. Script, for Bakhtin, is only one marker among others in the dialogism of the novel; but the many examples he draws from Russian novels (Tolstoy and Turgenev, in addition to Dostoevsky) repeatedly offer instances of a double-voicing of words, manifest in the shifting from Cyrillic to roman letters (which then—like the word "principle" for Turgenev[79]—lead to a marking of voice). In Bakhtin's theorization of novel form as "novelization," the dialogization of words, the heteroglossia of voices, and the hybridization of language is also a problem of romanization, a "novelization" (**романизация**; *romanizacija*) that takes place across scripts, opening the double-face of Russian romanization (Cyrillic and roman script; Russian and Western European texts) to a multifaceted process of transcription, transliteration, and translation.

The function of the letter K in both Conrad and Kafka draws attention to the key place of roman letters in both *oeuvres*. Shifting attention to the role of script in Deleuze and Guattari's analysis of the "assemblage" of the Kafka writing machine, and the process of novelization implicit in Bakhtin's analysis of the "chronotopes" of novel form, a comparison between Kafka's K and Conrad's K suggests how both index the complexity of the sociolinguistic phenomenon of (lowercase) romanization across Central Europe. Although in both cases, the letter appears to stand for—or betray—a single, ethno-national identity aligned with a single script, the way that it functions (and the way it enforces a "monolingual paradigm") depends on its ambiguous relation to at least two scripts. For Conrad, K marks the shared and contested space of Cyrillic and Western European letters. For Kafka, K marks the crossover between German and Czech letters. Within the broader sociolinguistic horizon of language and script reform from the mid-nineteenth century through the first part of the twentieth century, one might generalize to say that, for Conrad and Kafka, this K marks both the universal worldscript of roman letters (of respectively English and German) and another Slavic scriptworld (of Czech and Russian) that is this worldscript's double and secret sharer. This is, in effect, the Russian face of romanization. The chronotope of romanization gives aesthetic form, not to the history or genealogy of one single script (whether worldscript or scriptworld). Nor is it only the timing and spacing (or assemblage) into novel form of two rival, opposing, or contested scripts (English and Russian, German and Czech). Rather, it concerns the convergence of multiple scripts in the appearance of a single language and a single script. The other Slavic face of the roman alphabet is not singular (Cyrillic as opposed to roman). Nor is it simply double (Cyrillic and roman). It is multifaceted. K marks the way in which roman letters mediate the interaction between the faces and features of all those languages and scripts of Central Europe.

3
The Chinese Character of Romanization: Conrad and Lu Xun

The contrast between English and Russian scriptworlds, as explored in the previous chapter, reveals not so much a rivalry of opposed languages, scripts, and national identities, but rather a shared history of attempts to align language, script, and national identity. Turning now to the relevance of the Chinese scriptworld for this shared history brings me back to the multimedia riddle raised in the first chapter's discussion of the case of English romanization. At the very moment when English provides a universal model for romanizing languages worldwide, Standard English participates in a global transformation of print media. The English alphabet becomes the vehicle for converting roman letters into alphanumeric code, mediating a far-reaching displacement of romanized print forms of literacy. Lydia Liu has described this moment as the "ideographic turn" ("the moment when alphabetical writing completed its movement toward total ideographic inscription"[1]). There is a complicated irony in adopting a term so often used to oppose the medium of the Chinese character to the phonetic principles of the roman alphabet. The ironic reversal whereby the "ideographic" principle, once attributed to Chinese characters, comes to govern the use of the roman alphabet, suggests a cultural reversal of priorities in Europe's long-standing fascination and obsession with the incomprehensibility of Chinese writing.[2] It also points toward the significance of Chinese romanization for the global transformation from print to digital media in the twentieth century.

In the context of avant-garde European modernism, a long-standing obsession with the medium of the Chinese written character gives particular form to the innovations in writing, media, and technology that characterize what Christopher Bush has called (echoing Liu's formulation) "ideographic modernism."[3] Bush draws attention to the role played by the "ideographic" character of Chinese writing in articulating modernist engagements with the new technologies of phonograph, photography, and film. Conceived broadly in terms of Lydia Liu's "ideographic turn," all these new media technologies, including the later turn to digital computing systems, may be seen to emerge from a combined European fascination for Chinese characters and Chinese engagement with script reform involving various systems of romanization. Following the implications of Bush's argument that the "China" of European modernism "hides in plain sight,"[4] it should be possible to trace the reciprocal effects of the "European hallucination" of Chinese writing on the timing and spacing of romanized print form. Chinese characters are everywhere present, if everywhere effaced, in the mediating role increasingly assumed by the roman alphabet.

There are two sides to what I call the *Chinese character of romanization*. On the one hand, there is the story of how romanization schemes played a substantial role in the language and script reforms of twentieth-century China. On the other hand, there is the story of how the Chinese script revolution shaped transformations in writing, technology, and media worldwide. What from one perspective looks like the Chinese chapter in a history of romanization, from another perspective looks like the romanization chapter in a history of Chinese script. It is both of these perspectives seen together that I am calling the Chinese character of romanization. My discussion of the Chinese character of romanization in this double sense will turn later to a comparison between the work of Conrad and Lu Xun (1881–1936), the iconic Chinese revolutionary modernist and self-styled pioneer of modern Chinese literature. Surfacing in those moments where roman letters appear in Lu Xun's work, the Chinese character of romanization appears in Conrad's work in those moments where Chinese characters disappear. The way that Conrad's Malay fiction is organized around the effacement of Chinese characters provides the overarching frame of linguistic and cultural reference for the chronotope of romanization in the rest of his fiction. Lu Xun presents an exemplary point of reference for the Chinese character of romanization in the paradox of his call to abolish Chinese script while continuously using Chinese characters to revolutionize modern Chinese language and literature.

The Chinese Script Revolution and Romanization

The story of modern Chinese script reforms has been told by a number of recent scholars, from a variety of different perspectives. In *Sound and Script in Chinese Diaspora*, Jing Tsu foregrounds the diasporic complexity of script reforms (both within China and overseas), exploring the often-contradictory efforts to govern relations between national identity and script. The problems of what she calls "literary governance"[5] present an interesting sociolinguistic counterpart to the "monolingual paradigm" by which script and identity came to be politicized and racialized in late nineteenth- and early twentieth-century Europe. Her more recent book, *Kingdom of Characters*, is very different in its teleological account of how (as the subtitle puts it) "the language revolution . . . made China modern," and tends to diminish the problem of national identity and script raised by the issues of "literary governance" discussed in *Sound and Script*. But it continues the earlier book's emphasis on the importance of technologies (the typewriter, telegraphy, and the computer), returning, too, to the foundational importance of diaspora in shaping the language revolution. Thomas Mullaney's *The Chinese Typewriter* expands on Tsu's account of writing technologies, reframing the story of Chinese language debates as a story of "technolinguistic" innovation and information systems. Yurou Zhong's *Chinese Grammatology*, more conventionally organized around a chronological account of all the various script reforms in twentieth-century China, develops an ambitious argument about how the Chinese script revolution effected a paradigm shift in the science of writing systems worldwide. Jing Tsu, Thomas Mullaney, and Yurou Zhong all draw attention to the central place of romanization debates in the story of China's "script revolution." Yet they do so in strikingly different ways.

For Jing Tsu, the question of whether to abolish Chinese characters had already been settled in the early twentieth century. As she notes throughout both of her studies, there were several competing schemes for converting to the use of roman letters. Debates about those schemes are inextricably woven into the range of reforms about language and script, especially (as Tsu explores more fully in the second book, and as Mullaney also explores in his study) in the effort to reinvent language and script to adapt to the new technologies of typewriter, telegraphy, and computer. According to Tsu, in the early 1900s the tide had already turned away from the question of whether to abolish Chinese script altogether in favor of the roman alphabet, and more toward the ancillary use of this or that proposal for a phonetic alphabet alongside Chinese characters. As she puts it in *Sound and Script*, "by the early 1900s, calls for Romanization quietly gave way to proposals for the phonetic alphabet [as ancillary system] . . . from new script to mere pronunciation aid."[6] In *Kingdom of Characters* she writes, "After the founding of the republic [in 1912], it was evident there would be no more open talk of abolishing the Chinese script."[7]

By contrast, for Yurou Zhong, the question of whether to abolish Chinese characters remained very much alive from the beginning of the "script revolution" in 1916 up until it was shelved with the definitive decision in 1958 to adopt *pinyin* romanization alongside simplified Chinese characters:

> With unprecedented state sponsorship and an avowed determination to end the reign of characters for good, the socialist script reform was meant to be the definitive script revolution. Therefore, its sudden suspension in 1958, when Zhou Enlai delivered his speech 'The Current Task of the Script Reform,' came as a genuine surprise and dealt a heavy blow to international script revolutionaries...[8]

These are two very different ways to tell the story of romanization. In Zhong's telling, it was only late in the twentieth century that the question of whether to abolish Chinese characters was decided. In Tsu's telling, that question had already been shelved around the year 1900. Although these appear to be irreconcilable accounts of the place of romanization in Chinese script reform, both perspectives together are important for understanding the Chinese character of romanization.

Thomas Mullaney hints at why this might be, when he notes that the "seductively quotable" calls to "abolish characters, or to replace Chinese writing wholesale with English, French, Esperanto, or one of a variety of competing Romanization schemes," have obscured the technolinguistic history of language reform.[9] Mullaney's argument suggests that the debates about romanization—including calls to abolish Chinese characters—were never really (and certainly never only) a binary choice between Chinese characters and romanization. Although, for all three scholars, the story of Chinese script reforms features a confrontation between alphabetic and non-alphabetic writing systems, what makes each version compelling is the mutual interaction at work. Romanization systems transformed hierarchies of Chinese language and script; but the use of roman letters was transformed, in turn, by the character-based Chinese writing system. This technolinguistic history of interaction makes it difficult to date the moment when the question of abolishing Chinese characters was shelved (whether in 1900 or in 1958). If romanization schemes never ceased to present an alternative to using Chinese characters, that ongoing process of abolishing Chinese characters also repurposed and changed the roman alphabetic system. What Liu styles as the "ideographic turn" marks a process of multimedia conversion that affects the roman alphabet as much as it does Chinese characters. Both are transformed by the Chinese script reforms of the twentieth century. Neither was abolished outright, but neither has assumed ascendancy over the other, because their interaction continues: the romanization of Chinese characters goes hand in hand with the Chinese character of romanization.

The figure who most fully embodies the paradoxical imperative to abolish and to keep Chinese characters is Lu Xun. Mullaney, Tsu, and Zhong all cite versions of his repeated call to abolish Chinese characters. In a series of epigraphs, used as headings for *Kingdom of Characters*, Jing Tsu cites a statement attributed to Lu Xun from 1936: "If the Chinese script does not go, China will certainly perish!" At the beginning of her study, Yurou Zhong cites from the very end of Lu Xun's celebrated 1927 essay "Voiceless China": "Truly, we have heretofore two ways forward: either we cling to the old script and die; or we rid ourselves of it and live."[10] Mullaney cites a still more colorful statement from "Reply to an Interview from My Sickbed": "Chinese characters constitute a tubercle on the body of China's poor and laboring masses, inside of which the bacteria collect. If one does not clear them out, then one will die. If Chinese characters are not exterminated, there can be no doubt that China will perish."[11]

Mullaney emphasizes the "easy iconoclasm" in Lu Xun's abolitionist rhetoric in order to direct attention toward the technolinguistic questions obscured by that rhetoric. The rhetoric itself usefully situates the question of script reform within the broader iconoclastic aims of the language revolution. From this perspective, the question of abolishing the writing system is subordinated to the more important question of reforming language to create a (spoken and written) vernacular, the so-called "plain speech" (*baihua*) championed by the May Fourth Movement. In the 1927 essay "Voiceless China," from which Zhong cites, Lu Xun distinguishes between calls to abolish the script and calls to write in the vernacular. At a key moment in the essay, he points out how reaction against the "extreme proposition" of abolishing Chinese characters meant that the "relatively mild literary renovation" (developing the vernacular *baihua*) came to be accepted and realized: "The vernacular was able to come into use at the time due only to the proposition of eradicating the Chinese script in favor of a Romanized alphabet."[12]

This argument raises a question about how "extreme" Lu Xun's own calls for the "eradication" of the Chinese script actually were. When Zhong translates the final line of "Voiceless China" emphasizing the iconoclasm of its call to abolish the "script"—"we cling to the old *script* and die"—that translation echoes the "easy iconoclasm" in the quotations from Jing Tsu and Mullaney. Yet most translations of this essay render the Chinese characters for what Zhong translates as "old script" (古文; *gu wen*) as ancient or classical "language" rather than script. The Chinese text reads:

我们此后实在只有两条路：一是抱着古文而死掉，一是舍掉古文而生存。[13]

Theodore Huters translates this sentence as follows:

> From this point on, there are two paths available to us: one is to cling to the classical language and die, and the other is to abandon the classical language and survive.[13]

The different nuances in translating 古文 (*gu wen*) "classical language," "classical script"—or even "classical literature," which might imply both language and script—suggest the extent to which all those debates about the reform of language, writing, and literature could retain the more "extreme" call for abolishing the script, while *also* presuming the "compromise" of reforming language, literature, and script.

This is what makes Lu Xun a touchstone for the otherwise opposed stories presented by Tsu and Zhong. Writing midway between the beginning of the "script revolution" at the beginning of the twentieth century and the final containment of that revolution in 1958, as Zhong historicizes it, Lu Xun's comments show how the calls for script reform were always part of the wider revolution in language and culture, and how debates about romanization were always overdetermined by the hybrid phonetic, ideographic, and grammatological imperatives of Chinese language and script reform. Lu Xun's iconoclastic rhetoric of abolishing Chinese characters belongs to a broader attack on all the old hierarchies of culture, language, and script. When I turn in the last part of this chapter to consider the Chinese character of romanization in Lu Xun's fiction, by comparison to Conrad, I will consider how the role of film works to revolutionize those hierarchies of culture, language, and script. Film, in its revolutionary potential to abolish the traditional forms of literature and print culture, will reveal how all those new media technologies (what Bush classifies under "ideographic modernism"; what Mullaney foregrounds as the technolinguistic side of language reform) promise to abolish both Chinese characters and roman letters.

Zhong's *Chinese Grammatology* begins by arguing that the nuances and contradictions in Lu Xun's position prefigure the course of the modern Chinese script revolution. Her reading suggestively links the technical questions of romanization with the technological and technolinguistic questions that interest Tsu and Mullaney. For Zhong those are already embedded within Lu Xun's rhetoric. Noting the sheer number of times Lu Xun wrote in support of romanization (especially late in his life, between 1934 and 1936), Zhong offers a close reading of an early essay, "Malevolent Voices," to explore how the key metaphors of "voice" and "sound" (that recur throughout Lu Xun's essays, including the essay "Voiceless China") complicate Lu Xun's (seemingly) unequivocal endorsement of alphabetization. Concealed within Lu Xun's explicit endorsement of alphabetization, Zhong finds a critique of the "phonocentrism" attending all the various movements to reform the Chinese script:

> Despite his consistent, phonocentric-sounding arguments against the old script, within his own writings on script and sound stirred a complex grammatological critique that belabored the definition of *sheng* 聲, which could be translated as 'voice,' 'speech sound,' or 'sound' in general.[14]

This nuanced sense of *sheng* 聲 is also found in "Voiceless China," where Lu Xun wrote (as Zhong cites it): "Only true sound can move people of China and people of the world; only after [we have] true sound can we cohabit the world with people of the world."[15]

Zhong's reading of the way *sheng* 聲 signifies in Lu Xun's work calls attention to a hidden problem of "speech sound" that runs through all the debates about Chinese language and script reform throughout the twentieth century—twinning, indeed, questions about the spoken language and the written language that challenge long-standing assumptions about the hierarchy of relations between language, speech, and writing. The technical question of "speech sound," as Zhong's analysis shows, lies at the heart of the role of romanization in China's script revolution. Zhong dates the "beginning of the modern Chinese script revolution" to the year 1916, with the publication of Yuen Ren Chao's English-language article "The Problem of the Chinese Language." Chao's elevation of the Roman Latin alphabet as the universal measure for representing speech sound "launched the Chinese Romanization movement"[16] and gave birth to the *Gwoyeu Romatzyh* (National Language Romanization Script) that went on to receive official recognition in 1928. This was only one among a number of other competing romanization schemes and claims to represent "the Chinese alphabet." An important part of the story of the "script revolution" in China, as told by all three scholars, turns on the rivalry between the Romanization movement that produced Gwoyeu Romatzyh and the so-called Latinization movement from which the "new script" (*Sin Wenz*) emerged (and it was this script that Lu Xun promoted in his essays on romanization in the 1930s). Already in the contest over what form of script might best replace the old character-based writing system, Zhong delineates the contradictions around which the phonocentrism of romanization schemes would collapse to produce what she calls a Chinese "grammatology," based on a hybrid phonetic, ideographic, and multiscript (and non-identitarian) understanding of the function of writing systems worldwide. To simplify her argument considerably, the earlier Romanization movement (which peaked around 1928) embodied the contradictions of an "alphabetical universalism" which the later Latinization movement sought to address by "using the same Roman-Latin alphabet to create different writing systems for various dialects."[17] Both, however, revealed what Zhong calls the "antinomies of phonocentricism"[18]: the contradictory imperative to reconceive the relation between language and script by imposing the phonetic system of the roman alphabet; and, on the other hand, to adapt the phonetic function of the roman alphabet to fit the needs of many different linguistic variations.

Zhong's overall argument is prefigured in the nuances and contradictions of Lu Xun's prose. The metaphor of *sheng* 聲 throughout Lu Xun's work, anticipates the "antinomies of phonocentrism" revealed by the romanization movements. It embodies each of the three phases of that revolution that Zhong traces beginning in 1916 and ending in 1958. Lu Xun embodies the turn *toward* phonocentrism that characterizes the beginnings of the "script revolution" in 1916—with the "extreme" call to replace Chinese characters with romanization. Yet he also anticipates the concluding containment of that revolution with the "compromise" reform of a romanized writing system (*pinyin*) coexisting with the simplified reform of Chinese characters. In between, Lu Xun anticipates that middle turning point, when the contradictions inherent in the phonocentrism of all the main romanization movements led to a critique of the "alphabetic universalism" on which the script revolution was premised, leading to the Chinese "grammatology" Zhong sees emerging as a consequence of the history of the script revolution.[19] Lu Xun embodies—arguably in each and every articulation—that overall historical turn "first toward Latinization, and then back to grammatology"[20]; first elevating the phonetic ideal of roman alphabetization and then critiquing its phonocentrism.

All of these scholars, especially Tsu and Zhong, raise the question of whether it is even possible to talk about there being a single Chinese scriptworld. The enormous variations that exist in languages throughout the sinophone world, along with the specific linguistic and technological features of Chinese language reform lead them all, each in very different ways, to make arguments that have implications far beyond Chinese language debates. Even more clearly than with the sociolinguistic contradictions raised by Russification in Central Europe, efforts to formulate a standardized, modern Chinese script (whether using characters or roman letters) draw attention, not only to the sheer heterogeneity of languages converging in the formation and re-formation of written Chinese, but also to the constitutively diasporic coordinates of its standardized script forms. Given the enormous differences between various regional Chinese dialects or languages (*fangyan*), the imperative to create a fit between spoken and written language faces almost insurmountable difficulties. This is evident in that contest Zhong, Tsu, and Mullaney all refer to, between two different visions of how to unify a national Chinese language with a national script. The first, the so-called Romanization movement, dominated the earlier part of the twentieth century (promoting "National Romanization" [*Gwoyeu Romatzyh*]), whereas the second, the so-called Latinization movement (promoting the "Latin new script" [*Latinxua Sin Wenz*] from the 1930s on) came to dominate the later part of the century. The earlier "National Romanization" fell short of unifying language and script because of differences over which dialect to use for the "national pronunciation"[22]; whereas the later "Latin new script" succeeded in claiming to serve "every dialect and every class."[23]

This story is much more complicated, though, as both Tsu and Zhong illuminate in different ways. Zhong emphasizes the limitations for both of these movements of a phonocentric imperative (to make roman letters fit either one standard, national pronunciation [with Romanization] or fit a variable set of different linguistic variants [with Latinization]); and it is from those contradictory imperatives that the Chinese script revolution turned first toward, and then against, a phonocentric, Latin alphabet fetishism which Zhong terms "alphabetic universalism."[24] Tsu's story of the rise of Latinization over Romanization differs in its emphasis, complicating the national teleology that (arguably) inflects both Tsu's and Zhong's account of the Chinese script revolution, with an account of how Latinization emerged from encounters in Central Asia between Russian, Turkic, and, above all, Dunganese experiments with the roman alphabet.[25]

The idea that Chinese speakers inhabit a single scriptworld, misconstrues the extent to which the standardized Chinese worldscript (refracted across multiple other worldscripts and scriptworlds) serves a multitude of different variant languages or dialects, relating in different ways to a writing system of Chinese characters, closer to the way French, German, Polish, Russian, and English speakers relate to the writing system characterized by roman letters. Jing Tsu's focus (in *Sound and Script in Chinese Diaspora*) on the diasporic, and especially Southeast Asian reach of romanization debates, is especially interesting for my focus here on Conrad, if only to draw attention, from a sociolinguistic perspective, to the ways in which Conrad's Malay world forms a key site of interaction between worldscripts.

Rather than constituting a rivalry or opposition, the historical interrelation of roman alphabet and Chinese character (and the long and complex histories of each) reveals a much more varied and complex multiplicity of coexisting scripts. As worldscripts, neither the roman alphabet nor the writing system of Chinese characters has ever been as exclusive as claims have made them appear to be. The very claim to universalism, indeed, depends on recognizing the mediating role that these worldscripts have played (and continue to play) between a range of other languages and scripts. The full range of those other languages and scripts has an important bearing on the fiction of Joseph Conrad, as I will explore in a moment.

Two sociolinguistic examples serve to emphasize the ongoing significance of the Chinese character of romanization. Contemporary English characteristically confronts multiple ways of writing Chinese names, places, and words, revealing a layered history of different efforts to come up with a romanization system for Chinese. So, for example, we have "Beijing" and "Peking." Read from the perspective of linguistic debates about romanization, this presents a historical cross section of different moments in the standardization of Chinese (language and script)—recalling the history that Jing Tsu so richly explores, a history that positions the sinophone scriptworld (or rather the range of different sinophone scriptworlds) within a diaspora of linguistic and cultural interactions.[26] That diaspora also shapes the history of English. From this perspective the romanized form of "Beijing" coexists with "Peking" in ways that open the space of romanized print form to multiple possibilities in rendering the same place, name, or word. Everyday English, then, confronts readers with multiple effects of a process of romanization, bringing multiple histories of contact between Chinese characters and roman letters to bear on the everyday act of reading. Between "Beijing" and "Peking" the reader negotiates a reading experience that is not so distant, either from the Conradian "blank space" on the map (filled up now with names and places), or from the "iSpace" of Joyce's *Finnegans Wake*. The disappearing K-effect in adjusting from "Peking" (using the standard form set by the Chinese Postal Map Romanization system in 1906) to *pinyin's* "Beijing" (settled in 1958 with the ratification of the National People's Congress) is simply taken for granted. English readers likely pay as little attention to the Chinese character of romanization that it represents as they do to the K-effect in the way "Knights" is spelled with a silent K.

Another contemporary example is the near-ubiquitous use of the roman alphabet as a medium to access Chinese characters in the everyday texting of messages. In this case, the keyboard arrangement of roman letters (already anticipating the transcoding of alphabet into a different kind of media network[27]) serves an ancillary function in accessing and producing a Chinese scriptworld. This is, in some respects, analogous to the way ASCII and Unicode use the basic twenty-six letters of the English alphabet (plus the twenty-seventh letter—the space—that turns it into alphanumerical code) as building blocks. The analogy offers a concrete embodiment of the digital ideal of alphanumerical coding that gives access to any and all scripts. As an ideal, it makes the roman alphabet a kind of neutral space for a potentially unlimited switching to and from different scriptworlds. This ideal of instant script conversion, without the imposition of any one dominant script, and in which the roman alphabet becomes merely the ancillary instrument, allowing access to all the world's scripts, remains (of course) an ideal. The particular embodiment of that ideal in the everyday use of QWERTY keyboards to access Chinese characters, does nothing to do away with the complications of having to negotiate the particular challenges of script conversion.[28] Indeed, the way the user is given a choice of characters to correspond to the romanized text, reproduces precisely the kind of multiplicity found in the different, standard ways of romanizing names, places, or other word-forms.

What both examples together demonstrate, is how the romanized space of reading English, no less than the digitized space of reading Chinese today, involves a multimedia experience shaped by at least two centuries of reciprocal influence, exchange, and intermediation across a wide variety of languages and scripts. This involves not only English and all the various Chinese regional languages, and not only roman letters and Chinese characters. It also involves a technolinguistic transformation in forms of print media worldwide. Conrad's work traces the effects of this transformation in its effacement of Chinese characters. Seemingly marginal to the settings and diasporic movements of the cultures and peoples depicted in his novels, the influence of Chinese language and culture is everywhere present. Conrad's effacement of Chinese characters (both in the sense of protagonists and script), in fact, foregrounds their framing significance for the chronotopes of romanization in his fiction. This is most evident in the Malay settings, where Chinese characters are typically (indeed stereotypically) effaced.

Conrad's Chinese Characters: *Almayer's Folly* to *Victory*

Conrad's fiction is populated by more Chinese characters than one might initially imagine. The memorable examples—the coolies in "Typhoon"; Wang in *Victory*—tend to be memorable for their peripheral status, and the way that their characters are effaced in their respective narratives (the coolies collectively so in "Typhoon"; and Wang paradigmatically so as part of the stereotype of his "Chinese" character: "the Chinaman had gone in his peculiar manner, which suggested vanishing out of existence rather than out of sight, a process of evaporation rather than of movement" [*Victory*, 188–89]). Without either excusing, ignoring, or diminishing the obvious anti-Chinese prejudice in these characterizations, I read this effacement of Chinese characters as an index of the far more extensively discussed engagement with racialized identity and identification throughout Conrad's work. Indeed, Conrad's effacement of Chinese characters provides a kind of key to understanding how racism generates all of the most characteristic features of Conradian narrative. As a generative principle of narrative, moreover, this racism emerges from a constitutive misfit between language, script, and identity. In Chapter 1, I introduced this as a matter of those minute lexical effects of the "accusative case": what connects the full range of racialized resentments embedded in Cornelius's sarcastic mistranslation of "Tuan Jim" into "Lord Jim," and the almost textbook eruption of racism around the roll call that introduces the title character and racist epithet of *The Nigger of the 'Narcissus'* around the unreadable naming, spacing, and timing of the letters "Wait!" In examining the effacement of Chinese characters in Conrad—and the misfit between Chinese character as script and Chinese character as national, cultural, or racial identity—I want to explore how the narrative timing and spacing of this effacement frames all the chronotopes of romanization found throughout Conrad's work, from the beginning to the end of his literary career.

Almayer's Folly

The opening words of *Almayer's Folly* ("Kaspar! Makan!"), the first effect of delayed decoding in Conrad's *oeuvre*, also introduce the first riddling knot of romanized transliteration, transcription, and translation that inaugurates Conrad's entire writing endeavor. I have already discussed how this opening introduces the chronotope of romanization through a rivalry that mirrors, sociolinguistically, the alternative ways to transcribe Malay—between *jawi* (Arabic) script and *rumi* (roman) print forms. I now want to explore how this rivalry is itself situated within a problematic entanglement of romanization and Chinese script.

Conrad's first published words present a riddle of transcription, transliteration, and translation at several different levels. As an instance of dialogue, they introduce, within the fictional space of narrative, a distinction between diegesis and mimesis that complicates the basic question as to what these words signify. Eventually, the meaning of the Malay word "makan" will be decoded, or rather deduced, from the manner in which Almayer's thoughts return to "a hazy recollection of having been called some time during the evening by his wife. To his dinner probably" (*Almayer's*, 11). But the full significance of this dialogic exchange will likely never be decoded, as is emphasized by the text's own return to Almayer's being "deaf to the shrill cries of his wife calling him to the evening meal" at the end of Chapter Five (*Almayer's*, 74). The disorienting effect of the novel's first words introduce so many questions about the language spoken, the background of the speaker, and the emotional force of the call and its nonresponse, that the narrative will never be able to resolve all the discrepancies opened up by the utterance. Recalling the Aristotelian distinctions between plot (*mythos*), character (*ethos*), and diction (*lexis*) that I raised earlier, this inaugural example of delayed decoding is the premise for all those accusative cases yet to come in Conrad—lexical effects that break the illusion of any kind of faithful, reliable, or trustworthy fit between identity and script, *ethos* and character, lexicon and scriptworld.

The person speaking the opening words, Almayer's wife, represents precisely that instability of a relation between identity and scriptworld on which the novel turns. The range of linguistic possibilities inflecting Mrs. Almayer's use of Malay is already considerable: she is the "legacy" of a "boatful of pirates" described as "Sulu" and so, as Andrew Francis has noted, she is "someone for whom *makan* is therefore almost certainly a foreign word."[29] This applies to virtually *all* the characters in the novel. In a Bakhtinian sense, all Malay words are the words of another, the language all share as the language of their own native estrangement from speech itself. Within the diegetic coordinates of the plot, Mrs. Almayer's allegiances to this or that faction in the political plot is also linguistically encoded. Indeed, it might be possible to map out what Cedric Watts calls the novel's "covert plotting"[30] through the linguistic encoding of Mrs. Almayer's allegiances: her mixed loyalties to Lingard (English); the Dutch of the man Lingard has her marry; her alliance with Babalatchi (Malay, but as inflected by other languages not specified, e.g. Buginese); and her role in helping her daughter's lover, Dain Maroola (whose Buginese name is a linguistic disguise for the Balinese identity of his political and family romance, which then involves the conflicted linguistic and political allegiances of his affair with the daughter, Nina). These linguistic registers meet up with the rival claims over what script (or scripts) mediate this native language spoken (strangely) in common by all the characters. This, in turn, poses an important question about the framing significance of Conrad's use of Malay: in what sense does the covert plot of Conrad's novel register, in the form of the novel's opening address, the shift from Arabic script to the romanized print form of what Pramoedya Ananta Toer called "pre-Indonesian"?

Early on, the presence of Chinese characters marks the logic of this kind of Malay (whether conceived of as "bazaar Malay" or, in Ben Anderson's formulation "revolutionary Malay"—or, again, in Pramoedya's formulation, "pre-Indonesian") as a language that exists between scripts and that positions characters between languages, scripts, and national identities. Recalling "Hudig's lofty and cool warehouses" in Macassar, Almayer's memories conjure "the little railed-off spaces amongst piles of merchandise where the Chinese clerks, neat, cool, and sad-eyed, wrote rapidly and in silence amidst the din of the working gangs rolling casks or shifting cases to a muttered song, ending with a desperate yell" (*Almayer's*, 5). What is evoked here—in the very first reference to writing in Conrad's fiction—is that fateful convergence of capitalism, print, and linguistic diversity that suggests the resonant phrase "print-capitalism," coined by Benedict Anderson to capture the global conditions for the origin and spread of nationalism.[31] It might appear initially counterintuitive to apply Anderson's general term for this interplay between "fatality, technology, and capitalism"[32] to what is here, more narrowly, an evocation of the ledger books of global trade, juxtaposed with a language of labor. Whereas Anderson's phrase "print-capitalism" sums up the accidental fact that Latin becomes the script for global trade, Conrad's passage ascribes this global coincidence of print, capitalism, and language to "the Chinese clerks." Why give a specifically *Chinese* character to the globalizing models (print, capitalism, and the alphabet) usually contrasted most to the example of China? Anderson himself makes this contrast—"The contrast [of the "universality of Latin in mediaeval Western Europe"] with Imperial China, where the reach of the mandarinal bureaucracy and of painted characters largely coincided, is instructive."[33]

It is striking for various reasons, that this space of global trade positions the transfer of "Manchester goods" between a common (but unknown) language sung by "working gangs," whose work is recorded by the writing of "Chinese clerks." The narrative dwells on this space of international trade and exchange for some two pages—elaborating on, and indeed racializing, the clerks' Chinese identity by associating the Chinese ("other discreet Chinese"), metonymically, with the "continuous clink of silver guilders"—until by the end of the passage, the narrative performs again the scene as it was initially evoked: "the song of the workmen, the rumble of barrels, the scratch of rapid pens; while above all rose the musical chink of broad silver pieces streaming ceaselessly through the yellow fingers of the attentive Chinamen" (*Almayer's*, 6).

With the consolidation of a racist pattern of anti-Chinese prejudice (the words "chink" and "yellow" are unmistakably racist), the narrative simultaneously foregrounds, and then again effaces, the importance of Chinese characters in the overall setting of the novel. Especially interesting and important is the effacement of the script ascribed to the Chinese clerks. All at once the very script of the world of global trade—the worldscript of capitalism, if you will—the written form of what the passage initially figures as silent (they "wrote rapidly and in silence") and then conjures as sound ("the scratch of rapid pens") remains entirely hidden. What is the script of world trade, of this "print-capitalism"? How is this script related to the sound and voice of the language announced by the novel's opening Malay utterance? If, as Anderson's whole argument presumes, the script of "print-capitalism" is Latin or roman script, what, then, is the Chinese character of this romanized print form?

Although one can surely speculate as to what script and what language is being used (Dutch? Malay? numerals?), the most important point to emphasize here is that this is represented as a *gap* in the text. It is a gap, however, to which the character of the Chinese, as cultural, ethnic, and racialized identity, is assigned. Within the plotting of *Almayer's Folly*, these Chinese clerks play a negligible role, and the important coordinates of global trade they signal get displaced by a more stereotyped Chinese character, Jim-Eng the opium smoker. Introduced early in the novel as the "near neighbour" (*Almayer's*, 28) that Almayer envies (apparently for the leisure and ease that comes from opium), his function appears to be to provide a corresponding point of reference, next to Almayer himself, for an incomprehension of the political plotting and intrigue surrounding Almayer's house and household. Jim-Eng is described as being "baffled" (*Almayer's*, 60) by the appearance of Babalatchi (the "prime minister of Sambir") at Almayer's house, marking the central blind spot of the novel's "covert plot" (to borrow Watts's formulation again). As Watts notes, critics and readers continue to be baffled by the hidden details of a plot whose full significance continues to elude them.

Many of these covert details might be illuminated by a reading suggested by Indonesian novelist Pramoedya Ananta Toer. Arguing that there are "historical facts" in Conrad's work that "have not been recorded elsewhere," drawing particular attention to the struggles against colonialism not registered in Dutch historiography, he characterizes the main plot of *Almayer's Folly* as a story of decolonization: the "story about a Balinese prince who is smuggling guns to organize resistance against Dutch colonial rule."[34] This plot summary has the striking effect of resituating the novel—and by extension the projected trilogy that inaugurated Conrad's career—within a history of decolonization, not legible to Conrad or his readers at the time of writing. The ambivalence of Conrad's investment in the Malay world has made me ask, repeatedly, in what sense Conrad's fiction is engaged in a remembering or a forgetting of the politics of anti-colonial resistance. The novel's framing rivalry between Arabic script and romanized print already poses this political ambiguity: in what sense does the space of English print appropriate and contain the Arabic scriptworld of Abdulla's concluding invocation of the bismillah; and in what sense does the plot's ironic unraveling of Almayer's English investments point to a displacement and unraveling of the space of English print itself? I want to return to this open-ended question by considering the framing function of the effaced Chinese presence of a script—whatever it actually is that almost seems paradigmatically that of "print-capitalism"—in governing the conceit of that rivalry between Arabic script and romanized print.

The role of Chinese characters in organizing the chronotope of romanized print form in *Almayer's Folly* emerges from a stratification of different levels of plotting in the broadest possible sense of that term—not only the plot of the single novel; nor only the plotting of the trilogy it begins (or rather, in a fictive-plot sense, ends); nor again the novels Conrad would go on to write; but also— moving simultaneously toward the opposed poles of "history" and "fiction"[35] (more specifically, the history of print media and geopolitical fiction of world literature)—the various strands of a plot that precedes the writing of Conrad's first novel and then follows from it (most concretely in terms of the multitude of readings, critical and creative, including readings such as Pramoedya Ananta Toer's, in whatever media, it has engendered).[36] Within the compass of the single novel itself, the covert plots anticipate all the chronotopes of romanization to be developed through Conrad's later narratives. Those chronotopes of romanization are organized by the ironic nesting of roman letters within Arabic script—and the nesting of that rivalry, in turn, within a Chinese scriptworld from which most of the characters and readers of the novel are excluded. This Chinese script appears, at the end of the novel, in the renaming of "Almayer's Folly" according to the Chinese lettering on the "long strip of faded red silk" (*Almayer's*, 205) Jim-Eng has fastened to one of the pillars and that Ford, whose perspective closes the narrative, cannot read.

A reading of *Almayer's Folly* on its own might recognize the ironic nesting structure of the governing chronotope of romanization. The "half obliterated words" of the roman lettering "Office: Lingard and Co." (*Almayer's*, 15) anticipate the "folly" the Dutch soldiers see when they give the name "Almayer's Folly" to the house Almayer is building in the false hope that the British will come to colonize Sambir (*Almayer's*, 36–37). The entire Lingard enterprise is buried—along with Almayer's body—by the end of the novel, whose concluding invocation (in Arabic) suggests the ascendancy of an Arabic scriptworld over the romanized scriptworld figured by the English lettering of "Lingard and Co." The irony, though, cuts many ways. It prefigures an ironic and still unresolved interrelation between British and Arabic legacies of multinational capitalism. Just as Lingard's many titles borrow from the prestige of the older Arabic Malay scriptworld, Abdulla's trading interests are secured by the prestige and legal paperwork of modern romanized print form (in the registration of his shipping company and in the form of his own British citizenship). The open-ended, unresolved ambiguity of this ironic reversal in the rivalry between Arabic and romanized scriptworlds, is the open-ended, unresolved ambiguity of that "revolutionary Malay" articulated in the opening words of the novel. The ironic structure of the novel—like the deliberately ironic ring of the novel's title-reference to Almayer's house—situates this reversal and chiasmus of Arabic and romanized scriptworlds within another scriptworld—that of Chinese characters. Thus, the final renaming of Almayer's house according to the illegible Chinese script, "the crazy-looking maze of the Chinese inscription," positions this rivalry (and the projected past and future of its genealogy) under the sign of a Chinese scriptworld whose future legibility is presented as the condition for understanding the full irony of all those nested and embedded ironies encoded in the novel's title: "Had he asked Jim-Eng, that patient Chinaman would have informed him with proper pride that its meaning was: 'House of heavenly delight'" (*Almayer's*, 205).

The character who perhaps most fully captures the problem of unfolding narrative consciousness, both for *Almayer's Folly* and for the Malay (or Lingard) trilogy as a whole, is Babalatchi, the "prime minister" (*Almayer's*, 38) of Sambir. The novel's archetypal covert plotter, schemer, and archetypal villain (and not coincidentally an archetypal Orientalist racial stereotype), Babalatchi's name is itself a striking example of the effacement of Chinese script in the timing and spacing of Conrad's narrative. The repertoire of racialized stereotypes condensed in this name reenforces the function of his character as the "repulsive," (*Almayer's*, 38) distorted perspective through which the narrative is organized.[37] The sheer number of possible markers of identification and disidentification converging on this character (Malay, Sulu, Bugis, Muslim, and Chinese) indexes a highly volatile point of reference for reading both this novel's unfolding plot and the reverse chronological sequence projected by the whole Lingard trilogy. Read chronologically, from the perspective of that history of decolonization that is the premise for Pramoedya's plot summary—specifically the history of Indonesian anti-colonial nationalism—Babalatchi is a proto-nationalist native insurgent, allied (albeit unpredictably) with the Balinese prince "smuggling guns to organize resistance against Dutch colonial rule." Read in the reverse chronological order, in which Conrad planned and executed the trilogy (and deferred over the course of his entire publishing career), Babalatchi is the unpredictable ally in Lingard's failed attempt to rescue a romance of political adventure that would align English and Malay interests. As a character, he is central to the unfolding political plot, while also marking the limit of the narrative's ability to develop anything but an ironic consciousness of Malay politics. In the second novel, *An Outcast of the Islands*, the standoff between him and Lingard refers to a shared piratical past of heroism, adventure, and betrayal whose story will never be told. Babalatchi is nowhere to be found in the third novel, *The Rescue*.

As a clue to the overall timing and spacing of the novel sequence that frames Conrad's entire literary career, Babalatchi's character and function is especially interesting. The problem of narrative consciousness he embodies reveals the way that Conrad truncates and fragments epic and novelistic form, laying bare a fragmentary narrative form. Babalatchi's name itself encodes these broader narrative and aesthetic concerns through a riddling effacement of Chinese. "Baba" (usually "babah") is the Indonesian term for "an elderly Chinese man"; or the title used in addressing such a person. And if one spaces out the letters of Babalatchi's name as a romanization of the kind of name one might expect to encounter in the Malay archipelago at this time, what emerges is the romanized transcription of a Chinese name—"La-Tchi."[38] I am not claiming that Conrad intends for Babalatchi's character to be recognized as ethnically Chinese, in any way comparable to the Chinese "clerks" referred to at the beginning of the novel, or the character of Almayer's neighbor Jim-Eng (whose interaction with Babalatchi seems precisely to hinge on a *mis*recognition of Babalatchi's character). Yet the name registers a detail that recalls Pramoedya's point about the "historical facts" recorded in Conrad's fiction. A bill of lading found among Conrad's possessions shows goods shipped by "Babalatchie" on the west coast of Sulawesi. Whatever Conrad may have known about the person referred to on this bill of lading, the linguistic register of the name itself underscores a historical fact of some considerable importance: namely, the emergence of a sociolinguistic space of reading, exchange, and communication populated by various Chinese readers and writers making use of romanized print Malay.

This sociolinguistic space which Pramoedya calls "pre-Indonesian" is the template for that lingua franca, "market Malay" or "bazaar Malay" (*pasar Melayu*), that would become the language of anti-colonial nationalism, adopted as such in the "Oath of Youth" of 1928. The name Babalatchi, moreover, read as a Malay romanization from the Chinese, registers (historically) the mediating role of Chinese characters in that form of "print-capitalism" that links the opening call of the novel ("Kaspar, Makan!") with the script of the Chinese clerks. Indonesian-born Chinese (*peranakan* Chinese) played an important mediating role in the sudden increase in print publications in romanized Malay at the end of the nineteenth century (see Salmon, Maier [1993 and 2004], Siegel, Anderson, and Pramoedya).[39] Claudine Salmon suggests that this mediating role also involved the transition from the circulation of Malay manuscripts in Arabic script to that of books in romanized print form. The full history of this script conversion from Arabic to romanized print Malay is a complex matter. There is certainly no direct representation of this shift in *Almayer's Folly*. Its significance, however, for the creation of that sociolinguistic space of interaction producing "revolutionary Malay," is marked everywhere in the text—and, as I have already discussed, seems to underwrite the rivalry between Lingard and Abdulla. To the extent that this rivalry might also be read as a rivalry over the shared space of "print-capitalism," "Babalatchi" marks the effaced role of

Chinese characters in that history. Itself a miniature chronotope of romanization, then, the name "Babalatchi" spells out an effacement of Chinese characters that frames the covert plotting of the whole Malay trilogy and, by extension, all of Conrad's work. Certainly, each return to the scene of the trilogy's Malay setting may be re-read in light of the coded effacement of Chinese, marking the temporal and spatial arrangement of romanized print form. The effaced forms of Chinese characters appear everywhere in Conrad's Malay narratives. It is in those very effects of effacement (legible in names such as "Babalatchi" or the "Nan-Shan" of *Typhoon*) that I read the Chinese character of romanized print form.

Victory

Victory thematizes the form of this Chinese effacement in multiple ways, most prominently in the figure of Wang, Axel Heyst's domestic servant on the remote island of Samburan where the English-educated, Swedish entrepreneur continues to live after the collapse of his short-lived Tropical Belt Coal Company. When Wang is introduced, in Part III, his presence on Samburan is explained as a leftover remnant of Chinese laborers, since vanished, who were brought to the island to work for the Tropical Belt Coal Company:

> Of the crowd of imported Chinese labourers, one at least had remained in Samburan, solitary and strange, like a swallow left behind in the migrating season of his tribe. (*Victory*, 178)

Wang's appearance here, midway through the novel, serves as a reminder of this disappearing trace of Chinese coolie labor in the development of the now-decayed central station for the defunct coal company. Associating Wang with this effaced history of Chinese coolie labor, the narrative enacts a kind of double-effacement of Chinese by noting, immediately following the above passage: "Wang was not a common coolie. He had been a servant to white men before" (*Victory*, 178). The ghostly revenant of a disappearing labor force, Wang *also* appears as the revenant of a different kind of Chinese labor, the domestic "servant to white men." Doubling as the ghostly return of two different kinds of social labor, he will reiterate them both later, in a kind of contemptuous, self-effacing accusation with the still more precise formulation "mine coolie turned houseboy" (*Victory*, 348). Wang reenacts a trope, repeatedly used earlier in the novel, when the omniscient narrator, recounting things from Captain Davidson's point of view, sums up the ubiquity of Chinese people throughout the Malay Archipelago by negation: "Not a soul was in sight, *not even a China boy*" (*Victory*, 35; emphasis mine); and again a few pages later: "Otherwise *the very Chinamen* ignored her existence" (*Victory*, 39; emphasis mine). These designations, in both cases metonyms for "servant," figure Chinese, rhetorically, as the most negligible sign of human community. Yet the distance between the social labor of "servant" and that of "coolies" signals the effacement of a whole history. In the case of *Victory*, this is the effaced history of racialized forms of social labor in the capitalist development in Southeast Asia, as represented by the Tropical Coal Belt Company. In the case of Conrad's overall career (most especially read in light of the work of Pramoedya Ananta Toer), it is the effaced history of the East-Indies born *peranakan* Chinese in the formation of Indonesian anti-colonial nationalism.

"He had been a servant to white men before." The sentence that introduces Wang might be read in several, rather different ways. On the one hand, it presents the prior work experience that explains what Wang now does for Heyst. The passage goes on to explain the conditions of his work as domestic servant to Heyst, describing Wang's relationship with an "Alfuro" woman, and the way he divides his time between serving Heyst and tending the vegetable garden that also produces the food he provides for Heyst. These conditions, however, seem very different from the kind of work ascribed to the Chinese servants in Sourabaya (as suggested by Lena's comment "He's like those waiters in that place [Schomberg's hotel]" [*Victory*, 182] to which Heyst responds, "One Chinaman looks very much like another ... We shall find it useful to have him here"). In fact, Wang's character functions as a kind of perpetual effacement, both of the stereotype of Chinese coolie, and the stereotype of the Chinese servant figured by the earlier references to the Chinese in Surabaya. Wang himself will offer a third stereotype, that of "a merchant with a big hong in Singapore" (*Victory*, 348). An alternative reading might then emphasize Wang's role by *contrast* to his prior experience—i.e. "He had been a servant to white men before [*and was wiser for the experience*]." Although this reading is not developed by any of the characters, or the omniscient narrator for that matter, the whole passage exaggerates the extent to which Wang is *neither* a coolie *nor* the sort of servant that Lena recalls from Schomberg's hotel. He appears enigmatic to Lena and Heyst (and to the omniscient narrator)—an unreadable riddle of the social labor that determines the circumstances of their own existence on Samburan. This is one way to explain the "vanishing" trick repeatedly ascribed to Wang's character ("which suggested vanishing out of existence rather than out of sight, a process of evaporation rather than movement" [(*Victory*, 188–189]). The social labor he performs is literally unreadable to those around him. Its unreadability, indeed, seems like an extended, exaggerated spinning out of the racialized trope of the "inscrutable" Chinese (*Victory*, 184).

In one particularly striking exchange between Heyst and Lena, the offensive racialization of Wang's "vanishing" is made explicit:

> "That's it—he vanishes. It's a very remarkable gift in that Chinaman."
> "Are they all like that?" she asked with naive curiosity and uneasiness.
> "Not in such perfection," said Heyst, amused. (*Victory*, 217)

A particular example of Conrad's racist treatment of Chinese characters, the effacement of Wang's Chinese character in *Victory* also stages a key turning point in the novel's denouement. Terry Collits's reading of the novel offers an especially useful way to recognize Wang's importance for this denouement, which turns on the discovery that neither Heyst nor Lena—nor, for that matter, the omniscient narrator—has understood Wang's position. Collits focuses on the revelation of a depth of perspective in Wang's character that stands in stark contrast to the racialized stereotypes of "coolie" and "servant." The moment when Wang's character is suddenly seen to be endowed with a full social and historical complexity reveals the novel's "political unconscious": everything that the "white couple" (*Victory*, 307) fail to see in their racialized construction of the world around them.[40]

What makes this reading all the more interesting and important (as a reading of Conrad's work in general, and one of the few critical assessments of *Victory* that refuses to dismiss the novel) is its valorization of Wang's character. While this would appear to turn on precisely the opposite of an effacement of the novel's most important Chinese character, the moment Collits emphasizes is the moment when the Chinese stereotypes—"coolie" and "servant"—are negated. It is quite precisely a moment when the narrative negates Wang's "tie" to any form of Chinese community the novel can imagine: "The graves of Wang's ancestors were far away, his parents were dead, his elder brother was a soldier in the yamen of some Mandarin away in Formosa. . . . He had been for years a labouring, restless vagabond. His only tie in the world was the Alfuro woman" (*Victory*, 307).

This reading, indeed, meets up with Wang's own self-effacing, self-accusatory characterization of himself, in the moment when he threatens to shoot Heyst if Heyst insists on seeking shelter for Lena amongst the "Alfuro" community: "If I were a wise man, I would be a merchant with a big hong in Singapore, instead of being a mine coolie turned houseboy" (*Victory*, 348). Here, Wang not only reiterates the repertoire of different Chinese stereotypes that frame the novel's overall plotting. His rejection of Heyst's measure of what is "foolish" and what is "wise" is itself premised on a communal identity set against all of those stereotypes: his relation to the "Alfuro" community that Heyst (along with the narrator) dismisses.[41] The function of Wang as character in *Victory* draws attention to the framing function of the effacement of Chinese characters in all of Conrad's work, going back to the very first novel, *Almayer's Folly*. If, as Collits's reading emphasizes, it is really Wang's perspective that enacts the turning point in the novel, precipitating readers' recognition of a world Heyst, Lena, and the seemingly omniscient narrator all misrecognize, the logic of the novel's plot might be distilled in terms of this reversal of perspective, whereby Wang's "Chinese" character turns out to be something entirely different from what the narrative seems to be presenting. The "covert plot" of *Victory* depends on Wang's perspective, not unlike the way the covert plot of *Almayer's Folly* depends on Babalatchi's.

I trace three ways in which Wang, as character, functions as anchor for the covert plot of *Victory*; and this points to the threefold way Chinese characters, throughout Conrad's fiction, formulate a relation between script and identity that organizes narrative sequence in terms of the timing and spacing of romanization. First, and at the simplest level of Chinese stereotype, Wang's character reinforces the basic, ironic structure of plotting found in *Almayer's Folly*, whereby the "folly" of European characters is represented through their subordination to the more ancient civilization of a primitive, atavistic Chinese (simultaneously represented as civilized and primitive). The renaming of "Almayer's Folly" graphically presents this in the Chinese renaming of the house "House of heavenly delight," completing the ruin of European imperialist dreams, represented by the decaying roman letters of the company sign "Office: Lingard and Co." A similar plot sequence is legible—albeit as covert plot—in *Victory*, signaled early on by the reference to the Chinese owner of Davidson's ship. The fact that Davidson serves Chinese interests is worth noting, as is the fact that the narrator feels compelled to explain its significance by way of a stereotyped dismissal of Chinese ("To serve a Chinese firm is not so bad. Once they become convinced you deal straight by them, their confidence becomes unlimited. You can do no wrong." [*Victory*, 30]).[42] This Chinese owner, moreover, takes an interest in Heyst's story that makes him a privileged reader of the whole novel. Effaced though that hypothetical Chinese reading of *Victory* may be (Davidson, in retelling the end of Heyst's story, is figured as addressing a European dignitary, not his Chinese owner), such a reading cannot easily be dismissed, especially in light of the central role Wang plays in disposing of all the remaining bodies left in the wake of Heyst's affairs. Davidson's final account leaves the reader's judgment suspended between the two rather different Chinese perspectives of Wang, on the one hand, and Davidson's Chinese owner on the other. Especially given the way Davidson offers the story as a kind of racial allegory—"there are more dead in this affair—more white people, I mean—than have been killed in many of the battles of the last Achin war" (*Victory*, 408)—suggests an ironic political allegory of white racial identity framed by a non-white, and perhaps specifically Chinese reading.

Victory does not give us quite the same ironic juxtaposition of roman letters and Chinese characters as *Almayer's Folly*, unraveling the "folly" of a European character (Almayer) according to the fading romanized print sign of a defunct European business ("Lingard and Co."), now rehoused and renamed according to an illegible Chinese script. Yet the plot of *Victory* does unfold according to a similar chronotope of roman lettering as with the "half obliterated words" "Lingard and Co." from *Almayer's Folly*. In *Victory*, "the most conspicuous object was a gigantic blackboard raised on two posts and presenting to Heyst, when the moon got over that side, the white letters "T. B. C. Co." in a row at least two feet high" (*Victory*, 5). The symbolic arrangement of those roman letters, moreover, is read successively in relation to all three of the different kinds of Chinese perspectives or stereotypes that unfold during the course of the novel, and that are summed up in Wang's later, self-accusatory reading of his own character: Chinese business owner (Wang notes that he is not a "big hong in Singapore"), coolie ("mine coolie"), and domestic servant ("houseboy") (*Victory*, 348). Each is figured as a different form of labor in relation to the T. B. C. Co.'s enterprise (and perhaps in that sense the covert clue to an understanding of economic "development") and without specifying a relation to literacy (and so without specifying a relation of Chinese identity to Chinese script). Wang reinforces the sense in which all the Chinese characters of the novel are presented as outside the decaying framework of those redundant "white letters." Although no alternative Chinese scriptworld is represented as such (by contrast to *Almayer's Folly*), whatever space of reading remains after the ultimate collapse and decay of the symbolic roman letters, will be Chinese.

That Chinese reading, however, is effaced from view, leading me to the second way in which Wang functions as anchor for the novel's covert plot (and for the effacement of Chinese characters throughout Conrad's work). Even without representing Chinese script in the way that *Almayer's Folly* does—indeed precisely in the absence of, or through, the effacement of a space of Chinese reading—one of the functions of Wang's character is to represent the riddle of the European characters' folly as a problem of reading. This is evident already in the chronotope of those "white letters" of the "T. B. C. Co." It emerges in the striking image of Heyst's inability to read Lena's character: "His mental attitude was that of a man looking this way and that on a piece of writing which he was unable to decipher, but which may be big with some revelation" (*Victory*, 222). The very terms of this reading imagery emerge from a confused formulation of the relation between script and language. The extended figure of this bewildered attempt to decipher an illegible piece of writing emerges from the beginning of the paragraph: "That girl, seated in her chair in graceful quietude, was to him like a script in an unknown language, or even more mysterious: like any writing to the illiterate" (*Victory*, 222). The narrative's own bewildered attempt to find the right "mysterious" simile is part of the confusion that produces something much more unsettling or estranging than the chronotope of romanization in the "white letters" of the T. B. C. Co. Is the "script" of this simile *known* while the language is *unknown*; or is the language *unknown* because the script is unknown as well? Forced to read this allegorically (as readers are compelled to do everywhere in this novel), one way to resolve the mystery is to read Heyst's inability as the mirror image of Lena's inability to read, in which case the first simile can be explained as her facing the script of his Swedish language (a more or less familiar script, using roman letters), the second, in terms of her relatively illiterate relation to the world of print, in the most general of senses.

That reading is shadowed by another, and specifically by the presence of Wang as a Chinese character who, by stereotyped association, might suggest contradictorily both a foreign script (Chinese writing) and an experience of illiteracy. The effacement of Chinese characters, here then, might be read as part of that mystery the narrator is invoking to articulate the problem of Heyst's relationship with Lena. In this case, the function of Wang as Chinese character serves to frame and reinforce an estrangement of identity (and specifically European "white" identity), figured as an estrangement of identity and script. This has already been prefigured in the moment when Heyst renames Lena as part of the domestic arrangement of their living conditions on Samburan. At the beginning of Chapter II of Part III, Heyst's return to the island with Lena is presented—from Wang's perspective—as follows: "Hanging on the arm of the white man before whom [Wang] stood was the girl called Alma; but neither from the Chinaman's eyes nor from his expression could any one have guessed that he was in the slightest degree aware of the fact" (*Victory*, 182). Even more circuitous and far-fetched than the extended figure of a script in a foreign language, this exaggerated emphasis on the impossibility of reading Wang's "aware"ness of Heyst's appearance with Alma, is itself a kind of impossible exercise in deciphering something that is either unreadable or simply a condition of illiteracy. A few pages later, this bizarre effacement of Wang's "aware"ness of "the fact" is echoed and explained through the renaming of "Alma" as "Lena," a rearrangement of letters that enacts a miniature, yet far-reaching reiteration of the chronotope of romanization in the "white letters" of the Company's sign-board: "still without looking at the girl—to whom, after several experimental essays in combining detached letters and loose syllables, he had given the name Lena" (*Victory*, 186).

The entire sequence describing Heyst's return to Samburan with Alma / Lena is staged as a problem of reading, that might itself more closely be read—letter for letter, sentence by sentence—as an extended metaphor of the relation between script and language, of experimental combinations of letters and syllables in which Wang's character is presented as, all at once, the mystery and the solution to the riddle of Heyst's relationship with Lena. Here, Wang's character stages the sort of effect that leads Christopher Bush to coin the phrase "ideographic modernism" to explain how "China" is invoked as the repressed sign of Europe's own multimedia estrangement of global and globalizing identity. Heyst's experiment in "combining detached letters and loose syllables" suggests a phonocentric grasp of the relation between sound and script, script and language, not to mention language and identity, that nonetheless unravels according to a hidden, symbolic logic unreadable to Heyst himself. This second way of understanding Wang's function in *Victory* illustrates the "ideographic" turn in European modernism: a foregrounding of the space of roman letters as enigma, mystery, and mark of European "folly."

This enigmatic space of reading points to a third sense in which Wang's character functions as anchor to the covert plot of *Victory* and all of Conrad's Malay tales. Simply put, Wang's appearance foregrounds the significance of Malay as the lingua franca of all the various characters in the novel, by contrast to English as the medium of the novel's own space of print. There is nothing simple about this point, since there is no way that Conrad could have articulated what might seem obvious from the perspective of an Indonesian reading of Conrad's Malay tales: namely, that the form of Malay shared in common by all the characters in this imagined community is that form of "pre-Indonesian," as Pramoedya called it, or "revolutionary Malay," as Anderson called it, that will give shape to the social and political articulation of anti-colonial nationalism. Nonetheless, in a quite fundamental sense, the covert plot of all Conrad's Malay tales turns out to be what can now retrospectively be understood as the emergence of Indonesian anti-colonial nationalism. The question of why it is the Chinese character of Wang that calls attention to the linguistic dimension of this covert plot is intimately linked to the role of romanization in transforming Malay into the vehicle of Indonesian anti-colonial nationalism.

In *Victory*, all the narrator's excessive figurative formulations of script are prefigured by the way in which Wang marks a disjuncture between speech and writing. First, there is the representation of Wang's speech as pidgin

English—"All finish?" are the first words attributed to Wang, referring to the end of the Company's operations and the departure of all its employees and laborers, and then leading to a conversation between Wang and Heyst settling the terms of Wang's staying on as Heyst's "boy" (*Victory*, 178). Wang's pidgin English is perhaps most notoriously represented by the phrase "Catchee one piecee wife" (*Victory*, 179)—and this reference to Wang's domestic arrangement prefigures the domestic arrangement Heyst will attempt to set up with Lena. It also provides the key to unlocking one crucial feature of the novel's covert plot—the fact that Wang's agreement to act as Heyst's servant is motivated by interests antithetical to Heyst's own, premised on an alliance with the "Alfuros" community who continue to resist the encroachment of Europeans in Samburan. This pidgin English is highly significant, not only in racializing the depiction of Chinese language, character, and identity, but also in registering a specific set of derogatory terms that simultaneously efface Chinese characteristics and make them ubiquitous in a sociolinguistic environment that extends beyond the reach of the novel's own ability to imagine its multiple communities.

Wang's pidgin English, however, is only one part of the way that the novel depicts his linguistic presence—and indeed it is unclear whether this pidgin is meant as a direct transcription of the way Wang communicates to Heyst in English, or as a looser translation from whatever language it is they speak together. This ambiguity itself (and the way the pidgin English troubles a reader's sense of the way all speech is rendered throughout the novel) is foregrounded in the first moment when Malay is revealed to be the everyday language of communication:

> It was easy to be taciturn with Heyst, who had plunged himself into an abyss of meditation over books, and remained in it till the shadow of Wang falling across the page, and the sound of a rough, low voice uttering the Malay word "*makan*," would force him to climb out to a meal. (*Victory*, 180)

This early description of "the shadow of Wang falling across the page" confirms the point that Wang characterizes a problem of reading. Indeed, all the various, later figurative images of script and writing are haunted by the "shadow of Wang falling across the page." What this passage *also* reveals, however, is a disjuncture between the space of the written and the space of the spoken word—the spoken language marked here (in print of course) by "the Malay word '*makan*.'"

From this point on, not only will the "shadow of Wang" fall over each turn in the extended figurative play on reading, language, and script. The hidden

Chinese character of that interrupted space of reading will also signal the importance of Malay as a language shared by Heyst and Wang but occupying a different space and time from that of the novel's readers. In a series of subsequent scenes, whenever Heyst or Wang speak in Malay, it signals some key turn in the plot's denouement: first (*Victory*, 224) when Wang announces the arrival of the "white men" (Jones, Ricardo, and Pedro); later, when Wang is instructed to reopen the Company's living quarters to provide the "white men" with lodgings; and finally in the standoff between Wang and Heyst when Wang threatens to shoot Heyst if he insists on Lena joining the "Alfuros" (*Victory*, 348). In this last exchange, Heyst himself reveals what kind of shared language Malay represents for himself and Wang—"We were talking in such Malay as we are both equal to" (*Victory*, 348). This moment also complicates the spell of "pidgin English"—or rather reverses the prejudices embedded in all those moments of pidgin English—by making spoken Malay the mirror image of whatever derogatory implications are embedded in each pidgin English phrase. Retrospectively, this reveals how Malay, as a language (and its leveling effects within a hierarchy of languages and scripts), produces what I explored in Chapter 1 as the function of the accusative case in Conrad's fiction, in the use of the word "Tuan" (above all in *Lord Jim*). It is not at all incidental that this is the very moment when Wang repeats the derogatory terms of racialized Chinese labor in a sort of self-accusatory, self-effacing, but also sarcastic retort to Heyst's claims that Wang's fears are "foolish." Here, the covert plot is revealed in a leveling, revolutionary form of Malay that overturns the derogatory epithets applied to the Chinese ("big hong," "mine coolie," "houseboy").

If "the Malay word '*makan*'" marks a key turning point in the timing and spacing of this novel's denouement, it also reveals the long-delayed decoding effect built into the very first words of Conrad's career. "Kaspar! Makan!" reproduces the same sociolinguistic effect of Malay as a lingua franca, shared among people who speak a whole range of languages and who inhabit a whole range of different scriptworlds. What this moment in *Victory* makes clearer is the Chinese character of this form of Malay—hinted at in *Almayer's Folly* but, to an important extent, effaced precisely through the exaggeration of that novel's contrast between the decaying form of roman letters and the ironic ascendancy of Chinese script.

In this third sense, then, the function of Wang in the plotting of *Victory* reveals the Chinese character of that form of Malay that has, from the very beginning of Conrad's writing career, encoded the chronotope of romanization as the delayed decoding effect (in a word—*makan*) of all Conrad's narratives. While not minimizing the extent to which Conrad's effacement of Chinese characters involves a racialized negation of Chinese language, culture, and identity, I, nonetheless, want to argue that this effacement leaves the imprint on all of Conrad's narratives of precisely those experiences that the narrative seeks to efface. In particular, the historical experience of the Chinese diaspora throughout Southeast Asia, distorted though this may be in the stereotyped caricatures of the Chinese articulated by Wang—"a big hong from Singapore"—"mine coolie"—and "houseboy"—leaves its mark, not only in the covert plot of Wang's successful containment of the harm Heyst brings to the island tale of *Victory*, but also in the linguistic register with which the derogatory English stereotypes, translated into their contested Malay counterparts, offer an alternative way to read the chronotope of romanized print form (whether the printed page of Heyst's book or the "white letters" of the T. B. C. Co.'s advertising billboard). What, from the narrator's seemingly omniscient perspective, appears to be a mutual incomprehension of different scriptworlds and worldscripts ("white" versus "Chinese"), becomes, with the reversal of perspectives enabled by Wang's role in the covert plotting, an alternative spacing and timing of reading. This is the spacing and timing of romanized print Malay (*makan*)—also of "print-capitalism"—in a constant process of translation, transliteration, and transcription across different worldscripts and scriptworlds. From *Almayer's Folly* to *Victory*, this form of romanized print Malay reveals the Chinese character of romanization framing Conrad's Malay fiction.

Conrad and Lu Xun: The Interface of Chinese and Roman Characters

One of the consequences of this reading of Conrad's effacement of Chinese characters is to confirm Pramoedya Ananta Toer's assessment of Conrad's work as providing an archive ("facts") for understanding decolonization. It confirms this assessment while also supporting the historical and political importance of Chinese Indonesians (*peranakan* Chinese) as key figures in the development of a romanized form of print Malay—"pre-Indonesian" or "revolutionary Malay"—that became the vehicle for imagining Indonesian nationalism. Both points together, underscore the sociolinguistic significance of romanization more broadly. Romanization, seemingly the imposition of European forms of language, script, and identity in the service of colonization, historically becomes the medium for contesting and decolonizing European forms from the perspective of non-European languages, scripts, and identities. This is one of the key points to emerge from a study of romanization, both as a feature of transnational modernism, and as a sociolinguistic phenomenon. In both cases, what is revealed is the broader historical context of decolonization within which romanization should be positioned. Adapting Peter Hitchcock's formulation for describing transnationalism and postcolonial form, one might call this the "long space"[43] of narrative and history, within which to situate both transnational artistic modernism and the modernizing imperatives of language and script reform.

There is, however, another side to this same argument, which I associate, by contrast to the "long space" of decolonizing narrative and history, with reference to the short, or even fragmentary, space of the individual passage of literature or text. This side of the argument, while still recognizing the reversal of colonial into decolonial imperatives, pays closer attention to the difficulty presented by any reading experience. Rather than simply demystifying the reading process—say, for example, by adopting a Jamesonian, interpretive key that unlocks the metaphors of writing and script as so many ideological ruses[44]— this approach seeks to recognize the fullest possible complexity involved in any short passage of text at all, including the problematic medium of the text itself: above all, the fact that it is the product of multiple (and still unfolding) effects of transcription, transliteration, and translation across many different languages and scripts and in the transformation of print media. There is no one hermeneutic that will decipher the political unconscious of decolonization. Far from it, in fact. The very imperative that revolutionizes hierarchies of languages and scripts, and that reverses colonizing fixtures of language, script, and identity, opens up the reading of any individual passage of text to the multiple, possible philological traditions that accompany all the languages and scripts registered in that passage of text.[45] Both sides of this argument (but especially this second question of the media fragmentation of the space of reading, of romanized print form, and of "print-capitalism"), I now explore through a comparison between Conrad and Lu Xun.

Lu Xun is the iconic figure of Chinese modernism, the literary voice of the May Fourth movement, and the universally recognized founding figure of modern Chinese literature. If Lu Xun's work is universally recognized as such, even by readers and critics who evaluate and interpret his work in very different ways, one of the most iconic of his stories (next to "Diary of a Madman") is "The Real Story of Ah-Q," which Lydia Liu describes as "the climactic event" in "May Fourth literary discourse."[46] The appearance of the roman letter Q in Lu Xun's story stands, in revealing counterpoint, to the effacement of Chinese characters in Conrad's fiction. A graphic mark of the betrayal of a Chinese sense of character (as well as the traditional use of Chinese characters), it might be read as an accusation of self-abnegation in Lu Xun's call to modernize and revolutionize China's cultural identity (a complex fictional counterpart to those iconoclastic calls to abolish Chinese characters discussed earlier). Whereas Conrad points to the sociolinguistic role of diasporic Chinese actors in revolutionizing the scriptworld of romanized print form—and so, to the work of script conversion from Chinese (and also Arabic) scriptworlds—Lu Xun points in a rather different direction, toward a revolution in language and script that reframes romanized print form within a Chinese scriptworld. The use of the roman letter Q marks a foreign presence, a loss of identity that calls for the reassertion of an appropriate modern form of Chinese identity, bound to revolutionizing Chinese language, writing, and script.

These two paradigmatic examples may appear to be diametrically opposed: the one subordinating Chinese letters within a romanized scriptworld; the other subordinating roman letters within a Chinese scriptworld. Yet it is the interface between the two, seemingly opposed, scriptworlds that is the most revealing. What it reveals, moreover, emphasizes the other side of my argument about the Chinese character of romanization as a revolutionary imperative to decolonize hierarchies of language, script, and identity. If the "long space" of decolonization follows a temporal and spatial elaboration of narrative forms that are still unfolding (still legible in the chronotopes of romanization to be found in twenty-first-century narratives, from Ha Jin's *War Trash* to Xu Bing; from Haruki Murakami's *1Q84* to Ted Chiang's short stories; in television shows or films like *Blade Runner* and *Arrival*), those narrative forms are themselves dependent on a fragmentation inherent in the phenomenon of romanization, whatever scriptworld one inhabits. Simply put, despite the long-lasting literary legacies of both Conrad and Lu Xun, each writer's grasp of the chronotope of romanization is premised on the way romanization itself enacts the disappearance of the space (and time) of literature, literary form, and print literacy. All the chronotopes of romanization to follow constitute afterimages of that space-time of print—including Anderson's "print-capitalism"—whose eclipse may be traced back to the moment in which Conrad and Lu Xun came to write (what I characterized in the Introduction, following Ha Jin's formulation, as Conrad's "timely appearance in print").

A theoretical point of reference for these claims is provided by Walter Benjamin's celebrated argument in "The Work of Art in the Age of Technological Reproducibility." Benjamin's dialectical account of the material history of different forms of "technological reproducibility" positions print as only one (albeit "particularly important") form among others in the transformation of different forms of technological reproducibility, from the "woodcut" through engraving and lithography, finally to photography and film. "Around 1900," Benjamin famously argues, describing the birth of film, "technical reproduction had reached a standard that . . . permitted it to reproduce all transmitted works of art and thus to cause the most profound change in their impact upon the public . . ."[47] In short, film eclipses the literary form of print. It is, in part, on the basis of this thesis that Christopher Bush develops his argument about "ideographic modernism," tracing the potent link developed from the entanglement of modern conceptions of China—above all, focused on the Chinese "ideographic" writing system—and the new media. Bush recognizes Benjamin's privileging of film, while emphasizing the multimedia context within which "the ideographic topos" emerged:

> Eisenstein's account of cinematic montage is perhaps the best-known instance of the ideographic topos being used to describe a modern technological medium, but from the telegraph (1837), through the daguerreotype (1839), the typewriter (1874), the phonograph (1876), the cinema (1895), and well into the twentieth century, critics would continue to associate new writing technologies with the writing systems of the ancient Orient.[48]

Bush focuses on the moment of Europe's fetishization of "China"—and above all, the Chinese character as "ideograph"—in this emerging new media network that Benjamin traces around the transformative effects of film. Seen from a slightly different perspective—but still retaining the range of Bush's argument—this presents that other side of what I have been tracing as the process of romanization. The K-effect in Conrad—as well as the effect of the letter Q in Lu Xun—is, in a number of senses, the mirror image of the European fetishization of the Chinese character. Here, more broadly, the Chinese character of romanization surfaces as the "ideographic" moment of transnational modernism. Following Benjamin's analysis, I want to consider the revolutionary agency of film in the media system that appropriates and displaces the space of print.

Film is the new media system that both Conrad and Lu Xun shared. Both retrospectively argued that film played a decisive role in the formation of their literary ventures. In notes used as the basis for a talk delivered to employees of his publisher, Doubleday, on his visit to the United States in 1923 (the year before he died), Conrad wrote of the affinity, and also rivalry, between the writer and cinematography. Entitled "Author and Cinematograph," these notes open with the argument that novelists have long claimed the same narrative ambition ascribed to cinematography today.[49] Although Conrad begins by distinguishing the author's work from that of the camera—"the author unlike the camera had the power to react not only to light, shades and colour but also to form"—he goes on to insist that novel writing and filmmaking share something "fundamental": "That fundamental condition of visuality, of animation, applies to all the masters of creative art"—and a little later, "fundamentally the creator in letters aims at a moving picture—moving to the eye, to the mind, and to our complex emotions."[50]

Lu Xun's retrospective account of the significance of the new media system of film is more famous. In the 1922 "Preface" to his collection of stories, "Outcry" (sometimes translated "Call to Arms"), Lu Xun recalls the moment, as a medical student in Japan, when he decided to become a writer. He recounts the effect of seeing a film (or slideshow—different translations create an interesting ambiguity about the precise nature of the media system)[51] that depicted a Chinese man about to be executed as a spy by the Japanese, during the Russo-Japanese war: "The man tied up, the caption informed us, had been caught spying for the Russians and was about to be beheaded by the Japanese as a public example for the appreciative [Chinese] mob."[52] Reflecting on this moment, he goes on to explain why he gave up studying medicine in order to become a writer: "For I no longer believed in the overwhelming importance of medical science. However rude a nation was in physical health, if its people were intellectually feeble, they would never become anything other than cannon fodder or gawping spectators, their loss to the world through illness no cause for regret. The first task was to change their spirit; and literature . . . I decided at the time, [was] the best means to this end. And so I reinvented myself as a crusader for cultural reform."[53]

In her extended discussion of this much-cited passage, Lydia Liu redirects attention away from "straightforward biographical" readings and toward the problem of representation it poses ("Who represents and who gets represented? Who views the representation?"[54]). Focusing both on the "cinematic spectacle" of the passage and the role of "Lu Xun the narrator," Liu illuminates how it reproduces the conflicted and ambiguous position on Chinese national character found elsewhere in Lu Xun's fiction, and most notably in "The Real Story of Ah-Q."

Rey Chow, discussing this paradigmatic autobiographical account of Lu Xun's beginnings as a writer (and hence the beginnings of modern Chinese literature), writes, "Lu Xun's story is not simply part of a famous writer's autobiography about his writing career but a story about the beginning of a new kind of discourse in the postcolonial 'third world.' This is a discourse of technologized visuality."[55] Connecting this episode with the theories of Benjamin, Chow writes, "This episode of an emerging 'modernity' that is specifically grounded in visuality would find many parallels elsewhere in the world. Lu Xun's experience anticipated the ways European intellectuals such as Martin Heidegger and Walter Benjamin were to write about modernity . . ."[56] Chow's argument is especially interesting for drawing attention to a contradiction written into Lu Xun's account itself, and repeated in later comments on the significance of this account for modern Chinese literature: the contradictory fact that the spectacle of visuality that has displaced literary form, leads to a "call to arms" to return to the medium of literature that film has displaced: "If this story is indeed the foundational story about the "origins" of modern Chinese literature . . . then these origins are illuminatingly self-contradictory."[57] As she later points out, expanding on this contradiction: "Besides a radical conversion from medicine to literature . . . the *other* conversion in Lu Xun's story is a reconversion to tradition, a reaffirmation of culture as literary culture, which is to be centered in writing and reading, in opposition to the technology that includes film as well as medicine."[58] And again: "If the lantern slide convinced Lu Xun of the need to revitalize national culture through writing, this return to writing—the "original" practice of the Chinese tradition—would henceforth be haunted by the implications of an erasure. What is erased is precisely the violence experienced through the technologized decentering of "China" into a screen image. The written text, in which the erudite male intellectual seeks refuge, thus becomes a cover-up that veils the vulgar and brutal exhibition of Chinese men being slaughtered in the midst of transnational imperialism . . ."[59]

Chow's reading of the contradictory origins of modern Chinese literature in the visuality of the screen image extends to a reading of the style and form of Lu Xun's own stories ("verbal texts that deliver *condensed, pointed* messages . . . the short story . . . like a snapshot, a quick capturing of life with minimal background detail within a frozen span of time"[60]). Relating this reading to the chronotope of romanization in "The Real Story of Ah-Q," the visual image of the roman letter effects an estrangement of the space of print, analogous to the forms of estrangement found everywhere that the scholar confronts the disrupted space of the traditional Chinese character. Indeed, the roman letter Q itself, from the very beginning, may be nothing other than the visual mark of that traditional order of Chinese writing, now, forever displaced by the regime of "technologized visuality." In the "Preface," too, Lu Xun puts himself in the compromised position of outmoded scholar "copying out ancient stone inscriptions."[61]

Whether the technology Lu Xun refers to is a slideshow or a film, points to a hesitation in defining the technology of the media system of film itself, built as it is on the photographic image turned into moving images. The relation of photography to cinematography is part of Benjamin's argument, set as it is, within the wider dialectical grasp of the history of technological media from woodcut through lithography to cinematography (and including the printing press). It is also part of Christopher Bush's argument about the emergence of "ideographic modernism," which adds to Benjamin's predominantly European frame of reference the fetishized emphasis on the visual image of Chinese writing. Rey Chow's reading resituates those arguments within what she describes as a "new kind of discourse in the postcolonial 'third world.'" Much of the argument of Chow's *Primitive Passions* is concerned with complicating the tired binary logic of East-West constructs to show how the coupling of visuality and modernity displaces the colonial hierarchies of European "West" and Orientalized "East." Implied in all these approaches to understanding the new media networks of 1900, then, is something analogous to what I have been exploring with respect to romanization—now with the additional point that the roman letter and the Chinese character *both* undergo what Lydia Liu calls the "ideographic turn."[62]

The ambiguity in Lu Xun's autobiographical recollection is not, however, the ambiguous status of writing in either roman characters or Chinese characters (whether romanized according to a Japanese system or using the Japanese system [kanji] of Chinese characters). It is, more fundamentally, the displacement of any and all scripts in relation to the visual image: the displacement of writing, however, that nonetheless retains the form of script in the very medium of the screen image—and even more specifically in the fundamental effect of the transformation from the single frame to the moving image. Here is Lu Xun's description of the film or lantern slideshow: "The man tied up, *the caption informed us*, had been caught spying for the Russians *and was about to be* beheaded by the Japanese as a public example to the appreciative mob."[63] To repeat, then, the key points. There is a "caption" (in some translations this is given as "commentary" [the Chinese is quite vague, simply indicating "it was explained": *jie shuo* [解说]]—*writing* of some kind, then (presumably in Japanese kanji, possibly in romanized print). And there is a screen image (possibly a sequence, either in slide form or as a moving film image) representing something *about to happen*. Narrative is given both as sequence and in the arrested still image. The visual technology is both freed from words and prescribed or bound to script.

Benjamin's argument about the development of film from photography concisely underscores the logic of this riddle, whereby the power of script is encoded in the medium of film in the moment when film eclipses the space of the printed word. As Benjamin puts it, describing the "incomparable significance of Atget, who, around 1900, took photographs of deserted Paris streets" that become "like scenes of crime":

> They demand a specific kind of approach; free-floating contemplation is not appropriate to them. They stir the viewer; he feels challenged by them in a new way. At the same time picture magazines begin to put up signposts for him, right ones or wrong ones, no matter. For the first time, captions have become obligatory. And it is clear that they have an

altogether different character than the title of a painting. The directives which the captions give to those looking at the pictures in illustrated magazines soon become even more explicit and more imperative in the film where the meaning of each single picture appears to be prescribed by the sequence of all the preceding ones.[64]

Benjamin's argument here, taken together with Lu Xun's famous account of the effect of the visual image from the Russo-Japanese war footage, might be read as a description of the way that film has fundamentally altered the way that we read today. The timing and spacing of words, no longer bound by the space and time of print, follows the logic of film sequence. That is not to say that scripts, words, and language vanish altogether. On the contrary, "captions" "become even more explicit and more imperative." They are subordinated, however, to a logic of the moving image—"each single picture appears to be *prescribed* by the sequence of all the preceding ones."

This argument has consequences far beyond merely suggesting that the new visual technologies influence the way in which writers compose literature. For sure, the works of both Conrad and Lu Xun may be described in filmic terms. Rey Chow notes the way that Lu Xun composes scenes "like a snapshot." There are many different critical accounts of the way that Conrad's work has cinematic elements (including Conrad's own comments, which enable a rereading of Conrad's famous articulation of the "task" of the writer—"before all, to make you *see*"—as fundamentally cinematic[65]). Benjamin's formulation that "each single picture appears to be *prescribed* by the sequence of all the preceding ones" suggests a cinematic imperative in Conrad's famous delayed decoding technique. What Benjamin's formulation also suggests, when set side by side with such contrasting examples as those from Lu Xun and Conrad, is how fundamentally this cinematic imperative reorganizes the hierarchies of language and script, prescribing a temporal and spatial arrangement of letters according to a new filmic sequence. In some respects, this is simply the logical extension of the way romanization mediates the timing and spacing of print culture, but now in two rather different senses that might appear, at first, to stand opposed. First, there is the transcription of all languages and scripts into the same scriptworld, following the linearity of romanized print form, but spaced out on screen (read from left to right—even if the script happens to be Chinese characters, or Japanese kanji, as might well be the case with Lu Xun's example). Second, there is the juxtaposition of the word on screen (roman letter or Chinese character), literally subordinated as caption, read (whether legible or not) in relation to the sequence of images. The first suggests a romanization of all scripts. The second accentuates the

Chinese character of that romanization—first, in the application of linear (left to right) reading of script; second, in the turning of all letters, and/or words, into the "ideographic" filmic image.

What the logic of film sequence shows, then, is the ideographic turn in the process of romanization as the new technologies of writing cross over languages and scripts, at the same time rearranging the hierarchies of those languages, scriptworlds, and worldscripts. Lu Xun's memory of the film reel or lantern-slideshow is organized around a profoundly translingual, transcriptural scene—a scene of betrayal. The Chinese man about to be executed as a Russian spy by Japanese soldiers. If this is the moment that inaugurates a revolutionary commitment to Chinese literature, as Rey Chow points out, it scripts that simultaneously modernist break from and traditional return to Chinese letters across multiple languages, scripts, and worldscripts (Chinese, Japanese, Russian), all of which are captured by the visual image, and whose significance might best be understood as emerging from the gap between languages, scripts, and national identities (the illegibility of the blank faces of the crowd). The scene of looking, of traumatic witness, is a scene of filmic reading, premised on a hierarchy of languages and scripts about to be undone forever (in fact, already cut off, decapitated by the caption or commentary explaining what is about to happen).

Lydia Liu's chapter on Lu Xun in *Translingual Practice* relates the multiple languages and scripts implicated in this "cinematic spectacle" to the translingual practices at work in "The Real Story of Ah-Q," which ends with a similarly public spectacle of execution. The concluding public spectacle Liu emphasizes, though, is the "unforgettable scene" that mirrors the opening account of Ah Q's name: "an almost symmetrical episode in which Ah Q not only is incapable of signing his name on a piece of court paper that probably contains his own death sentence but, when asked to draw a circle instead of his signature, fails to accomplish that task as well."[66] As Liu goes on to explain, "If Ah Q had drawn a perfect circle, it would have resembled the English letter O, not far in the alphabet from the letter Q. But since the power of naming and writing is in the hands of the narrator, Ah Q's failure to draw the miraculous circle is not surprising."[67] The story itself emerges from the conflicted position between Ah Q's illiteracy and the narrator's knowledge of both traditional Chinese writing and roman characters, as Liu's reading of the story itself shows, with its focus on the importance of the role of the narrator (by no means the same as the position of Lu Xun as author). The translingual practices Liu finds at work in the story turn on the significance of the "erased presence of the narrator,"[68] an effacement of perspective Liu links to the complex, translingual practice of Lu Xun's own attempts to negotiate the question of China's national character.

There is something very different in the way that Conrad organizes the problem of reading around the effacement of his Chinese characters. The filmic element, however, draws attention to similarities—large and small. Conrad's notes on "Author and Cinematograph," from his 1923 visit to the United States, were designed to accompany a reading of passages from *Victory*. The recently filmed version of that novel prompted his retrospective account of the "fundamental" affinities between novelist and cinema. Yet the way in which Wang's character functions to organize the narrative denouement of that novel draws attention to filmic elements already embedded in the novel. As Cedric Watts has noted, in a parenthesis that makes the claim itself a little cryptic, "Wang's habit of materialising and vanishing anticipates the devices of film-cartoon."[69] Watts's formulation draws attention to several different ways in which Wang's character reflects the "devices of film-cartoon." First, and perhaps foremost, it describes the racialized, visual depictions with which all the Chinese characters are presented, everywhere in Conrad's fiction. Prescribed by the racist epithets that appear so frequently throughout *Victory*, the labeling (or accusative naming) enacts a reversal and contestation of the significance of those epithets, becoming switch words, marked by the turn from pidgin English to Malay. At one of the key moments, later in the novel, when Wang makes it clear that the alignment of his interests with the "Alfuros" and against the "white" intruders, he is described as appearing to Lena/Alma as if through a form of visual entertainment, recalled from East London: "It was Wang's face, of course, with no suggestion of a body belonging to it, like those cardboard faces at which she remembered gazing as a child in the window of a certain dim shop kept by a mysterious little man in Kingsland Road. Only this face, instead of mere holes, had eyes which blinked. She could see the beating of the eyelids" (*Victory*, 345). This becomes a film image (a paradigmatic example of the racialized use of early forms of cinematography[70]) a few lines later: "she saw Wang's unreal cardboard face moving its thin lips and grimacing artificially" (*Victory*, 345).

As Terry Collits's reading of *Victory* shows, this racialized, "cartoon" image is not simply incidental to the way the narrative works, which Watts laments in "resembling a Hollywood melodrama."[71] It is part of the timing and spacing of the narrative, whereby Wang's "habit of materialising and vanishing" (to use Watts's words) problematizes the space of reading itself (in the image of "the shadow of Wang falling across the page" of the book that Heyst is reading [*Victory*, 180] repeated later in Heyst's estrangement before the "crowded, parallel lines" of the pages of the book before looking up to see Wang [*Victory*, 310]). The metaphors of writing, script, and reading, as already discussed, all turn on the "shadow of Wang" whose "trick" of appearing and disappearing—part of the film apparatus of trick photography—provides an alternative script to the one Heyst and Lena, each in their rather different ways, have learned to read. If the chronotope of romanized print is reframed, then, by Wang's Chinese character, it is the character of *film* that reframes the visual image of those "white letters"—T. B. C. Co.—and that space of reading print—the "crowded, parallel lines" of the pages of Heyst's father's book—not to mention Heyst's experiment in arranging the letters of Alma/Lena's name. Wang's appearance, halfway through the novel, rearranges the way in which the whole sequence of the narrative is to be read. One way to conceive this (and arguably this is both Watts's and Collits's presumption, albeit in very different ways) is to recognize in Wang's "trick" the "covert plot" of the novel. His character possesses the "keys" to unlocking the hidden narrative, which none of the white characters will ever see. And this has been my reading of *Victory* as revealing the "covert plot" of all Conrad's Malay fiction, the key to decoding the delayed effect of Conrad's opening words—"Kaspar! Makan!"—as the opening of the space of print-capitalism, via the mediation of *peranakan* Chinese writers and publishers, to a romanized form of "revolutionary Malay" or "pre-Indonesian." Another way to conceive this, however, is to recognize a more fundamental disruption of the spacing and timing of narrative sequence, in which the reader is compelled to see the non-linear sequencing of letters, words, and images that surface everywhere that the chronotope of romanization appears.

Each of those moments, after all (going back over all of Conrad's texts), is prescribed by a logic of romanization that fragments the space-time of "print-capitalism"; that undoes linear sequence; and that compels a reading, attentive to a whole range of disruptive K-effects such as those already discussed in Marlow's abrupt shift from (uppercase) Romanization to (lowercase) romanization, from "Knights" to "nights," in the *mise-en-scène* of *Heart of Darkness*. If montage is the technique most commonly associated with this fundamental feature of film—and indeed, montage is the key device that Benjamin discusses in his essay—the K-effect may itself be an effect of montage. The use of montage has sometimes been called the "Kuleshov-effect" (or, again, K-effect), referring to filmmaker and film theorist Lev Kuleshov.[72] In Conrad's texts, this elementary technique of montage may be seen at work at the level of images (descriptions of faces), at the level of words ("coolie," "houseboy"), and at the level of letters. At all levels, the juxtaposition of images, words, and letters enacts that constant process of crossing over language and script inherent in the process of romanization. Comparing this to Lu Xun's "Preface," a similar process may be found in the way that the medium of "film" (*dian ying*, 电影) governs a whole set of juxtapositions at different levels of his own text: in the description of the visual image; the caption, or commentary, and even in the casual inclusion of roman letters to mark Japanese place-names.

The "film-cartoon" of Wang's disappearing "trick" (conceived now as a kind of montage K-effect) calls attention to a third feature of the film logic, indicating the way in which Conrad's Chinese characters function (in *Victory* and also elsewhere). As already suggested by the silent image of "Wang's unreal cardboard face moving its thin lips and grimacing artificially," the visual image implies a relation to *sound* that is a part of the film logic of sequentiality—here, in the delayed decoding trick of recognizing that Lena has no idea what Wang is saying; his speech is entirely effaced by the fetishized appearance of the animated, cartoonish face. The sense in which sound is bound to script, indicates a phonetic logic (indeed, a phonocentrism) that is both philosophically overdetermined (as Derrida's entire work demonstrates) and also (seemingly obviously) the premise of romanization (the effect of the letter K turns on its phonetic significance—whether the letter is spoken or unspoken, for example, in the word "Knights"). This last fact draws attention to a point foregrounded by the example from *Victory*: that the K-effect in cinema, premised on a technology of the silent visual image, nonetheless presupposes (and to some extent fully anticipates), technologically speaking, the emergence of sound. Yet at the same time, the logic of film sequence enacts a thoroughgoing rupture in the relation between sound and script, writing and speech. The example from *Victory*, as already noted, hinges on the revelation of a language of communication, shared by Heyst and Wang, that has been effaced by the space of English print: the lingua franca Malay, given by the single word *makan*, in the passage that juxtaposes, through contrast, the space of reading and the space of speech. The situation is no less complicated—and no less revolutionary in its implications—in the example from Lu Xun. The complexity with which the visual image implies a reorganization of the hierarchies of speech to language, sound to script, may be gauged, simply by considering the function of the "caption" (the Chinese term arguably foregrounding this all the more through the phrase *jie shuo* [解说]— literally, "according to what was said"). The scene implies at least three languages—Russian, Japanese, and Chinese—and also implies a scene of crossing-over (indeed *double-crossing*) of languages. All these languages—again, *silently*—presume the traumatic recognition of a Chinese identity within this silent visual image. The typeface of Lu Xun's own Chinese prose reproduces the K-effect of this film logic, both in the "Preface" and throughout the stories.

At the level of the letter, the word, the sentence, as well as at the level of the narrative ambition of all their works, Conrad's and Lu Xun's fiction shares a fundamentally similar logic, even though their work occupies very different scriptworlds. Whether emphasizing the Chinese character of romanization in Conrad's English, or the effect of the roman character in Lu Xun's Chinese, the problem of sequence, implied by this visual film logic, effects a far-reaching disruption in the hierarchies of language to speech, sound to script, scriptworld to worldscript.

4
Sanskritization, Romanization, Digitization

The title of this concluding chapter is meant to suggest a chronological succession of three different ways of scripting world literature and print culture. Sanskritization refers to the spread of a Sanskrit form of literacy that Sheldon Pollock has described in terms of the "Sanskrit cosmopolis," a universalizing, political model reproduced in a range of scripts throughout South and Southeast Asia.[1] Romanization refers to the historical spread of roman letters as the standardizing, near-universal alphabet for modern literary print form. Digitization refers to the recent revolution in media technologies that reproduces all forms of literature via computer code. To the extent that this three-part template suggests a succession of different forms and technologies of writing, print culture, and world literature, it is meant, also, to signal the broader historical context within which to situate the phenomenon that has preoccupied me in this book: proliferating forms of romanization (with a lowercase "r"), above all print romanization; that is, romanization as the timing and spacing of print culture. I propose here a speculative, dialectical grasp of writing systems through these three forms, beginning with the early Sanskrit model for disseminating world literature; turning then to the print forms that came to dominate Europe, and through Europe the world, coinciding with what Benedict Anderson has suggestively dubbed "print-capitalism"[2]; and turning finally to the digital forms of representation that circulate today and reproduce (or displace) any and all literatures of the world.

Speculative though it certainly is, this dialectical grasp of the history of worldscripts and scriptworlds sets in perspective the more narrowly conceived historical phenomenon of (lowercase) romanization (around the turn of the century) that has been the focus of this book. The broader historical scope of this speculative dialectic provides useful tools for explaining some of the characteristic riddles of romanization, tools that might then be applied elsewhere in literary and cultural studies. If the K-effect of romanization at work in Conrad's fiction is part of a characteristic chronotope of avant-garde transnational modernism, that chronotope itself might prompt future comparative readings of literary form within a more fully multilingual and multiscript perspective. Such readings might, in turn, further illuminate the striking paradox that the time-space (chronotope) of print romanization comes into view as the eclipse of the traditional medium of print itself. Just as oral forms of recitation are inscribed in the very origins of world literature (as told by the Sanskrit epics), and just as the rise of print media depends on older hierarchies of prestige scripts (the interrelation between scriptworlds and worldscripts), with the conversion of roman letters into alphanumerical code, the printed letter remains (often as a flickering afterimage, a K-effect) in the temporal and spatial forms of contemporary digitized reading, writing, and coding.

Situating the romanization of world literature and print forms within the historical perspective of ancient Sanskrit literary form, on the one hand, and the digital recoding of all forms of text on the other, I want to review some of the key turns in the argument that I have been following. Contrasting Sanskritization with Romanization (as Pollock's work helpfully does) revisits a riddle of romanized print form that I have explored using the terms *worldscript* and *scriptworld*. While in the initial stages of Romanization, the roman alphabet becomes the medium for imposing a single worldscript wherever it goes, the "Sanskrit cosmopolis" spreads throughout South and Southeast Asia without the domination of a single script, leaving its imprint on a range of scriptworlds. I will return to the details of this contrast in a moment. The key point to emphasize here, however, is a historical reversal in this contrast between Sanskritization and Romanization. With the waning of the Sanskrit cosmopolis, Sanskrit does come to be associated ("ironically," as Pollock will put it[3]) with a dominant worldscript: Devanagari. With the emergent, worldwide hegemony of romanized print form, by contrast, the single worldscript of the roman alphabet confronts, and seeks to adapt to, multiple scriptworlds, marking that global historical shift that I have characterized as the shift from (uppercase) Romanization to (lowercase) romanization. The historical moment when the standardized print form of English letters gets used as the premise for cybernetic theory and computer coding reformulates, again, this dialectical interplay between worldscripts and scriptworlds. The Latin alphabet, initially imposed on the world as the single hegemonic worldscript (uppercase Romanization), now serves as a template for providing universal access to any and all scriptworlds (lowercase romanization). The "ideographic turn"[4] that precipitates digitization, reproduces a multiply ironic effect, intensifying the dialectical interplay of worldscript and scriptworld. The digitized world of coding presumes (simultaneously) a universal worldscript (the basis of coding) and a multiplication of scriptworlds. It is this ironic effect that I have been tracking in the K-effect of Conrad's work, of avant-garde modernism, and in the ambivalence with which the *Oxford English Dictionary* repositions English within a changing hierarchy of worldscripts and scriptworlds. Within the dialectical trajectory of this broader historical relay from Sanskritization to Romanization to Digitization, the effects of (lowercase) romanization reveal an inflection point in the shift from Romanization to Digitization: that moment when the extreme ideal of Sanskritization (a universal form of literature for all scriptworlds) meets the extreme ideal of Romanization (a universal worldscript for world literature imposed to the exclusion of all other scripts), to produce the extreme ideal of Digitization (a single code of worldscript to unlock access to all scriptworlds).

Before exploring Sanskritization with a little more attention to detail, I want to consider an anecdote that illustrates this speculative dialectic of worldscript and scriptworld, while also standing in counterpoint to the main examples of romanized print form that I have been discussing (notably, Conrad's fiction, its reception, and the OED). This anecdote comes from a mid-nineteenth-century Malay text, the *Hikayat Abdullah*, written by author and munshi (or language teacher) Abdullah bin Abdul Kadir. The text itself, an important precursor of modern Malay (including modern Indonesian), is positioned between older and newer forms of script. Written in Malay in the 1840s by a writer who taught some of the key British colonial figures in the early nineteenth century, an Arabic (*jawi*) script version was lithographed in 1849 and this became the prototype for later print versions beginning in 1880, a romanized version appearing in 1939, and a full English translation appearing in 1955. (See Figure 8 for the Arabic form of the manuscript, reproduced as illustration in the later romanized print translation.)

Abdullah himself may be viewed ambiguously, as both an agent and critic of British imperial interests, his innovations in modern Malay forming something like an intermediary between older, traditional Malay literary forms and modernizing imperatives.[5] Although it coincides with the period during which Malay was being assimilated and appropriated by European colonizing interests, the text of his autobiography itself, preserves the writing system (*jawi*, or Arabic) that was already being displaced (especially in the Dutch East Indies) by romanized print forms of Malay. A fascinating document for many reasons, including its first-person account of the founding of Singapore, it recounts an anecdote that stands in counterpoint to the various examples of romanization

Figure 8. Arabic (*jawi*) script from *Hikayat Abdullah* (reproduced from Abdullah bin Abdul Kadir, *Hikayat Abdullah*).

discussed so far. The anecdote concerns the discovery of a marvelous "chiseled inscription":

> It was then that they found at the point of the headland a rock lying in the bushes. The rock was smooth, about six feet wide, square in shape, and its face was covered with a chiseled inscription. But although it had writing, this was illegible because of extensive scouring by water. Allah alone knows how many thousands of years old it may have been. After its discovery crowds of all races came to see it. The Indians declared that the writing was Hindu but they were unable to read it. The Chinese claimed that it was in Chinese characters. I went with a party of people, and also Mr. Raffles and Mr. Thomson, and we all looked at the rock. I noticed that in shape the lettering was rather like Arabic, but I could not read it because owing to its great age the relief was partly effaced. . . . it was [Mr. Coleman . . . then engineer in Singapore] who broke up the stone; a great pity, and in my opinion a most

improper thing to do, prompted perhaps by his own thoughtlessness and folly. He destroyed the rock because he did not realize its importance. Perhaps he did not stop to consider that a man cleverer than he might extract its secrets from it, for I have heard it said that in England there are scholars with special knowledge who can easily understand such writing, whatever the language or race. As the Malays say "If you cannot improve a thing at least do not destroy it."[6]

This marvelous discovery of an ancient, unknown form of writing that looks like Devanagari to Indians, Chinese characters to Chinese, and Arabic lettering to the author, offers a kind of parable about the riddling appearance of worldscripts that define the way in which peoples inhabit scriptworlds.

Although illegible to everyone ("crowds of all races"), the writing is identified by each of the groups described (the Indians, the Chinese, and the author's) as their own script. This is, among other things, a useful reminder of the way that I have repurposed David Damrosch's definition of the term "scriptworld": the idea that people come to view the world through the particular writing system that happens to be the dominant form of their upbringing and/or cultural environment. Each scriptworld specified here, corresponds to a worldscript as defined earlier: a writing system that has given shape to a widespread, global historical formation, such as Devanagari, Chinese, or Arabic. In providing illustrations for these notions, the anecdote also enacts a riddling confrontation of scriptworld and worldscript—of the various scriptworlds inhabited by each group and the presumption that the stone inscription represents its own worldscript. Each group is able to recognize as its own worldscript what, nonetheless, has become illegible to the scriptworld each inhabits. Put another way, each group is able (initially) to read the script as belonging to their own scriptworld, and yet each discovers that the script belongs to an alien worldscript.

The author's own position, as observer of this reading encounter, participant in the reading, and as writer recording the event, all play a crucial role in drawing attention to the puzzling disconnect between the scriptworld each group inhabits and whatever worldscript the stone's inscription presents. Within the context of the *Hikayat Abdullah*, this anecdote is a very rich and complex reflection on the medium of Malay as a global language, as a vehicle for mediating between other global languages, and as the linguistic-literary form for recording a particular historical moment (the founding of Singapore). The way that the author finds the lettering of the inscription "rather like Arabic," resonates in quite complicated, and specific, ways with other passages throughout the *Hikayat*, where the author reflects on the Malay language, and, most notably, in the comparisons made to English (especially, as Sanjay Krishnan has discussed, the need to reform Malay the way the English "have been improving their language day by day"[7]). One striking thing is that this anecdote seems nowhere to be interested in either the worldscript or the scriptworld of roman letters. In this sense it stands in revealing counterpoint to the inaugural example of romanization for Conrad (the opening to *Almayer's Folly*: "Kaspar! Makan!"), and for my analysis of the phenomenon of romanization more generally. Whereas Conrad's fiction begins with the riddle of romanized Malay— the riddle of encountering a language alien to English within the scriptworld of romanized print form—the whole of the *Hikayat Abdullah* is entirely composed within the scriptworld of a Malay written (and then printed) in Arabic letters, or *jawi* script.

In part, then, this anecdote stands in historical and linguistic counterpoint to the primary focus of this book. Whereas I have been concerned with the historical moment following the script conversion from Arabic script to romanized print—the moment after Malay has been transcribed, transliterated, and translated into romanized print form—the *Hikayat Abdullah* is written prior to that moment of script conversion. Abdullah's text inhabits an Arabic scriptworld. Conrad's text can only invoke that scriptworld in the medium of romanized print form. This difference suggests—even from within the limits of a romanized scriptworld—the possibility of conceiving the question of romanization from outside the perspective of a romanized scriptworld, and from the perspective of another worldscript. Whereas Conrad's novels frame a linguistic comparison between Malay and English through the chronotope of romanization, the *Hikayat Abdullah* frames a similar linguistic comparison through a different chronotope—that of the Arabic lettering he thinks he sees in the stone inscription, and the Arabic lettering of the text he is writing.

There is more to this counterpoint of Malay and English, and it is in fact more of a contemporaneous phenomenon than a matter of historical shifts. The writing of the *Hikayat Abdullah* may be dated historically before Conrad begins writing, but its appearance in print coincides, much more proximately, to that "timely appearance"[8] by which Ha Jin marks (as noted in the Introduction) the significance of Conrad's own emergence as a non-English writer of English. The rivalry between different forms of writing Malay—whether in *jawi* or *rumi*—extends throughout the nineteenth century (and unevenly across British and Dutch areas of colonial control), reaching back (at least) to the historical moment that makes the *Hikayat Abdullah* such an interesting and important archival record. Perhaps Abdullah's reflections on the stone inscription are also indirectly (and through the medium of the Arabic *jawi* scriptworld in which it is composed) a reflection on the timing and spacing of romanized print form. Before entertaining that possibility, I want first to consider how the anecdote situates itself in relation to the Sanskrit cosmopolis.

According to Pollock, the Sanskrit cosmopolis involved the spread of a literary form of political inscription that depended on no one script but could be recognized across a range of different, local scripts. That all the people from different scriptworlds should recognize this inscription as their own, might suggest this cosmopolitan Sanskrit model, although what is crucially lacking here is an actual understanding of what it is that the inscription conveys. Given the specific form of this ancient inscription in stone (and what scholars have concluded since), Abdullah's anecdote does, indeed, seem to evoke what Pollock calls the ancient Sanskrit cosmopolis. It evokes the Sanskrit cosmopolis, however, as forgotten riddling afterimage. The world of multiple scripts described in the anecdote may seem to have little to do with the model of Romanization, as Pollock compares that to the Sanskrit model, since Romanization, in this view, involves the imposition of a single script to the exclusion of all others. At the end of the quotation above, however, Abdullah dwells on the unfortunate fate of the inscription that might be read as a reflection on just this model. The destruction of the rock, by the engineer Mr. Coleman, is presented as mere thoughtlessness and "folly" rather than a systematic assault on a model of language. Yet precisely this "folly" might be seen to prefigure a form of disregard for writing and script associated with romanized print form. If the Sanskrit ideal (one linguistic-literary form, many scripts) is captured as a forgotten afterimage, perhaps the imperial Roman ideal (one alphabet imposed to the exclusion of all others) is captured as a prefiguration of English engineering "folly." The anecdote certainly seems to be presented as a comment on the emerging, new, colonial order of relations with the arrival of the English.

This anecdote is more fully ambiguous, though, both with respect to the lost Sanskrit cosmopolitan ideal, and with respect to the future fate of Romanization under English colonial rule. The end of the passage (quoted above) brings out this fuller ambiguity by countering the "folly" of the English engineer with the wisdom of those "scholars" whose "special knowledge" might have deciphered the inscription. Although the passage pays no direct attention, either to the forgotten ancient Sanskrit, linguistic-literary form of the stone inscription, or to the romanized print culture of the English, it implicitly brings both together—at least as a possibility—in invoking the philological expertise of those "scholars" in England he has heard about. It provides an intriguing, non-European, glimpse of the emerging profile of European, comparative philology and the important place of Sanskrit in the formation of that philology. One might speculate that the author sees himself, and the *jawi* Malay form of his *Hikayat* itself, as mediating between the two faces of the new colonial order, the one premised on English engineering "folly," and the other premised on a comparative study of all the world's literature ("whatever the language or race"). If so, the Malay saying, cited at the very end of the anecdote, sums up an ideal reconciliation between the future modernizing form of romanized print culture and the forgotten cosmopolitan Sanskrit past.

By contrast to Joseph Conrad's "timely appearance" in print, it is tempting to describe Abdullah's as an "untimely" appearance. Whereas Conrad invests in the now-dominant global medium of romanized print form, Abdullah invests in an increasingly outmoded medium (Arabic, or *jawi* script). The reason to dwell on this contrast, however, is to note a constitutive interrelation between the "timely" and the "untimely" qualities of each kind of investment. Both authors, after all, invest in an English ideal (an idealized sense of English that both figure as "folly"). Both invest that idealized English in a relation to Malay. Although they seem to occupy opposed positions within the rival claims of Arabic and roman forms of scripting Malay, that very rivalry structures each writer's relation to the form of script in which they appear. Each writer's scriptworld allows access to the worldscript of the other. Conrad's Malay fiction, as I have explored, evokes the Arabic scriptworld of the *Hikayat Abdullah*. The very end of *Almayer's Folly* concludes with its Abdulla pronouncing, over the grave of Almayer, the words of the *bismillah*, the spoken formula whose transcription provides the formulaic inauguration of the *Hikayat Abdullah*. Abdullah's reflections on Malay, as already noted, are premised on a model of improvement in grammar and structure, found in the example of English; and, more generally, the *Hikayat* is a record of an experience of working alongside English administrators (notably, Sir Stamford Raffles), a work of collaboration between Malay and English, expressed in the material medium of the *jawi* print form of the *Hikayat* itself.

Conrad's "timely" appearance in romanized print form, then, may be seen as the reversed mirror image of Abdullah's "untimely" appearance in the printed form of the *Hikayat*'s Arabic script. The anecdote of the illegible inscription in stone provides a kind of inverse, miniature reflection of everything that I have been exploring in terms of the timing and spacing of romanized print form in Conrad. The inverse form of its Arabic lettering may reveal (and decode) the long-delayed distortion of that chronotope of romanization that frames Conrad's entire career. Malay and English, together, share the same fate, a past entanglement and future investment in a multiscript world where people "of all races" encounter a worldscript, simultaneously legible and illegible as their own scriptworld.

Sanskritization

Turning from Abdullah's *Hikayat* to a foundational text in the formation of European comparative philology, Wilhelm von Humboldt's *Über die Kawi-Sprache*, I want to expand upon the non-European glimpse of European comparative philology, offered in the *Hikayat*, to reconsider the importance of Sanskrit for the foundations of European linguistics. European comparative philology, as is well known, was founded on a colonial appropriation of Sanskrit. There are many important accounts of how Sanskrit became an idealized point of reference for the formation of a new science of language, redefining the human sciences (as Michel Foucault tells the story in *The Order of Things*), and consolidating the discursive formation of Orientalism (as Edward Said retells that story in *Orientalism*).[9] This story involves the colonial English appropriation of Sanskrit by some of the figures that appear in the *Hikayat* (like Sir Stamford Raffles) who provided the basic insights that later German scholars (like Schlegel, Bopp, and Humboldt) based their foundational theories of comparative linguistic study upon. Abdullah's non-European glimpse of European philology offers another perspective on this story, illuminating a foundational blind spot in European philology's idealization of Sanskrit. As with Abdullah's assessment of the universally legible, illegible script, European philology is also premised on the forgotten ideal of a Sanskrit cosmopolis. In the case of European philology, this active forgetting becomes a key premise for comparative historical study.

Abdullah's anecdote may be read as a parable about the persistence into modernity of the old forgotten ideal that Sheldon Pollock describes as the "Sanskrit cosmopolis." The roughly thousand-year span of this "quasi-global formation" came into being "around the start of the Common Era" in southern Asia "and at its height a thousand years later extended across all of South and much of Southeast Asia."[10] Pollock's account of the spread of Sanskrit is too long and detailed to do justice to in summary, but something of the scope of its comparative global claim may be gauged in considering the contrast he makes between Rome's imposition of an alphabet on the world, and the "linguistic symbiosis of Sanskrit and local language" that forms the heart of the "Sanskrit cosmopolis."[11] As Pollock argues, "Latin carried the Roman script with it wherever it went and tolerated no fundamental deviation from the metropolitan style for centuries to follow (no later development, of uncial, minuscule, or anything else, ever constituted a cognitive break). And the script was indivisible from the literature: Vergil could have written the opening words of the *Aeneid, arma virumque cano*, only in a single alphabet, and from then on, the words would be written only in that alphabet."[12]

The contrast to Sanskrit is striking, as he goes on to write:

> In southern Asia, no writing system was ever so determinative of Sanskrit (until, ironically, Devanagari attained this status just as the cosmopolitan era was waning). Whereas early Brahmi script ultimately shaped all regional alphabets in South Asia and many in Southeast Asia (Burmese, Lao, Thai, Khmer, and probably Javanese), that script tolerated modification, often profound modification, wherever it traveled. Through this process, which appears to have occurred more or less synchronously across the Sanskrit world, scripts quickly began to assert a regional individuality in accordance with local aesthetic sensibilities, so much so that by the eighth century one self-same cosmopolitan language, undeviating in its literary incarnation, was being written in a range of alphabets almost totally distinct from each other and indecipherable without specialized study.[13]

Two things make Pollock's argument relevant for Abdullah's anecdote. First, as later philologists have attested, that stone inscription is (likely) precisely the kind of incarnation of the "self-same cosmopolitan language" that made its way "across the Sanskrit world" in a variety of scripts—in this case, according to the Javanese scholar N. J. Krom, "the inscription was in Majapahit Kawi, older than 1361."[14] The second point to emphasize is that this Sanskrit, cosmopolitan ideal is long since ancient history—equally ancient, and equally distant, and perhaps equally as forgotten for each of the peoples that Abdullah invokes in his parable of encountering the riddling legibility of an illegible script: Hindus, Chinese, and all those who, like the author, use Arabic script.

Abdullah's anecdote, then, shows how Sanskrit provides the shared model for a whole set of rival scriptworlds, all of which measure the ideal of a universal worldscript against an ancient, lost cosmopolitan ideal. Sanskritization—seen from the broad historical perspective of this *longue durée* (or long-*lost* duration)—might then be redefined, by contrast to the historical formation of what Pollock calls the "Sanskrit cosmopolis," as the dissolution of that cosmopolis and its long-lasting aftereffects. For convenience, I will call this lowercase sanskritization by analogy to lowercase romanization. The idealized, *lost* cosmopolitical origin of Sanskrit offers the contradictory point of reference for measuring the reach of any worldscript (e.g., Arabic, roman, Chinese) according to an identification with, and affiliation to, the experience of its own scriptworld.

It is this (lowercase) sanskritization, in an idealized, but lost, cosmopolitical sense, which becomes a defining feature of European comparative philology, anchoring its science of linguistics in a kind of willed forgetfulness, or grammatological blindness, with implications for both historical linguistics and the linguistic turn toward structural linguistics. This is, perhaps, nowhere more evident than in one of the foundational texts of comparative philology, Wilhelm von Humboldt's preface to *Über die Kawi-Sprache*, an ambitious argument about the "diversity of human language forms" published posthumously in 1836. One of the key premises of European comparative philology is the presupposition that the spirit of a language develops itself most fully in literary form; and that literary form is most fully, and most spiritually, manifest in the form of literary texts. As Humboldt puts it in *Über die Kawi-Sprache*, "For reasons having to do with the inner foundations of the development of language itself, a true literature can only emerge from a given script in common use" ("Eine wahre Litteratur kann, und zwar aus inneren Gründen der Sprachbildung selbst, nur mit einer zugleich gegebenen und in Gebrauch kommenden Schrift entstehen").[15] The specific example Humboldt is discussing here, concerns the influence of Sanskrit on Malay literary forms. It is the Malay form of Old Javanese, or Kawi, which gives Humboldt the ideal point of reference for elaborating a comparative study of the diversity of all human language forms. As Hans Aarsleff explains, as a "mixed language"—"its vocabulary . . . largely Sanskrit, while its [grammatical] form was Malayan"—Kawi gave Humboldt the "global vantage point" he had long sought.[16] The long title of the work indicates the importance of this focus: *On the Kawi Language on the Island of Java alongside an Introduction on the Diversity of Human Language Forms and its Influence on the Spiritual Development of Humankind* (*Über die Kawi-Sprache auf der Insel Java nebst einer Einleitung über die Verschiedenheit des menschlichen Sprachbaues und ihren Einfluß auf die geistige Entwickelung des Menschengeschlechts*).[17] The term "Kawi" (referring both to the language and the script) holds in place the linguistic-literary premise of the entire work, making its specialized discussion of Old Javanese the pretext for a wide-ranging set of claims about the scientific principles of comparative philology.[18]

Humboldt's emphasis on the Kawi script, or "alphabet," is significant precisely as evidence of the linguistic and literary influence of Sanskrit. Immediately following the assertion about language, literature, and script cited above, Humboldt goes on to write that, "It is therefore of momentous importance for the cultural relations of Southeast Asia that precisely this area of the Malay archipelago [i.e. Java] . . . possessed an alphabetic script"—going on to note: "But there is an important distinction to be made here that should not be overlooked. The alphabetic script in this part of the world is *Indian*" ("Es ist hierbei doch ein nicht zu übersehender Unterschied. Die alphabetische Schrift in diesem Theile der Erde ist *Indische*" [x]).[19] In many respects, the lineage linking Kawi script to other Indian scripts offers the philological evidence that might allow Humboldt to answer the riddle of Abdullah's universally legible, illegible inscription (likely in Kawi script) found (and destroyed) with the foundation of Singapore. Both register the aftereffects of that long-lost, forgotten Sanskrit ideal of a cosmopolitan language expressed in many variant scripts. If Abdullah's anecdote both preserves and forgets that ideal, Humboldt does so as well, but with a theoretical and practical reversal of the relation between language and script, implied by that older Sanskrit ideal.

In this respect, Humboldt's whole treatise exemplifies the importance of the discovery of Sanskrit for European comparative philology. Foregrounding the importance of "alphabetic script," Humboldt's idealization of Sanskrit dramatically reverses the relation of language and script at the heart of the Sanskrit cosmopolis. Classifying Kawi as constituting a variation of the "Indian" alphabet, Humboldt goes on to speculate on how Kawi shaped a Malay scriptworld related to, but distinct from, Sanskrit. Humboldt's interest in the relation between Kawi and Sanskrit reveals a central dilemma, and generative problem, of European comparative philology: how writing determines the link between the form of a particular language and the spirit of a particular national formation: "In the early epochs to which our current reflections refer back, we know of nations only through their languages, but we cannot tell exactly what people—which branch, or which offshoot—to think of in relation to each language" ("In den frühen Epochen, in welche uns die gegenwärtigen Betrachtungen zurückversetzen, kennen wir die Nationen überhaupt nur durch ihre Sprachen, wissen nicht einmal immer genau, welches Volk wir uns, der Abstammung und Verknüpfung nach, bei jeder Sprache zu denken haben.")[20] Here, a problem of historical scale formulates what will become a foundational historical principle, the scientific premise for the comparative study of languages measured against a projected, distant Indo-European (or Aryan) origin. This particular example of the (contradictory) foundational principles of comparative philology is interesting, not only because it shows the process of what I have called (lowercase) sanskritization. It provides a classic European instance of the far-reaching influence of a Sanskrit philological model going back to the Sanskrit cosmopolis, but premised on a *post*-Sanskrit cosmopolitical grasp of the relation between language and script, and one that anticipates the ethno-nationalist imperative to align language and script (as I discussed in Chapter 3). What Pollock calls the historical irony of coming to identify Sanskrit with Devanagari, makes the identification of language and script a kind of permanently destabilizing irony at the foundations of European comparative philology.

Although Humboldt classifies "Kawi" script as an "Indian" alphabet, he is certainly aware of the difference between that script and Devanagari. The book's prefatory note on the "method" of transliteration, explains the way that the two scripts—described as the "Sanskrit alphabet" ("Sanskrit-Alphabet") and "the Javanese alphabet" ("Javanisches Alphabet") respectively—are transliterated into roman letters.[21] Already in the naming of these scripts, Humboldt simultaneously recognizes, and then reverses, the point that Pollock makes when he explains that "no writing system was ever as determinative" as the roman alphabet for the development of Sanskrit. Recognizing the adaptability of Sanskrit across a range of writing systems from South to Southeast Asia, Humboldt, nonetheless, posits a determinative relation between language and script, naming Devanagari the "Sanskrit" alphabet and noting, through romanized transliteration, the variations in orthography between the "Sanskrit" and the "Javanese" alphabet. Recognizing those differences through a romanized transliteration, notably mediated by "English writers," Humboldt's text projects the way in which "Kawi" (as language and script) derives from "Sanskrit."

In referring to Sanskrit as a script, and identifying it with Devanagari, Humboldt combines a forgetting of the old Sanskrit cosmopolitical model, with an English practice of romanized transliteration, to produce a classic instance of what Derrida identifies as phonocentrism. Writing is elevated above speech (as with Humboldt's emphasizing the priority of literature in expressing the development of language), and yet writing is secondary to the system of sounds ("Lautsystem") which constitutes the inner orientation of any linguistic development.[22] So, Humboldt claims:

> *Sanskrit* is happier and more creative than any other language; it has a wordform and possesses an alphabet that is able, more perfectly than our own, to represent the exact expression both for the ear and graphically for the eye.[23]

Humboldt's emphasis on the Sanskrit "alphabet" privileges a particular worldscript, the terms of whose relation to spoken language must have been forgotten in order to provide us with the model of writing that all languages aspire to. Humboldt calls this worldscript *Sanskrit*, spacing out the letters according to the German convention of emphasis (which in English might either be underlined or italicized), but without any identificatory mark of its transliteration from some original script. It is only later (at the beginning of the study of Kawi proper) that Humboldt will identify this script (with diacritical marks to signal the sound of its original written form) as "*Dêwanâgarî*," naming the script that is described in the preface on transliteration, simply as the "Sanskrit-Alphabet."[24] According to the logic of sanskritization, this worldscript is both a particular, historically specific worldscript (*Dêwanâgarî*) and, simultaneously, an idealization of the relation between sound and script (*Sanskrit*) that manifests itself in a variety of scripts (potentially, indeed metaphysically, the infinite variety of scripts that attests to the whole history of humankind).

This idealization of Sanskrit not only sanskritizes *Dêwanâgarî* as "the Sanskrit-Alphabet" (graphic illustration of Pollock's "irony"). Embedded in that idealized, European sanskritization is a practice of transliteration that orchestrates the vast comparative reach of Humboldt's philology. The romanized transliteration represents that more perfect relation of spoken to written language, first as "*Sanskrit*" and then as "*Dêwanâgarî.*" The theoretical centrality of Sanskrit, for Humboldt's ambitious comparative study of the diversity of languages throughout the world and throughout history, depends on a practice of romanized transliteration that first recalls the forgotten ideal of Sanskrit's relation to multiple scripts and then reverses that relation between writing and script by determining Devanagari as the alphabetic writing system for Sanskrit. Humboldt's emphasis on the role of script and writing systems, then, provides an especially striking formulation for the convergence of sanskritization and romanization in constructing the grammatological blindness shaping European comparative philology. This is how European comparative philology embodies the riddle of the universally legible, illegible script in Abdullah's anecdote. Positing a distant Indo-European origin for all the world's languages, the comparative philologist turns Sanskrit, through a practice of romanized transliteration, into the idealized form of a writing system against which to measure all the variety of language formations throughout human history.

More might be said about the theoretical and practical significance of Humboldt's comparison between the "Sanskrit-Alphabet" and the "Javanese Alphabet." The methodological note on transliteration alone poses important questions about the interrelation between the theoretical weight given to Sanskrit in comparative philology and the practical importance of romanized transliteration in developing its comparative scope. One point to consider is how that idealization of Sanskrit as worldscript supplements the grammatological blindness that Derrida outlines, following the work of Madeleine V.-David, about the history of alphabetic writing.[25] On the one hand, the discovery of Sanskrit simply confirms the phonocentrism of those earlier European "prejudices" (the theological prejudice, the Egyptian prejudice, the Chinese prejudice), sanskritization constituting the latest, most up-to-date European prejudice—with the important difference that Sanskrit and Javanese are assimilated into the linguistic family of phonetic writing systems. On the other hand, the historical scale of reference implied by Humboldt's idealization of Sanskrit, along with the geographical variation brought to the notion of alphabetic writing systems, adds a further complication to the problem of historicizing alphabetic, or phonetic writing systems. The "irony" of identifying Sanskrit with one "alphabet" (the Devanagari script) suggests this complicating factor in ways that invite reconsideration of Walter Ong's assertion that there are "many scripts, but only one alphabet." Humboldt's idealization of Sanskrit (a sanskritization premised on a practice of romanization) reveals that there are many alphabets, but only one mediating script—the use of roman, or Latin letters—to transliterate between those alphabets, as Humboldt does between Sanskrit and Javanese.

If sanskritization lies at the theoretical heart of European comparative philology and historical linguistics, its theoretical and practical convergence with romanization is carried over into the so-called linguistic turn from historical to synchronic, or structural linguistics. In *Of Grammatology* Derrida refers to the foundational principles of European comparative philology, but without commenting on the place of Sanskrit in the philosophical tradition he repeatedly characterizes in terms of "Western metaphysics." In a number of important ways Derrida's bracketing of Sanskrit repeats the way that Ferdinand de Saussure brackets Sanskrit in the *Course in General Linguistics*, that touchstone for the shift from historical to structural linguistics. *Of Grammatology* repeats the way that Saussure delimits the model of writing in order to deconstruct its presumptions about the relation of writing to speech. In doing so, however, it also reenacts Saussure's own strategic forgetting of the model of Sanskrit. Outlining the two "limitations" that Saussure sets on the number of possible writing systems by which to define writing, Derrida notes, first, Saussure's division between "two" writing systems—ideographic and phonetic. This first limitation is important and deserves a more patient deconstruction in order to see how it, too, enacts a forgetting of Humboldt's interest in the whole variety of different scripts attested to in the history of linguistic development (and most especially the "ideographic" principle of Chinese characters).

It is the second limitation, however, that elides Humboldt's perfect Sanskrit model: "I shall limit discussion to the phonetic system and especially to the one used today, the system that stems from the Greek alphabet" ("Nous bornerons notre étude au système phonétique, et tout spécialement à celui qui est en usage aujourd'hui et dont le prototype est l'alphabet grec.").[26] Saussure models an idealized "phonetic system"—*the* alphabet—around an erasure and forgetting of Humboldt's idealization of the phonetic system of Sanskrit. Humboldt's reversal of the cosmopolitical Sanskrit model of a relation between language and script is forgotten twice over, as it were, and the practice of romanized transliteration becomes a kind of programmatic reenactment of sanskritization. Where the presumptions of a "phonetic" logic are at work—most especially where that is delimited to the operation of a "phonetic system" most commonly used today, i.e. the Greek-derived roman or Latin alphabet—there, too, Humboldt's Sanskrit model is at work: the model of an alphabet perfectly (by happy accident) adapted to the needs of any language. As with sanskritization, so with romanization: it is easy to forget (and indeed both the practice and the ideal *depend* on this forgetting) that what makes it so ideally practical a "phonetic system," is precisely its adaptability to any and all relations of language to script. The practice of romanized transliteration aspires to the old Sanskrit cosmopolitical model it actively forgets in the positing of a single, ancient, perfectly phonetic writing system. This active forgetting shapes the "Latin alphabet fetishism" that I have discussed in earlier chapters, a disavowal that lodges sanskritization at the heart of romanization, especially as expressed in McLuhan's and Ong's insistence on there being only "one alphabet."

When Derrida cites Saussure's "massive" limitation to just the one, Greek-derived phonetic system, he is (following the painstaking care in carrying out a deconstruction of Saussure's text) simply repeating Saussure's bracketing of Humboldt's idealized Sanskrit model. Knowing the importance of Sanskrit for the foundational principles of historical linguistics (Saussure's "Preface" provides what might be called a classical version of this story), Saussure deliberately displaces Humboldt's idealization of that perfect fit between sonic and graphic elements ascribed to the Sanskrit "alphabet." In the passage immediately following the one Derrida cites, Saussure ascribes to Greek (more specifically "primitive Greek") the kind of harmony that Humboldt ascribes to Sanskrit: "With respect to logic, the Greek alphabet is especially remarkable . . . But this harmony between the written form and pronunciation does not last." ("Au regard de la logique, l'alphabet grec est particulièrement remarquable . . . Mais cette harmonie entre la graphie et la prononciation ne dure pas.")[27] Saussure's emphasis on the "Greek-derived" alphabet makes more explicit what is mostly implicit in Derrida: namely, that the narrower sense of writing ("the phonetic system we use today") emerges from a process of increasing discord between the original "logic" and harmony of primitive Greek. The later discussion of the "genius" of the Greek alphabet, "inherited by the Latins,"[28] reproduces the kind of idealized harmony of graphic and phonemic signs that Humboldt ascribes to Sanskrit, and traces the history of its development (or fall) with some interesting attention to particular effects that primitive Greek handled better than "our" alphabet.[29]

The whole question of Sanskrit (raised at the outset of the *Course*) has been bracketed in Saussure's turn to these problems of writing and phonology. The reason for this appears much later in the *Course* (in the Conclusion, 5th Part, Chapter 2), when Saussure argues that Sanskrit has been accorded too privileged a place by linguistics (notably comparative philologists), as the most ancient of (and hence the prototype for) all other languages. As part of his overall revision of the paradigm of historical linguistics, Saussure reframes the metaphysical idealism of Humboldt's privileging of Sanskrit. He never entirely abandons the importance of Sanskrit in the development of comparative linguistics, but he faults the historical method for confusing Sanskrit with the more distant, Indo-European origin reconstructed according to the model of Sanskrit. The qualification crucially retains a historical perspective, albeit one that can never be recovered. This points to what synchronic, structuralist linguistics (after Saussure) still has in common with the diachronic, historical, and comparative linguistics of the nineteenth century. The turn from the one to the other might be described as a turn from the idealization of Sanskrit to a practical emphasis on the Greek-derived roman script. Implied already in Humboldt, this shift from sanskritization to romanization is not so much a historical sequence as it is a recalibration of perspective in the comparative study of the relation between languages and scripts.

Saussure's reorientation of the historical perspective on the relation between sound and script accorded to Sanskrit in European, nineteenth-century comparative philology constitutes, then, from one point of view an entire paradigm shift: from diachronic to synchronic linguistics; from privileging Sanskrit to privileging Greek in explaining the relation between sound and script. From another point of view, however, this reorientation of historical perspective effects a reversal of (linguistic) figure and (historical) ground that retains (still) all the essential presumptions (and above all, those of phonocentrism) on which comparative philology was founded. For both Humboldt and Saussure, Sanskrit defines a crucial point of reference for all attempts to account for the history of language in relation to writing systems. Humboldt idealizes it as embodying the perfect alignment of language and script. Saussure brackets it as remaining too distant a historical point of reference for measuring the relation between language and script.[30] In this sense, sanskritization produces the vanishing point of historical, linguistic perspective around which both diachronic and synchronic linguistics get formed.

The narrowest, technical sense of romanization (the OED's "transliteration into roman letters") helps illuminate in what sense both Humboldt's comparative philology and Saussure's attempt to reorient that philology share the same problem of grammatology. For both, the spacing and timing of roman letters is all at once a subordinate, side issue (the written form being merely an illustration of the spoken language) *and* the primary vehicle for gathering and presenting the fundamental evidence (either for Humboldt's comparative study of all languages or for Saussure's analysis of language as a structure of signs). Grammar, for comparative philology (and linguistics generally), is more important than the writing system used to represent language; and yet it is the written mark, sign, or "gram" ("grammè"[31] in Derrida's romanized transliteration) that anchors the laws of grammatical change in comparative philology (or the structuralist reorientation of linguistic study). Relying on the written sign to trace the grammatical significance of phonetic changes opens up an abyss between the historical scale, not only of the changing relation between language and script, but also (and as part of this very question) between languages in translation and transliteration across multiple scripts.

Sanskritization and Romanization in the OED and in Pramoedya Ananta Toer

Two contrasting examples help illuminate the significance of the problem of historical perspective that sanskritization embeds within romanization. They are drawn from the two contrasting historical archives on which this book has relied: the OED and the work of Indonesian novelist, Pramoedya Ananta Toer. The first example is the etymology of Sanskrit as given in the most current, online OED entry. The second example concerns the historical and linguistic place of Sanskrit in Pramoedya's work.

The OED's entry for "Sanskrit" provides a revealing supplement to the contrast between Humboldt's "Sanskrit" (unburdened by diacritical marks) and "*Dêwanâgarî*" (where the diacritical marks signal the determining world-script for Sanskrit). The OED's etymology renders "Sanskrit" as coming from the "Sanskrit *saṃskṛta*." Its romanization follows a different system from the one used by Humboldt to render *Dêwanâgarî*. The etymology recalls the problems discussed in Chapter 1, arising from the transcription, transliteration, and translation of the Malay word "Tuan." While more precise in its use of diacritical marks that imply a particular system of transliteration, as with "Tuan," the etymology does not explain what *script* is involved. It would appear to follow the system for romanizing Devanagari, proposed at the Tenth International Congress of Orientalists in 1895 by the Committee appointed "to select a system for the transliteration of the Sanskrit and Arabic Alphabets."[32]

The etymological silence on the question of script introduces an ambiguity reminiscent of the ambiguity about the written origin of the word "Tuan," providing another miniature example of sanskritization: the positing of a forgotten relation between Sanskrit language and script. Once again, we see the implied Sanskrit ideal of a relation between sound and script spelled out in the spacing and timing of roman letters: sanskritization, that is, as romanization. In the case of "Tuan," as discussed in Chapter 1, the etymological elision of script points toward a shift in the hierarchical relation between Arabic script and romanized print form. In the case of "Sanskrit," there is nothing directly analogous. The OED rarely attempts to represent any of the variety of scripts from South and Southeast Asia in which Sanskrit might be written. In the absence of an identifiable worldscript, the act of romanized transliteration measures the adoption of the English word "Sanskrit" according to a shifting, historically quite unstable relation between worldscript and scriptworld. More graphically than "Tuan" (in the form of the word's diacritical marks) the etymology for Sanskrit positions English in relation to a dizzying historical set of shifting hierarchies of language and script—from the most ancient (even before the consolidation of the Sanskrit cosmopolis), to the most modern (the deliberations amongst German, French, English, and Swiss Orientalists in Geneva in 1895), and up to the most current online revision of the OED's entry on Sanskrit.

If the disappearance of Arabic script from the OED registers a specific historical shift in the relative prestige of Arabic script and romanized print form, the absence of any specific script form attributed to Sanskrit creates an open-ended succession of possible, shifting interrelations between multiple scriptworlds and worldscripts. In the romanized form of *saṃskṛta*, the OED simultaneously projects a distant world of script forms (more ancient, perhaps even more worldly than the Latin alphabet) and a contemporary practice of transcription, transliteration, and translation among multiple languages and across multiple scripts, all now regulated by the spacing and timing of roman letters.[33]

A very different example of this convergence of sanskritization and romanization is provided by the Indonesian novelist Pramoedya Ananta Toer (whose work has set the precedent for my reading of Conrad). Writing in the modern form of romanized print Malay that came to shape the revolutionary anti-colonial language of Indonesian, Pramoedya's fictional engagement with legacies of colonization and decolonization involved multiple reflections on the role of language and script in the changing hierarchies of social relations. The Indonesian scriptworld of his fiction (which is also, as Benedict Anderson's *Imagined Communities* famously elaborated, the anti-colonial vehicle for imagining community) is premised on a historical shift between all three of the worldscripts that I have been considering so far over the course of this chapter: the Kawi-script that Humboldt takes as his model for Sanskrit and that remained the script that defined the Javanese scriptworld of Pramoedya's father; the Arabic Jawi-script of the *Hikayat Abdullah* that had largely been replaced by the time Pramoedya came of age (but still held an important prestige through the influence of Islam); and finally the romanized print form of *bahasa Indonesia* (whose own orthography underwent important changes during Pramoedya's lifetime).

The great cycle of historical novels that Pramoedya composed in the Buru prison camps during the 1970s, looks back on key turning points in the shifting hierarchies brought with the conversion from one script to another. *Arok Dedes* (set in the thirteenth century) turns on the shift in the status of Sanskrit from being a foreign elite language and literature to becoming an indigenized Javanese linguistic-literary form. From one perspective, this is the moment when Java gets absorbed into the Sanskrit cosmopolis. It is the historical moment, indeed, from which the stone inscription of the *Hikayat Abdullah* likely comes. It is also the moment that provides Humboldt a starting point for his comparative study of linguistic diversity. Pramoedya has described this era as a turning point—"a major historical shift ... from a Hindu to an indigenous Javanese outlook"—or, as he puts it elsewhere, "the Arok revolution, the opening of a new era, from Hindu-Java to Java-Hindu" (*"Revolusi Arok, pemuka kurun baru, dari Hindu-Jawa ke Jawa-Hindu"*).[34]

What interests Pramoedya in this "major historical shift" is the transformation in linguistic, literary, and political hierarchies: the confrontation between an elite, caste-bound, literary consciousness and a subaltern, revolutionary rejection of caste. An important complication in this vision (central for all Pramoedya's fiction) is that the "indigenous Javanese" perspective, valorized as part of this shift in the hierarchy of language and script, is pitted against the later historical formation of a literate class of elite Javanists (whether Indigenous literati or European Orientalists). Pramoedya's interest is in the revolutionary sweeping away of oppressive hierarchical structures of language and script; in the revolutionary potential of those moments of script conversion.[35] This is true for each of the great historical novels. In *Arus Balik*, the arrival of Arabic (and also, with the Portuguese, romanized print form) precipitates an overturning of the hierarchies of Javanese. In the Buru tetralogy (most famously) the medium of the newspaper and the romanized print form of *bahasa Indonesia* become the vehicles for mass organizing against Dutch colonial rule.

The reversals of historical perspective built into these shifts in the hierarchy of worldscripts and scriptworlds, are not only projected in the chronological sequence of each historical novel (*Arok Dedes* in the thirteenth century; *Arus Balik* in the sixteenth century; the Buru quartet in the early twentieth century). They are also implied in the linguistic effects of what Pramoedya does with contemporary Indonesian in its romanized print form. Both *Arus Balik* and the last novel in the Buru quartet, *House of Glass*, are framed by chronotopes of romanization in the sense that I have been exploring with respect to Conrad. While the main center of narrative consciousness in *Arus Balik* is the political consciousness of the Arab harbormaster with a command of a range of languages and scripts (Javanese, Malay, Arabic, Portuguese, and Spanish), the concluding coda of the novel marks a shift from that character's Arabic Malay scriptworld to the roman scriptworld of a Portuguese traveler, who recounts the story of the harbormaster's murder at the hand of his illegitimate son, a Christian convert. *House of Glass* frames its narrative (and by extension the whole quartet of Buru novels) around a citation from the Vulgate *Magnificat*: "*Deposuit Potentes de Sede et Exaltavit Humiles* (He has brought down the mighty from their thrones and raised up the lowly)."[36] The Latin text will turn out to be, at the very end of the novel, the parting words with which the first-person narrator (the French-educated, Catholic, native Menadonese chief police commissioner) delivers the notes confiscated from the narrator of the first three volumes of the tetralogy. As Benedict Anderson succinctly puts it, "In a brilliant, unexpected move, Pram has the narrator of the fourth novel be the senior native intelligence-officer assigned by the Dutch to watch the hero and hound him to his end."[37] If the Latin epigraph foregrounds a specifically Christian, exegetical tradition, far from enclosing the documentary conceit of the novel (and the tetralogy as a whole) within a Christian hermeneutic, the passage of Latin text stages a *mise-en-abîme* of textual and philological traditions, opening interpretation to a dizzying hybridization of worldscripts and scriptworlds. It opens the romanized print form to a constantly dialogized space of print literacy, translating from Latin (the Vulgate), to French (the language of Pangemanann's education), to Dutch (the language used by the Javanese first-person narrator of the first three novels whose notes the police have confiscated), to Javanese (the language Minke rejects and the script of European Orientalist scholarship), and then Indonesian (the language Pramoedya writes in). This constitutes a constant process of transliteration, transcription, and translation across languages and scripts, a constantly changing conversion of worldscripts and scriptworlds, reading across the range of religious traditions involved (which include at least Christian, Islamic, Brahminic, and Buddhist traditions). The native police commissioner's conflicted Catholic conscience (itself split between the Catholic and Protestant sides of his family background) is counterpointed against the awakening of a modernizing Islamic political consciousness—the narrative consciousness of the first-person narrator of the first three volumes, Minke, based on the historical figure of the Javanese journalist and anti-colonial activist Tirto Adi Suryo.

The way that Pramoedya opens every passage of romanized text to a contest of philological traditions, resonates across all the worldscripts involved in shaping Indonesian history and across all the scriptworlds of contemporary Indonesia. This recalls the way that Conrad's chronotopes of romanization unfold a set of embedded rivalries and contests between worldscripts and scriptworlds. Indeed, it is precisely what Pramoedya does with the "revolutionary Malay" and with "pre-Indonesian" texts—including his own reading of Conrad (as I discussed in Chapters 1 and 3)—that reveals how the Conradian chronotopes of romanization are invested in a timing and spacing of romanized print Malay.

For the OED, sanskritization posits—in the absence of an original worldscript against which to compare the roman lettering of *saṃskṛta*—a proper form of writing and speaking that must necessarily be too distant to verify. The OED's definitions for "sanskritize" and "sanskritization" conveniently capture what happens with the emergence of (lowercase) sanskritization by focusing on "mistakes" in sanskritizing or "an erroneous" sanskritization. Differences in pronunciation, and the different grammatical inflections (so central for the entire project of European comparative philology, and, as Humboldt attests, so centrally bound to an idealization of Sanskrit) are differences marked by the roman lettering. *Saṃskṛta* offers a characteristic case study in the problem of Derridean "différance," opening up the entire text of the OED (each and every passage) to a deconstruction, both in the classic Derridean sense, and with the narrower focus that I am suggesting on the process of romanized transliteration.

Sanskritization shadows romanization in each and every entry of the OED. Alongside each absent, written form of the word—whether *saṃskṛta* or *tuan*, *tuwan*—there is a grammatical form that affects whatever case the OED claims for its English romanized print form. Sanskrit (almost by definition—the word means "well-formed ... perfected") embodies an ideal grammar (codified, famously, by the grammar of Pāṇini). As Haun Saussy notes, it was this Humboldtian idealization of this ideal grammar that enabled European comparative philologists to claim a typological contrast between all the languages of the world, according to which Chinese—in Saussy's succinct words—"lost its grammar": "All their divisions of languages into types according to grammatical structure have as their 'degree zero' the Chinese language, the absence of grammar."[38] Whatever effect this effacement of Chinese grammar may have on the OED (built, as it is, on the presuppositions of European comparative grammar), its entries can only regulate such a hierarchy of languages through a shifting, historically quite unstable, relation between worldscript and scriptworld. Grammatical precision can only ever appear (at best) as a lost ideal—lost in the transcription across multiple scriptworlds—and, perhaps more usually, as mistakes (sanskritization itself, almost by definition, a mistaken application of Sanskrit models). The problem of grammar posed by any romanized transcription of a word from another language and another script (let alone across multiple languages and multiple scripts) forms the point of reference for a far-reaching deconstruction of the ongoing act of romanization (and sanskritization) in the OED. The OED's definition of the "accusative" case has already provided a deconstructive model for reading how Conrad crafts (in aesthetic form) the case of English romanization.

Pramoedya's interest in the grammatical mistakes of Sanskrit offers a postcolonial philological model for considering the interrelation between sanskritization and romanization. Sanskritization, in the historical root form in which he explores it in *Arok Dedes*, is a kind of necessary grammatical error, the adaptation of "Hindu" forms to indigenous "Javanese" forms. The mistaken mixing of categories of language, speech, and writing opens up the possibility of a social and political revolution in the caste system. If the turn from Hindu-Java to Java-Hindu in the thirteenth century involved an overturning of systems of caste, that provides a model for the ongoing struggle against the regulation of a caste system according to linguistic categories: notably in the use of *bahasa Indonesia* against the rigid hierarchies of Javanese. So, for Pramoedya, each passage of text is the site of a contest over the hierarchies of social class and caste, regulated by hierarchies of language and script: an ongoing contest with its roots in much older moments of reversal in the crossing over from worldscript to scriptworld. Pramoedya's vision—the vision of romanization (and sanskritization) as the ongoing work of "revolutionary Malay" (i.e., writing in Indonesian)—sees a contestation of linguistic hierarchies, stitched into the use of roman letters throughout the world and across history. This is the shifting hierarchies of language and script that I have been tracing in Conrad's chronotopes of romanization measured in relation to other transnational writers as varied as Joyce, Kafka, and Lu Xun.

Digitization

Those sudden reversals in perspective, opened up by the crossing over from one worldscript to another (or the conversion within a scriptworld from one worldscript to another), are what indicate the convergence between sanskritization and romanization (both as a phenomenon of romanization in the narrow sense and as part of the long historical duration in the interaction between worldscripts and scriptworlds). Digitization intensifies the processes of sanskritization and romanization, even as it appears to eclipse entirely the world of durable print, the very medium in which the timing and spacing of roman letters takes place, showing how to spell out Sanskrit (*Dêwanâgarî* or *saṃskṛta*), and how to track the difference (and *différance*) between them.

The OED already shows us the effect of digitization in its erasure of all the forms of Arabic script once used to mark the etymology of certain words. Contemporary culture furnishes many more recent examples. A common trope, or topos, of contemporary television and film titles is to present the digital image of letters—or numbers—and display the flickering image of their disappearance on the screen. Even the simplest of these (the binary appearance and disappearance of letters), presents what might be called a chronotope of digital romanization. Often though, such title sequences work by suggesting a richer depth of perspective in the crossing over from one script to another, or from lettering to numbering. The television crime show *Numbers*, for example, provides an example of the latter, evident in its stylized title **NUMB3RS**, (see Figure 9); and the television series *The Americans* gives an example of the former (in the alternation between Cyrillic and roman script in the cast credits, and also in the substitution of a hammer and sickle icon in place of the "c" of the title (see Figure 10). In films, too, the chronotope of digital romanization has become something of a commonplace framing device. In some cases, the chronotope extends to become a part of the plotting of the film itself.

Arrival (Denis Villeneuve's 2016 adaptation of Ted Chiang's "Story of Your Life") offers an especially interesting example. The conceit of its plot turns on the riddle of an alien script form (see Figure 11) that stands in interesting contrast to the universally legible, illegible script from the *Hikayat Abdullah*. With the arrival of twelve alien spaceships, the fate of the world depends on decoding the aliens' message, given in different parts to various different nations. Their language turns out to be the tool that can save humanity, the denouement of the plot hinging on the linguist heroine (Louise Banks) learning to understand the structure of the language and its writing. Presented in opposition to the linear timing and spacing of roman letters, the "non-linear orthography" of

Figure 9. Title sequence from the TV series *Numb3rs*.

Figure 10. Title sequence from the TV series *The Americans*.

Heptapod-B imparts a non-linear grasp of time, which allows linguist Banks to know the future and resolve the crisis of a divided, and hostile, international response to the aliens. The fantasy of a "universal language," written in a "non-linear orthography," is projected as a sci-fi solution to the time-space continuum (incidentally also the problem posed by Einstein, that Bakhtin draws from in formulating the term "chronotope"). This sci-fi fantasy is played out in the self-reflective medium of film's replaying all the technologies of human representation, a timing and spacing that does away with time in space. The aliens' message "there is no time," at first misinterpreted as a hostile ultimatum, is later decoded as a deep philosophical insight into the universal nature of time, embodied in the structure of the alien language and script. A science fiction fantasy of linguistic coding that projects the "ideographic turn" in language as a benevolent alien invasion, *Arrival* offers an extended riff on the dialectic of sanskritization, romanization, and digitization.

The logic of digital romanization is implied already in the Conradian "blank space" on the map of Africa. A moment of negation, it posits a degree zero of cartographic inscription, premised on the displacement and rearrangement of other names and places. Conrad later makes explicit some of those romanized names, when he rewrites Marlow's childhood passion for maps as his own autobiographical experience: first, in *A Personal Record*, where "*there*" is named "Stanley Falls"; and then again, in "Geography and Some Explorers," where the place-names "Tanganyika" and "Victoria Nyanza" are given. The chronotope

Figure 11. Alien script featured in Denis Villeneuve's film *Arrival*.

of the "blank space" in *Heart of Darkness* already anticipates the kind of cryptic coding with which Joyce's *Finnegans Wake* turns that "blank space" into a form of "iSpace": more specifically, into the degree zero (the Joycean "Nil" and "Nihil") of the way roman letters provide a worldscript for coding all scriptworlds. The negation implied by the absence of African place names may not, on its own, suggest the worldview of computer coding or the turn to alphanumerical coding made in Claude Shannon's invention of the twenty-seventh letter of the English alphabet, the letter that codes a space. Combined, however, with the phonemic and graphemic play on letters (the silent K-effect of "knights"), the "blank space" of a map yet to be color coded by Europe's colonization of Africa, is already a part of—indeed, is mediating—the eclipse of that durable form of print that is still constantly being transformed by what Hayles calls the "flickering signification" "underwritten by binary digits."[39]

Sanskrit grammar provides a model for considering the Conradian "blank space"—and the K-effect—in relation to computer coding. The "zero-degree"—"the absence of a linguistic feature" (as defined in the OED's 1891 entry for "zero")—provides an algorithm for grasping the linguistic significance of the "blank space" as degree zero of cartographic writing and the flicker effect of the silent K (or its binary substitution of C). Referring to Pāṇini's foundational Sanskrit grammar, the OED specifies the linguistic sense of zero as "The absence of a linguistic feature (such as an inflection, or a phonetic or syntactic element) in a position in which one previously existed, or where one is present in corresponding positions elsewhere." This "lopa" (as it is named in Sanskrit, according to the OED's reference to Pāṇini) corresponds, in striking ways, to the gap or blank opened up in the OED's own etymological transliterations, where the roman letters are given in place of whatever (spoken or written) inflection they may be intended to register. The linguistic dilemma—for which the Sanskrit "lopa" provides a solution—is explained by linguist Leonard Bloomfield:

> In describing the modulations and modifications which occur in syntax, we naturally take the absolute form of a word or phrase as our starting-point, but a bound form which occurs in several shapes will lead to several entirely different forms of description, according to our choice of a *basic alternant*. . . . In other cases there is not even a grammatical feature [to express a meaning]: a single phonetic form, in the manner of homonymy, represents two meanings which are usually distinguished by means of a linguistic form, as, singular and plural noun in *the sheep (grazes)* : *the sheep (graze)*. Here the Hindus hit upon the apparently artificial but in practice eminently serviceable device of speaking of a *zero element*: in *sheep: sheep* the plural-suffix is replaced by zero—that is, by nothing at all.[40]

The "zero element" marks where suffixes, affixes, or other inflected grammatical forms (to show the difference between cases) are absent. This "absence of a linguistic feature" is one of the examples where Pāṇini's Sanskrit grammar anticipates computational coding; or, rather, where computer programming catches up with ancient Sanskrit philology.

What Bloomfield calls the "eminently serviceable device" of the "zero element," also marks an especially interesting convergence between the principles of comparative philology (*à la* Humboldt), bound to the study of morphological change through history, and the principles of structuralist linguistics (*à la* Saussure) that displaced comparative philology. For the first, the "zero element" is put to the service of tracking morphological change. For the second, it marks that "zero degree" of a system of signs: "the zero degree testifies to the power held by any system of signs of creating meaning 'out of nothing.'"[41] The OED definition of this "zero" is already measuring the distance between its Sanskrit origin (in the word "lopa" in the citation from Pāṇini) and its more specialized meaning for "Linguistics" (which, in 1891, is poised to shift from historical to structuralist linguistics).[42] Tracking the sanskritization of Pāṇini's grammatical principle (that is, its adaptation to modern European linguistics), the OED's definition also reveals its relevance for romanization—not only in giving us the term "lopa," but, more consequentially, in suggesting the gap, or blank space (or "lopa") opened up wherever a "linguistic feature" from another language and/or script gets substituted in the spacing and timing of roman letters.

This "zero" degree—where sanskritization, romanization, and digitization all converge—is the common feature linking the Conradian "blank space," the Joycean "iSpace," and each and every entry in the OED. In each case, the timing and spacing of roman letters marks the "absence of a linguistic feature." The example of "tuan" stands out. The OED's definition illuminates this several times over: first in offering the alternate morphological forms *tuan*, *tuwan*; then in folding those italicized transcriptions (or transliterations) into the absence, marked simply by its "Malay" origin (although it is possible to note a gap in the difference of lowercase "tuan" and uppercase "Tuan"). When Joyce puts "Tuan" to use ("Tuan about whittinghim!"[43]), nothing but the play of roman letters invites us to pronounce the word variously "tu-an" and "turn" to measure the gap between the Malay word for "sir" (or Lord) and the English rhyme "turn again Whittington, Lord Mayor of London." Neither of these examples are what Bloomfield has in mind when he writes about the use to which the "zero element" of Sanskrit grammar might be put. These are not, properly speaking, the examples that either Sanskrit grammar or modern linguistics is designed to study. But it is precisely the *improper* grammatical and linguistic form that is revealed in the process of romanization.

This "zero" degree allows me to return to those cases of grammatical mistakes that I traced to the "accusative case" at the generative heart of Conrad's narratives. The mistaken ascription of "accusation" to the grammatical case (an early effect of romanizing the Greek form, as the OED studiously annotated) prompted me to consider the grammar of mistaken identity, accusation, and racialized naming around which Conrad's narratives turn. I would like to read this now, in light of the "zero" degree: where the "blank space" marks the absence of some prior linguistic form. Unlike the case of Bloomfield's "*sheep: sheep*," however, the missing element is something lost in the transcription, transliteration, and translation between languages and scripts. This, too, is the K-effect of romanized (sanskritized, digitized) timing and spacing that indexes a *blank* or *absence* where some prior grammatical form of inflection (or more likely *multiple* prior grammatical inflections) used to be.

Conrad's "Tuan" takes us back through the grammar of racialized accusations, self-accusations, and counteraccusations that I have explored in the chronotopes of romanization throughout Conrad's work—all the way back to the opening address of *Almayer's Folly* where Mrs. Almayer's "Kaspar! Makan!" might be seen to turn on an implied, but *absent*, form of respectful address to a European. So, the later appearance of the proper use of "Tuan," as respectful mode of address (to the extent that it *ever* appears in such a proper form) might be read as an inflection of that "zero" degree of utterance at the beginning of the novel, the beginning of Conrad's career: the accusative form of its absence.[44] Within that one utterance, but also over the arc of Conrad's entire *oeuvre* (from *Lord Jim* through *Victory*), what is at work in the romanization of "tuan" turns out to be a very long process of delayed decoding. Indeed, to the extent that "tuan" marks the "zero" degree of a grammatical form displaced in the process of romanization, there may be no end to this unfinished business of measuring what is missing—according to the work of sanskritization and digitization also converging on romanization.

Pramoedya's work, as a whole, calls attention to a missing term in the form of respect implied by the word "tuan" (missing, too, from the utterance "Kaspar! Makan!"). The term "nyai"—originally a respectful Javanese term for a woman—was a highly charged colonial term of denigration (and even abuse) used to designate a native woman's relation to a European "tuan." As I have discussed elsewhere, both the term "nyai" and the genre of the "nyai" narrative that flourished over the turn of the century, inform the overall arc of Pramoedya's Buru tetralogy (which begins with the main character's encounter with a "Nyai" figure who becomes a mother figure, his actual mother-in-law, and his "spiritual teacher"—and which ends with all the manuscripts of the first three novels being delivered to this same "Nyai" figure).[45] "Nyai"—the missing grammatical counterpart to "Tuan" in the colonial context of pre-Indonesian Malay—is itself, for Pramoedya, a kind of "zero" degree of linguistic utterance, the blank space of a form of Javanese respectful address turned into universal abuse: "All social classes had passed judgment on the Nyai, as well as all races: Native, European, Chinese, Arab" ("Semua lapisan kehidupan menghukum keluarga nyai-nyai; juga semua bangsa: Pribumi, Eropa, Tionghoa, Arab").[46] For Pramoedya, the term "nyai" constitutes a point of reference for a long, still unfolding process of decolonization, a struggle to undo the hierarchies of race, class, and caste embedded in the linguistic forms of successive languages and scripts. One of the earliest stories where the "nyai" appears as an enigmatic point of reference for such a war on Javanese hierarchies, "Houseboy + Maid," also offers one of the smallest, most succinct chronotopes of romanization: "The first generation of [slaves—those who will be figured as faithful *nyai* slaves to their *tuans*] became known because it was recorded in a big book with romanized letters: "native sergeant . . . [gazette number] . . ."[47] The archive of romanized letters is marked by ellipsis, a number, and blank space.

To read "nyai" as a missing part of the displaced grammatical form of address, romanized in the OED and Conrad's work, raises the possibility of a future reading of many more such gaps and silences in the archive that continues to emerge from an ongoing process of sanskritization, romanization, and digitization. This is related to what subaltern studies historian Ranajit Guha theorized in *Elementary Aspects of Peasant Insurrection* as the "zero sign of utterance," linking contemporary structuralist linguistics (Saussure, Jakobson, and Barthes) with the "grammatical *zero*" of Pāṇini's "lopa."[48] Rather than simply celebrating and applying the ancient Sanskrit principle to the problem of subaltern silence in the record of history, Guha lays emphasis on its historical relation to the enforcement of social inequity: "It was as if language was made to operate in a state of Paninian *lopa* and was known only by virtue of its elision so that the ban imposed by custom on various kinds of discourse could announce and display the subordination of junior kin to senior, of wife to husband, of low caste to high caste and generally of the underdog to the elite."[49] The way in which Guha draws on ancient Sanskrit philology to deploy against the hierarchies of caste that he sees encoded in its grammatical rules, has something in common with the way Pramoedya manipulates the relation between offensive colonial forms of address and Javanese linguistic hierarchies, pitting one against the other in an ongoing and far-reaching decolonization of tradition. The subaltern voice may never be retrieved, but the traces of its erasure may be measured in the "zero sign of utterance" marked by those forms of address—*tuan, nyai*—that signal global historical shifts in the hierarchies of language and script. Such forms of address, organized as chronotopes of romanization, may constitute small lexical units, or recurrent tropes (the trope of "tuan" or "nyai"/mistress), and may surface in either the accusative case or "zero sign of utterance" marked by names—the names of ships, for example; or names (of places or people), or designations ("coolie," "houseboy"). They may also unfold, however, into larger narrative patterns—the "long space," for example, of Pramoedya's classic, historical genealogies of Indonesian anti-colonial nationalism.

Especially in postcolonial literature, there are numerous instances where the chronotope of romanization can work, either according to the long space of novelistic form (as in Pramoedya's Buru quartet) or as a kind of fragmentary satirical algorithm (as in Pramoedya's short story "Houseboy + Maid" with the mathematical formula of the title). The poetics of naming is, perhaps, the most obvious place to turn to find both (as in the naming of the main character of Pramoedya's Buru quartet). Arundhati Roy's long novel, *The Ministry of Utmost Happiness*, offers a condensed chronotope of romanization in the opening description of its main character's name: "Long ago a man who knew English told her that her name written backwards (in English) spelled Majnu."[50] In the unraveling of this naming riddle (that can never fully be decoded), the narrative crosses all the main languages and scripts of postcolonial India to create a knot at the heart of the romanized English form of the reader's own experience to come:

> In the English version of the story of Laila and Majnu, he said, Majnu was called Romeo and Laila was Juliet. She found that hilarious. "You mean I've made a *khichdi* of their story?" she asked. "What will they do when they find that Laila may actually be Majnu and Romi was really Juli?" The next time he saw her, the Man Who Knew English said he'd made a mistake. Her name spelled backwards would be Mujna, which wasn't a name and meant nothing at all. To this she said, "It doesn't matter. I'm all of them, I'm Romi and Juli, I'm Laila and Majnu. *And* Mujna, why not? Who says my name is Anjum? I'm not Anjum, I'm Anjuman. I'm a *mehfil*, I'm a gathering. Of everybody and nobody, of everything and nothing. Is there anyone else you would like to invite? Everyone is invited."[51]

This offers a paradigmatic, postcolonial combination of both the long space of novel form, projected according to the spacing and timing of Anjum's unfolding experience in romanized English print, and the short space of an anagrammatical reversal of the spacing and timing of roman letters: in the condensed pun on "Romeo" as "Romi"; in the romanized transcription of the untranslated words "*khichdi*" and "*mehfil*"; and the anagrammatized engendering of Anjum's name as a place of transition across languages and scripts.[52]

There is something similar at work in Christina Sharpe's formula "blackness as, blackness is, anagrammatical":

> That is, we can see the moments when blackness opens up into the anagrammatical in the literal sense as when "a word, phrase, or name is formed by rearranging the letters of another" (*Merriam-Webster Online*). We can also apprehend this in the metaphorical sense in how, regarding blackness, grammatical gender falls away and new meanings proliferate; how "the letters of a text are formed into a secret message by rearranging them" or a secret message is discovered through the rearranging of the letters of a text. *Ana-*, as a prefix, means "up, in place or time, back, again, anew." So blackness anew, blackness as a/temporal, in and out of place and time putting pressure on meaning and that against which meaning is made. We see again and again how, in and out of the United States . . . *girl* doesn't mean "girl" but, for example, "prostitute" or "felon," *boy* doesn't mean "boy," but "Hulk Hogan" or "gunman," "thug" or "urban youth." We see that *mother* doesn't mean "mother," but "felon" and "defender" and/or "birther of terror" and

not one of the principal grounds of terrors multiple and quotidian enactments. We see that *child* is not "child," and a Coast Guard cutter becomes, in Brathwaite's hands, a Coast Guard gutter—not a rescue or a medical ship but a carrier of coffins, a coffle, and so on. As the meanings of words fall apart, we encounter again and again the difficulty of sticking the signification. This is Black being in the wake. This is the anagrammatical. These are Black lives, annotated.[53]

Almost all of Sharpe's references are to digital texts (including to the online OED for the prefix "ana-"), so this might be read as an "anagrammatical" theorization of what I annotated above as the chronotope of digital romanization. What it has in common with the novelistic play on Anjum's name in Roy's novel is a fundamental, critical dismantling of the hierarchies of language and script that also entails rethinking the acts of transcription, transliteration, and translation that underpin the phenomenon of romanization.[54]

Arundhati Roy and Christina Sharpe present two contrasting, if also complementary, examples of the contestation of hierarchies of language and script through an ongoing process of sanskritization, romanization, and digitization. Both recall (and reframe in turn) what the Conradian "blank space" and the Joycean "iSpace" each does with the timing and spacing of English. Both also invite a further reflection on what remains still to be thought through in the use of Bakhtin's terms "chronotope" and "novelization." The term "chronotope," in some respects, lends itself more to the "anagrammatical" analysis of the "wake" whereas the term "novelization" seems to privilege the "long space" of the novel form. And yet Roy and Sharpe suggest a need to rethink that privileging of either long or short forms, inviting a theoretical reconceptualization of each as the anagrammatical rescripting of the other. So, the privileging of the fragmentary trope in the chronotope of romanization (single names, single words—even such simple words as "girl" and "boy"—and perhaps, above all, the "blank space" or "zero" degree of absence) might unfold over the long space of a novelistic timing and spacing of roman letters yet to come. Novel form itself, after all, is what constantly unravels (as with all literary genres and hierarchies) through that process of "novelization" that is also, in an anagrammatical retranscription, transliteration, and translation from the Russian, an ongoing act of "romanization" across multiple languages and scripts.

Digitization makes evident (retrospectively) those effects of romanization that Conrad shapes into narrative form, which resonate across transnational modernism, and which the OED replicates in the work of transcription, transliteration, and translation often hidden in the blank spaces of its etymologies. These are the effects I have been calling the K-effect. Referring, first, to the signature K-effect hidden in Conrad's own authorial pseudonym, it registers a series of phonemic and graphemic distortions in the timing and spacing of roman letters that produce the chronotopes of romanization, organizing the temporal and spatial arrangement of all his narratives. These effects extend through the many readings and rewritings of Conrad that continue to shape the reception of his work, including those readings that have framed my own reading here (notably, Pramoedya's reading of *Almayer's Folly*, postcolonial readings in general, and anagrammatical Black readings in the wake of Conrad). These critical readings and rewritings of Conrad are themselves related to the second kind of K-effect that this book has traced as indexing a range of transnational, modernist experiments with letters, script, and writing systems (exemplified in the canonical examples of Joyce, Kafka, and Lu Xun). There are, indeed, many more chronotopes of romanization to be found throughout transnational, modernist experimentation (in literature, in theory, and in multimedia artistic practice). Not only does Bakhtin's term highlight the way in which a range of writers and artists use the letter K to abbreviate analphabetic distortions in the spacing and timing of print; Bakhtin's own term (variously romanized chronotope, xronotop, kronotop) itself turns on just such a K-effect, the "ch," "x," or "k" of its initial letter, indexing a range of different romanization systems across European languages. This points to the third sense of the K-effect, the sociolinguistic effect of romanization as a transformation in the global (and multimedia) timing and spacing of print culture. As an index of the difference in genealogies of the roman alphabet, as well as an index of the differences opened up in transliteration across the world's other writing systems, this K-effect illustrates the way in which roman letters mediate constantly shifting hierarchies of language and script in modern, global forms of print media.

Acknowledgments

This book has emerged over many years and from a number of related projects. I owe an enormous debt to all those who have helped me navigate the multiple issues that converge on the question of "romanization" considered here. From very early on, I recognized that my task was impossible. To write a history of romanization, properly speaking, would require a whole collective of scholars with expertise in all the languages and scripts in the world. I am, alas, a single, flawed scholar with a limited knowledge of only a few languages and scripts. In finding a way to broach the question of romanization, I have benefitted immensely from the rich and diverse experience and insights of many, many others—many more than I can name here. A very early version of this argument was presented at the Japanese Association of English Literature in Tokyo in 2011 and I would like to thank the organizers of that event for the invitation to deliver the talk, and for the rich and rewarding response I received from many of the attendees (with special thanks to Asako Nakai and Yasuko Shidara). I am also very grateful to Michelle Warren for inviting me to the conference on philology at Dartmouth in 2013, where I was able to explore some of these ideas among scholars with an impressive variety of linguistic expertise and an engaged and theoretical vision of the future of philology. This project has also been enriched by all the lively and fruitful debates with colleagues at Erfurt University, at events promoted by the ongoing work of scholarly collaboration between Erfurt and Fordham University (including the workshop on Bakhtin's chronotope with John Miele and Anna Förster). I have presented versions of this book's reading of Conrad at various conferences, and I thank the organizers of the Joseph Conrad Society, U.K., and the Joseph Conrad Society of America for hosting those events. As co-organizer of the Conrad conference at Fordham,

I want to thank all the participants of "Conradian Crosscurrents: Creativity and Critique," held in June 2017.

At Fordham, I have received invaluable collegial, critical, and scholarly support from the working group on questions of Race, Empire, and Coloniality. I'm immensely grateful to my colleagues Diane Detourney, Glenn Hendler, Robb Hernández, James Kim, Julie Kim, Fawzia Mustafa, Sasha Panaram, Dennis Tyler, Stephen Hong Sohn, and Jordan Stein for all their insights and suggestions. Their scholarship, the brilliance of their comments, and the antiracist vision of their collective scholarly work continue to inspire.

I owe my thanks to more individuals than I can list here, but I do want to thank, in particular, the following: John M. Archer, for many conversations on this topic over the years and for taking the time to read through final drafts at a few crisis moments in the revision process; Madeleine Brainerd for her critical insight and support; Fraser Easton, for unwavering support, helpful advice, and key insights at critical moments (early on and in the very last moments of the project); Holt Meyer for all of the many, ongoing, collaborative ventures (and for the constant stream of postcards from everywhere in the world); Fawzia Mustafa for the wealth of her experience and unbounded generosity and the critical model of her scholarship; and Matt Sommer for conversations early on in the process that made me realize how complicated the question of writing systems really is, and for his kind and patient response to earlier drafts of my argument about the Chinese character of romanization. I also owe special thanks to Julie Beth Napolin, Ben Tran, and Peter Hitchcock for conversations early in the process of imagining this book. And for the inspiration of intermittent conversations at conferences, as well as in more homely settings, thanks to Marco Formisano, Shari Goldberg, Mahlika Hopwood, Sarah Kay, Emily Sun, Peter Szendy, and Laura Odello. Thank you to friends and Conradians whose work has helped sustain my own—even if their work doesn't appear in direct citation: Katherine Baxter, Laurence Davies, Mark Deggan, Hugh Epstein, Daphna Erdinast-Vulcan, Robert Hampson, Nidesh Lawtoo, Jack Peters, Debra Romanick Baldwin, Kim Salmons, Jean Szczypien, Tania Zulli. Thanks also, to Fordham friends, students, and colleagues: Andrew Clark, Arnaldo Cruz-Malavé, John Bugg, Daniel Contreras, Tony D'Agostino, Anne Fernald, Anwita Ghosh, Sam Haddad, Tom O'Donnell, Cristiana Sogno, Vlasta Vranjes, Keri Walsh, and Sarah Zimmerman. Thanks to those ministering angels of Fordham's English department: Carole Alvino, Labelle De La Rosa, and MonaLisa Torres-Bates.

I am immensely grateful for the support and encouragement of a family that has, over the course of writing this book, increased its global reach. Thank you, Cai and Emily; thank you, Keir and Celeste. Thanks, as well, to the extended family of Ironclad; and to the extended family of AMOC. A special thanks to Keir for his judicious suggestions on revising the manuscript. To my father, thank you for the endless conversations about *Finnegans Wake*.

An early version of parts of Chapter 1 appeared in *postmedieval: a journal of medieval cultural studies* (Vol. 5 (4) Winter 2014) and I am grateful for permission to reproduce those here, albeit in a very different form. A version of the middle section of Chapter 1 appeared in *Conradiana* as "Conrad's Accusative Case"; and an early version of parts of Chapter 2 appeared in *Conrad and Language* (Edinburgh University Press, 2016), edited by Katherine Baxter and Robert Hampson. Thank you to Fordham University for a faculty fellowship in Fall 2015 that enabled me to make substantial progress on the book; and a fellowship in 2020–21 that enabled me to complete the manuscript.

Much appreciation for the anonymous reviewers at Fordham University Press, whose recommendations, criticisms, and encouragement helped substantially recast the final shape of the book. And thanks to Tom Lay and everyone at Fordham University Press for everything that they have done to help steer the book into published form. I don't know how best to acknowledge my debt to the late, much-missed, Helen Tartar, who was my first editor and whose editorial vision shaped so many important books at Stanford and then at Fordham. My thanks are not only to her and to the press that has been enriched by and enriches, in turn, her legacy; but also, to that constellation of authors that she helped bring together who continue to shape the way we read today.

Lastly, the person to whom I owe the greatest thanks, is the person who has nurtured this project the most, despite having suffered the most from its growing pains. Siu Li's constant encouragement, her wise interventions, and her scholarly (and anti-scholarly) insights, have all been indispensable. There is another book that should really accompany this, authored by Siu Li (with maybe some assistance from myself), in which examples of "romanization" would be given, simply, in illustrative form and perhaps without any words or letters at all: a collection of images of stairs and windows. With the thought of that shadow book, I dedicate this book to Siu Li, with all my love.

Notes

Introduction: Conrad's "timely appearance in English"

1. Merriam Webster defines "romanize" as "to write or print (something, such as a language) in the Latin alphabet" (with the example "romanize Chinese") *Merriam-Webster.com*. https://www.merriam-webster.com/dictionary/romanize (Accessed 9 Aug. 2022); the *Oxford English Dictionary* definition (to which I return in Chapter 1) reads "to transliterate into Roman characters"; *Chambers English Dictionary* reads "to represent by the Roman alphabet" (Chambers, 1990).

2. I. J. Gelb, *A Study of Writing*, revised edition (Chicago: University Chicago Press, 1963) is a classic and authoritative point of reference. Also see Peter Daniels and William Bright, *The World's Writing Systems* (New York: Oxford University Press, 1996), and Florian Coulmas, *Writing Systems: An Introduction to Their Linguistic Analysis* (New York: Cambridge University Press, 2003), especially important for the current study.

3. In addition to Gelb, Daniels and Bright, and Coulmas, see İlker Aytürk, "Introduction: Romanisation in Comparative Perspective," *Journal of the Royal Asia Society*, Third Series 20 (1) (2010):1–9, and John DeFrancis, *Nationalism and Language Reform in China* (Princeton: Princeton University Press, 1950).

4. See Coulmas, citing Battestini's critique of Gelb. Coulmas, *Writing Systems*, 15.

5. Even the critique of this condition (for example Derridean deconstruction) is bound to the biases imposed by the conditions of romanization. As Haun Saussy succinctly notes in reference to Derrida's discussions of "latinization" as "one dimension of globalization": "'Globalatinization' there may be, but it is well to remember that Latin is also a character-set, and one transmitted through particular technologies." Haun Saussy, *Great Walls of Discourse and Other Adventures in Cultural China* (Cambridge: Harvard University Press, 2001), 32.

6. Cited in note 2 to Part I, Chapter 3, of Jacques Derrida, *Of Grammatology*, trans. Gayatari Chakravorty Spivak (Baltimore: Johns Hopkins University Press, 1976), 330; "Sans doute notre qualité de scripteurs 'alphabétiques' concourt-elle puissamment aussi à nous dissimuler tels aspects essentiels de l'activité scripturale." Cited in Jacques Derrida, *de la grammatologie* (Paris: Editions de Minuit, 1967), 107.

7. While most such studies focus on the particular linguistic-literary context of particular authors, scholars who explore the broader implications of multilinguistic, multiscript interactions related to the phenomenon of romanization include Emily Apter, Christopher Bush, Rey Chow, Lydia Liu, Jing Tsu, Yasmin Yildiz, and Yurou Zhong.

8. Emily Apter, "Global *Translatio*: The 'Invention' of Comparative Literature, Istanbul, 1933," in *The Translation Zone: A New Comparative Literature* (Princeton: Princeton University Press, 2006), 41–64; see also Apter, "Auerbach's *Welt*-theology," in *Against Literature: On the Politics of Untranslatability* (New York: Verso, 2013), 193–210.

9. Each of these geographical and historical centers (Istanbul, Moscow, Tokyo) designates, not only the emergence of distinct genealogies of literary histories and theories. Those literary histories and theories emerge from their relation to other geographical centers which might be considered their displaced counterparts (Istanbul / Berlin; Moscow / Prague; Tokyo / Shanghai).

10. Walter Ong famously asserts what appears to be the absolute opposite. There are, he claims, "many scripts but only one alphabet." Although I will repeatedly be contesting Ong's claim, the book's argument about the way romanization constitutes the "timing and spacing of print culture" in many respects follows the lead of Ong's influential and important argument about the way print literacy attempts to fix in space, the temporality of oral practices. At the outset of this study, I propose the reader entertain both Ong's claim, and my claim, as counterfactuals. That both statements might be true, lies at the heart of the riddle of romanization. Walter Ong, *Orality and Literacy: The Technologizing of the Word* (New York: Routledge, 2002), 84.

11. Chinua Achebe, "An Image of Africa," in *Hopes and Impediments: Selected Essays* (Albany: Anchor, 1989), 1–20.

12. See the online *Oxford English Dictionary* (http://www.OED.com).

13. For an important and fascinating discussion of some of the debates among editors over how to mark the difference between "native" and "foreign" English words, see Sarah Ogilvie, *Words of the World: A Global History of the Oxford English Dictionary* (New York: Cambridge University Press, 2012), especially Chapter 5.

14. For an account of the complexity of this inaugural dialogue as a question of "modernist acoustics and narrative form," see Julie Beth Napolin, *The Fact of Resonance: Modernist Acoustics and Narrative Form* (New York: Fordham University Press, 2020).

15. Mikhail Bakhtin, *The Dialogic Imagination: Four Essays*, trans. Caryl Emerson, ed. Michael Holquist (Austin: University of Texas Press, 1981), 84.

16. "A global script forms the basis of a broad literary system—what we might call a 'scriptworld'—in which works that use that script are composed." David Damrosch, "Scriptworlds: Writing Systems and the Formation of World Literature," *Modern Language Quarterly* 68: 2 (June 2007): 195–219 (195).

17. Coulmas, *Writing Systems*, 35.

18. This is how the translator-editors explain the term in the Glossary to Bakhtin, *The Dialogic Imagination*.

19. Paul Gilroy, *The Black Atlantic: Modernity and Double Consciousness* (Cambridge: Harvard University Press, 1993), 4, 225.

20. The turn to digitization is usually ascribed to the middle of the twentieth century and credited to the mathematician Claude Shannon whose *A Mathematical Theory of Communication* was published in 1948. Lydia Liu describes this as "a specific historical moment in the evolution of alphabetical writing," emphasizing that Shannon added "a twenty-seventh letter to the English alphabet to code 'space'" precipitating what Liu calls the "ideographic turn." As Liu and others have noted, the beginnings of this digital turn may be traced back to the later nineteenth century, with the development of computer and telegraph technologies. As discussed in Chapter 1, Liu emphasizes the role of early twentieth-century modernist experimentation in the turn toward digitization. Lydia Liu, *The Freudian Robot: Digital Media and the Future of the Unconscious* (Chicago: University of Chicago Press, 2010), 27, 114.

21. Harold Love offers a useful set of warnings about the phrase "print culture," cautioning against using it as a historical category (Harold Love, "Early Modern Print Culture: Assessing the Models," *Parergon* 20 (1) (2003): 45–64). Throughout this book "print culture" is intended to stand (generally) for the place of "print" within a range of media (as suggested by media theorists as diverse as Walter Benjamin, Friedrich Kittler, N. Katherine Hayles, Lydia Liu, and Amaranth Borsuk). The later chapters of this book (notably Chapter 3) seek to specify this sense of "print culture" in terms of Benedict Anderson's suggestive formulation "print-capitalism." Chapter 4 offers a speculative way to situate "print culture" dialectically in historical relation to sanskritization, romanization, and digitization.

22. For the concept of "remediation" see Amaranth Borsuk's use of a term coined by Jay Bolter and Richard Grusin (Amaranth Borsuk, *The Book* (Cambridge: MIT Press, 2016), 202). See also Lisa Gitelman, *Always Already New: Media, History, and the Data of Culture* (Cambridge: MIT Press, 2006), especially 4 and 9–10.

23. Ha Jin, *The Writer as Migrant* (Chicago: University of Chicago Press, 2008), 42.

24. *The Collected Letters of Joseph Conrad*, 9 volumes, ed. Frederick Karl and Laurence Davies (New York: Cambridge University Press, 1983–2008), Volume 2, 322–23.

25. Salman Rushdie, *Joseph Anton: A Memoir* (New York: Random House, 2012), 165.

26. Fawzia Mustafa, "Gurnah and Naipaul: Intersections of *Paradise* and *A Bend in the River*," *Twentieth-Century Literature* 61 (2) (June 2015): 232–63, (242).

27. Ian Watt famously coins the term "delayed decoding" to explain Conrad's narrative method in Ian Watt, *Conrad in the Nineteenth Century* (Oakland: University of California Press, 1979), 175 ff.

28. Peter Nazareth, "Conrad's Descendants," *Conradiana* 22 (2) (Summer 1990): 101–9.

29. One of the most striking fictional renditions of this risk of betrayal is found in the opening sequence of Ha Jin's novel *War Trash* in the form of the roman letters tattooed onto the body of the Chinese Korean war veteran who narrates the novel. For analysis of this chronotope of romanization, see Jing Tsu, *Sound and Script in Chinese Diaspora* (Cambridge: Harvard University Press, 2010), 107–10; and my "Postcolonial Philology and the Transposition of 'Western Consciousness'" (forthcoming in *Transposing the West* [de Gruyter]).

30. Coulmas, *Writing Systems*, 102.

31. For Derrida's development of the term "mondialatinisation" (which Weber translates "globalatinization"), see Jacques Derrida, *Foi et Savoir: suivi de Le Siècle et le Pardon* (Paris: Editions de Seuil, 2000), and Jacques Derrida, *Acts of Religion*, ed. Gil Anidjar (New York: Routledge, 2002).

32. See Derrida, *Of Grammatology*, Part I, especially Chapter 2 ("Linguistics and Grammatology"), and most especially p. 68.

33. See especially Derrida, *Of Grammatology*, Part I, Chapter 3, 75–87.

34. Christina Sharpe, *In the Wake: On Blackness and Being* (Durham: Duke University Press, 2016), 76.

35. Gilroy, *Black Atlantic*, 4.

36. See my "Afterword" to Kim Salmons and Tania Zulli, eds., *Migration, Modernity and Transnationalism in the Work of Joseph Conrad* (London: Bloomsbury, 2017); and see also Julie Beth Napolin, *The Fact of Resonance*.

37. For a discussion of Shklovsky's concepts as chronotopes of romanization see my "Sklovskii's Key Concepts in Roman(*novel*)ized Time and Space," in *100 Years of Ostranenie*, ed. Holt Meyer [forthcoming, Sdvig Press]).

38. *Collected Letters*, Volume 8, 290.

39. Lydia Liu, *Translingual Practice: Literature, National Culture, and Translated Modernity—China, 1900–1937* (Redwood City: Stanford University Press, 1995).

40. The phrase is from the subtitle to Gilles Deleuze and Félix Guattari, *Kafka: Toward a Minor Literature*, trans. Dana Polan (Minneapolis: University of Minnesota Press, 1986) which is their adaptation of the terms Kafka elaborates in a diary entry from December 25, 1911. See Franz Kafka, *The Diaries of Franz Kafka*, ed. Max Brod (New York: Penguin, 1982), 148–51.

41. Cited in Russell Samolsky, *Apocalyptic Futures: Marked Bodies and the Violence of the Text in Kafka, Conrad, and Coetzee* (New York: Fordham University Press, 2011), 45.

42. The OED's entry for Q tracks a number of these K-effects, including its derivation from Phoenician via "the two *k*-sounds which exist in the Semitic tongues (Hebrew ק, Arabic ق)"; and also the tendency to use Q to substitute for K in certain

circumstances, a "tendency" that the OED attributes to "scholars" who "use Q by itself to transliterate the Semitic *kōph*, writing, e.g., *Qabbala, Qaraite, Qurán* for *Cabbala, Karaite, Koran*."

Chapter 1. The English Case of Romanization: From Conrad's "blank space" to Joyce's "iSpace"

1. İlker Aytürk, "Script Charisma in Hebrew and Turkish: A Comparative Framework for Understanding the Success and Failure of Romanization," *Journal of World History* 21 (1) (2010): 97–130, 102.

2. Other important cases of romanization include the romanization of Native American languages and scripts in the nineteenth century; the development of Vietnamese *quốc ngu* to replace Chinese script; the development of various romanization systems for Thai; and the formation of the International Phonetic Alphabet in the 1880s.

3. *Oxford English Dictionary* (http://www.OED.com). The revised second edition lists this definition first, shifting it from the fourth place it was accorded in the entry's first edition from 1909.

4. Florian Coulmas, *Writing Systems* (New York: Cambridge University Press, 2003), 32.

5. Coulmas, *Writing Systems*.

6. While the original OED entries rank the technical sense of transliteration beneath the historical and political sense, the revised entries put transliteration as the first meaning for "Romanization" and as a separately numbered meaning (number 3) for "Romanize."

7. Coulmas, *Writing Systems*, 198; see also 15–16.

8. Coulmas is citing Battestini's critique of Gelb's "common Latin alphabet fetishism" (Coulmas, *Writing Systems*, 15). Although Gelb's *A Study of Writing* usually makes the helpful and important distinction between the Latin alphabet and "English writing," the "teleological evolutionism" found throughout tends to conflate "the Latin writing" and "our writing" (i.e. English) even where he is offering illuminating contrasts between the two systems I. J. Gelb, *A Study of Writing*, revised edition (Chicago: University of Chicago Press, 1963), see especially 198.

9. Walter Ong, *Orality and Literacy: The Technologizing of the Word* (New York: Routledge, 2002), 84.

10. Yurou Zhong, *Chinese Grammatology: Script Revolution and Literary Modernity, 1916–1958* (New York: Columbia University Press, 2019), 5.

11. Ong, *Orality and Literacy*, 116.

12. Ong, *Orality and Literacy*, 119.

13. Marshall McLuhan, *Understanding Media: The Extensions of Man* (Berkeley: Gingko Press, 2003), 91.

14. McLuhan, *Understanding Media*, 43.

15. McLuhan, *Understanding Media*, 90–91.

16. Ong, *Orality and Literacy*, 164.

17. See especially Jacques Derrida, *Of Grammatology*, trans. Gayatri Chakravorty Spivak (Baltimore: Johns Hopkins University Press, 1976), 75–76, and Jacques Derrida, *de la Grammatologie* (Paris: Editions de Minuit, 1967), 108.

18. İlker Aytürk, "Introduction: Romanisation in Comparative Perspective," *Journal of the Royal Asiatic Society*, Third Series, 20 (1) (January 2010): 1–9.

19. Aytürk's own contributions to such a study, depending on this definition, introduce two very useful terms: first, the notion of "script conversion" (to describe the moment of enforcing the switch from one writing system to another); and then also the notion of "script charisma," above all to emphasize the hegemony of the roman alphabet over this historical period. In addition to the limitation discussed in what follows, it is worth noting, though, that Aytürk's approach emphasizes top-down reforms such as Turkey's, rather than less centralized changes such as the shift to romanized Malay in the Indonesian context. Aytürk, "Introduction."

20. In the special issue, edited by Aytürk, there is an especially interesting essay by Nanette Gottlieb devoted to this and other related Japanese language reform debates. Nanette Gottlieb, "The Romaji Movement in Japan," *Journal of the Royal Asiatic Society*, Third Series, 20 (1) (January 2010).

21. Coulmas, *Writing Systems*, 102.

22. Zhong, *Chinese Grammatology*, 41.

23. For an account of the OED's key role in "Standard English" see Tony Crowley, *Standard English and the Politics of Language*, second edition (London: Palgrave Macmillan, 2003).

24. Sarah Ogilvie, *Words of the World: A Global History of the Oxford English Dictionary* (New York: Cambridge University Press, 2012), Chapter 5.

25. See also the "General Explanations" section of the OED's "Introduction" for further discussion of the classification of words considered "adopted," xi.

26. The fact that the phonetic ideal depends on the authority of written evidence to support its prioritizing the spoken over the written word is a characteristic feature of Derrida's argument about the way "phonocentrism" and "logocentrism" characteristically work. See, in particular, Derrida, *Of Grammatology*, 88, and Jacques Derrida, *The Beast & the Sovereign*, Volume I, trans. Geoffrey Bennington (Chicago: University of Chicago Press, 2009), 347.

27. Addressing the fundamental, sociolinguistic question of the relation between language and writing, Coulmas notes: "Two questions linguists should not sidestep are: 'What happens when a language is written down, (1) in terms of linguistic description, and (2) in terms of linguistic evolution?'" (Coulmas, *Writing Systems*, 11). Both questions are relevant in the case of this (and indeed each and every) OED entry, and as applied all at once to transcription and transliteration: what happens when another language (Malay) is transcribed (into English); and what happens when that language is transcribed from one script into another?

28. For accounts of this historical shift see Henk Maier, "Boredom in Batavia: A Catalogue of Books in 1898," in *Text/Politics in Island Southeast Asia: Essays in Interpretation*, ed. D. M. Roskies (Athens: Ohio University Press, 1993), 131–56; Henk Maier, *We Are Playing Relatives: A Survey of Malay Writing* (Leiden: KITLV, 2004); and Claudine Salmon, *Literature in Malay by the Chinese of Indonesia* (Montreal: Association Archipel, 1981).

29. Benedict Anderson, *Language and Power* (Ithaca: Cornell University Press, 1990), 124.

30. Pramoedya Ananta Toer, *Tempo Doeloe: Antologi Sastra Pra-Indonesia* (Hasta Mitra, 1982).

31. The online edition dates this revised version of the entry to 1986, in Volume IV, the Supplement.

32. This might surely also be related to the decision to drop the double horizontal lines (called "tramlines") formerly used to indicate foreign loanwords from the 1933 Supplement. See Sarah Ogilvie's *Words of the World*, Chapter 5 for a study of the case of the "vanishing tramlines."

33. Ogilvie, *Words of the World*.

34. I develop such a reading in Christopher GoGwilt, *The Invention of the West: Joseph Conrad and the Double-Mapping of Europe and Empire* (Redwood City: Stanford University Press, 1995), Chapter 3. See also Robert Hampson, *Cross-Cultural Encounters in Joseph Conrad's Malay Fiction* (London: Palgrave Macmillan, 2000); Andrew Francis, *Culture and Commerce in Conrad's Asian Fiction* (New York: Cambridge University Press, 2015); Heliéna Krenn, *Conrad's Lingard Trilogy: Empire, Race, and Women in the Malay Novels* (New York: Garland, 1990); and Agnes S. K. Yeow, *Conrad's Eastern Vision: A Vain and Floating Appearance* (London: Palgrave Macmillan, 2009).

35. *The Collected Letters of Joseph Conrad*, 9 Volumes, ed. Frederick Karl and Laurence Davies (New York: Cambridge University Press, 1983–2008), volume 2: 60.

36. Aristotle, *On the Art of Poetry*, trans. S. H. Butcher et al (Indianapolis: Bobbs-Merrill, 1981), 10–11 (sections 1449 - 1551).

37. Cf. Ricoeur's theorization of the relation between all these different levels of narrative. Paul Ricouer, *Time and Narrative*, Volume 1, trans. Kathleen McLaughlin and David Pellauer (Chicago: University of Chicago Press, 1984).

38. *Collected Letters*, Volume 2, 59. Characteristically, Conrad's letter begins with complaints about his work (specifically about the difficulties in writing *The Rescue*): "Wrist bad again, baby ill, wife frightened, damned worry about my work and about other things, a fit of such stupidity that I could not think out a single sentence—excuses enough in all conscience, since I am not the master but the slave of the peripeties and accidents (generally beastly) of existence."

39. Restoring this phrase to the OED's original citation—from which it is dropped in subsequent editions—it is tempting to read this as "there is no Arab *script* here" and with reference to the disappearance of Arabic script from the OED.

40. McLuhan, *Understanding Media*, 144.

41. Ong, *Orality and Literacy*, 133.

42. Derrida, *Of Grammatology* (see esp. 27–73).

43. Lydia Liu, *The Freudian Robot: Digital Media and the Future of the Unconscious* (Chicago: University of Chicago Press, 2010), 113.

44. Liu, *The Freudian Robot*, 114.

45. Margaret Cezair-Thompson, "The Blank Spaces of *Heart of Darkness*," *Conradiana* 48 (2–3) (Fall/Winter 2016): 169–86.

46. Leila Aboulela's novel *The Translator* draws attention to the romanized form of Arabic African names in her rewriting of Marlow's map-pointing scene from the perspective of the Sudanese translator who, seeing "somewhere in [the] vast yellow" of a map of Africa "the life she had been exiled from," is "moved" by the "familiar names of towns, in black type against the yellow . . . Kassala, Darfur, Sennar. Kadugli, Karima, Wau." Leila Aboulela, *The Translator* (Shelter Island: Black Cat, 2007), 16.

47. N. Katherine Hayles, *How We Became Posthuman* (Chicago: University of Chicago Press, 1999), 103, 43.

48. N. Katherine Hayles, *My Mother Was a Computer: Digital Subjects and Literary Texts* (Chicago: University of Chicago Press, 2005), 33. Hayles expresses concern for the linear causality implied by "remediation"; but see also Amaranth Borsuk on the usefulness of this term, in Amaranth Borsuk, *The Book* (Cambridge: MIT Press, 2016), 202.

49. Tekla Mecsnóber, *Rewriting Joyce's Europe: The Politics of Language and Visual Design* (Gainesville: University of Florida Press, 2021), 80.

50. Mecsnóber, *Rewriting Joyce's Europe*, 81.

51. Mecsnóber, *Rewriting Joyce's Europe*.

52 See Moshe Gold, "Printing the Dragon's Bite: Joyce's Poetic History of Thoth, Cadmus, and Gutenberg in *Finnegans Wake*," *James Joyce Quarterly* 42/43 (1/4) (Summer 2006) for a discussion of the *Wake*'s elaboration of numerous different forms of writing and script.

53. As discussed by Mecsnóber, *Rewriting Joyce's Europe*, 74 ff.

54. Mecsnóber, *Rewriting Joyce's Europe*, 85.

55. Incidentally, the word English itself may be embedded in the final sequence of the sentence in which "iSpace" appears: "by pùnct! **ingh oles** (sic) in iSpace?" (my emphasis).

56. This is the punning allusion to "Basic English" in *Finnegans Wake*: "For if the lingo gasped between kicksheets, however basically English, were to be preached from the mouths of wickerchurchwardens and metaphysicians . . ." James Joyce, *Finnegans Wake* (London: Faber and Faber, [1939] 1979), 116.

57. Hayles, *How We Became Posthuman*, 43.

58. See also Garrett Stewart, *Between Film and Screen: Modernism's Photo Synthesis* (Chicago: University of Chicago Press, 1999).

59. Liu, *The Freudian Robot*, 47.

60. McLuhan, *Understanding Media*, 119.

61. McLuhan, *Understanding Media*, 152.
62. Laurent Milesi, "Metaphors of the Quest in *Finnegans Wake*" in *Finnegans Wake: Fifty Years*, ed. Gert Lernout (Amsterdam: Rodopi, 1990), 79–85.
63. Joseph Conrad, "Geography and Some Explorers" in *Last Essays: The Cambridge Edition of the Works of Joseph Conrad*, ed. Harold Ray Stevens and J. H. Stape (New York: Cambridge University Press, 2011), 14.
64. Adrian Wisnicki, "Victorian Field Notes from the Lualaba River, Congo" *Scottish Geographical Journal*, 129 (3–4) (2013): 210–39.
65. Cited in Milesi, "Metaphors of the Quest," 83.
66. Milesi, "Metaphors of the Quest," 84.
67. Milesi, "Metaphors of the Quest," 85.
68. See Liu, *The Freudian Robot*, 47.

Chapter 2. The Russian Face of Romanization: The K in Conrad and Kafka

1. *The Collected Letters of Joseph Conrad, 9 volumes*, ed. Frederick Karl and Laurence Davies (New York: Cambridge University Press, 1983–2008), Volume 7, 641.
2. *Collected Letters*, Volume 6, 77.
3. *Collected Letters*, Volume 4, 108.
4. *Collected Letters*, Volume 3, 492.
5. For discussion of the "Familiar Preface" (with particular attention to the K added to his signature) see Jean Szczypien, "Untyrannical Copy-Texts for the Prefatory Essays to Joseph Conrad's *A Personal Record*," *Conradiana* 9 (2) (1984): 81–89, and Jean Szcypien, "*Sailing Towards Poland*" *With Joseph Conrad* (Lausanne: Peter Lang, 2017), Chapter 8.
6. The Cyrillic script was modeled on the Greek alphabet at the beginning of the tenth century. In its origins, then, it shares a historical relation to that development of "the alphabet" as Ong articulates it in *Orality and Literacy* (Walter Ong, *Orality and Literacy: The Technologizing of the Word* (New York: Routledge, 2002), 84 ff). Later, under Peter the Great's reforms, Cyrillic was brought closer to Latin letters. See Roman Jakobson, *Slavic Languages: A Condensed Survey*, second edition (New York: King's Crown Press, 1955), 11.
7. Mikhail Bakhtin, *The Dialogic Imagination*, trans. Caryl Emerson and ed. by Michael Holquist (Austin: University of Texas Press, 1981), 250.
8. David R. Smith, ed. "The Hidden Narrative: The K in Conrad," in *Joseph Conrad's Under Western Eyes: Beginnings, Revisions, Final Forms* (North Haven: Archon Books, 1991), 39–81, and Szczypien, "*Sailing Towards Poland*," offer contrasting readings of the significance of Conrad's compulsive addition of K's in the margins of his manuscripts, Smith emphasizing their vexed psychological significance, Szczypien emphasizing their affirmation of his Polish identity. Johan Adam Warodell briefly discusses the "abundance" of K's in his study of Conrad's doodles, although he dismisses the significance Smith attaches to the letter K itself.

See Johan Adam Warodell, *Conrad's Decentered Fiction* (Cambridge: Cambridge University Press, 2022), 27.

9. Faith Hillis, *Children of Rus': Right-bank Ukraine and the Invention of Russia* (Ithaca: Cornell University Press, 2013), 3.

10. Laurence Davies notes that in the towns where Conrad grew up (Berdychiv, Zhytomyr and Chernihiv) "at least four secular languages were spoken—Ukrainian (then known as Ruthenian), Russian (the language of authority), Yiddish and Polish; three sacred languages were in ritual use—Hebrew, Latin and Church Slavonic; and in the Korzeniowski family there were books to read and to translate in French and English." Laurence Davies, "Afterword," in *Conrad and Language*, ed. Katherine Baxter and Robert Hampson (Edinburgh: Edinburgh University Press, 2016), 204–5.

11. Yasemin Yildiz, *Beyond the Mother Tongue: The Postmonolingual Condition* (New York: Fordham University Press, 2012), 2.

12. Yildiz, *Beyond the Mother Tongue*, 31.

13. Yildiz, *Beyond the Mother Tongue*, 34.

14. Walter Benjamin, *Illuminations: Essays and Reflections*, trans. Harry Zohn (New York: Schocken, 1969), 119.

15. Gilles Deleuze and Félix Guattari, *Kafka: Toward a Minor Literature*, trans. Dana Polan (Minneapolis: University of Minnesota Press, 1986), 18.

16. Yildiz, *Beyond the Mother Tongue*, 31.

17. Vladimir Yefimov, "Civil Type and Kis Cyrillic," in *Language, Culture, Type: International Type Design in the Age of Unicode*, ed. John Berry (Zürich: Graphis, 2002), 128.

18. Yefimov, "Civil Type," 140.

19. I. J. Gelb, *A Study of Writing*, revised edition (Chicago: University of Chicago Press, 1963), 240.

20. Hillis, *Children of Rus'*, 3.

21. See Andreas Renner, "Defining a Russian Nation: Mikhail Katkov and the 'Invention' of National Politics," *SEER* 81 (4) (October 2003): 659–82.

22. Hillis, *Children of Rus'*, 4–5.

23. Hillis, *Children of Rus'*, 66 ff.

24. Johannes Remy, "The Ukrainian Alphabet as a Political Question in the Russian Empire Before 1876," *Ab Imperio* 2 (2005): 167–90.

25. A recent graphic example of the politicization of scripts in the relation between Russia and Ukraine concerns the spelling of Ukraine's capital. Formerly Kiev, a transliteration from Russian Cyrillic Киев, U.S. newspapers now spell it Kyiv, a transliteration from the Ukrainian Cyrillic Ки́їв. For more on the contemporary politics of the relation between Russian and Ukrainian, see Timothy Snyder, "The War in Ukraine Has Unleashed a New Word," *The New York Times*, April 22, 2022.

26. David Damrosch, "Scriptworlds: Writing Systems and the Formation of World Literature," *Modern Language Quarterly* 68 (2) (June 2007): 195–219.

27. See Andrzej Busza's "Rhetoric and Ideology in Conrad's *Under Western Eyes*," in *Joseph Conrad: A Commemoration*, ed. Norman Sherry (New York: Macmillan,

1976), 105–18; Keith Carabine, *The Life and the Art: A Study of Conrad's Under Western Eyes* (Amsterdam: Rodopi, 1996); and Daniel Darvay, "The Politics of Gothic in Conrad's *Under Western Eyes,*" *Modern Fiction Studies* 55 (4) (Winter 2009): 693–715.

28. Mikhail Bakhtin, *Problems of Dostoevsky's Poetics,* ed. and trans. Caryl Emerson (Minneapolis: University of Minnesota Press, 1984), 74.

29. Mikhail Bakhtin, *The Dialogic Imagination,* trans. Caryl Emerson and Michael Holquist (Austin: University of Texas Press, 1981), 348.

30. For an excellent, succinct account of this multiple layering of texts see Shafquat Towheed, "Geneva v. St. Petersburg: Two Concepts of Literary Property and the Material Lives of Books in *Under Western Eyes,*" *Book History* 10 (2007): 169–91.

31. Jakob Lothe, *Conrad's Narrative Method* (Oxford: Clarendon, 1989), 263, 288.

32. For a rich assessment of the ("topodialogic") significance of this contrast for the structure of *Under Western Eyes,* see Paul Kirschner, "Topodialogic Narrative in *Under Western Eyes* and the Rasoumoffs of 'La Petite Russie'" in *Conrad's Cities: Essays for Hans van Marle,* ed. Gene Moore (Amsterdam: Rodopi, 1992).

33. This early semiotic link between faces and script is itself overdetermined by the fact that this description is ascribed to the "newspapers."

34. In *The Location of Culture,* Homi Bhabha's reading of *Heart of Darkness* emphasizes the importance of Marlow's discovery of the English book on seamanship (Homi Bhabha, *The Location of Culture* [New York: Routledge, 1994], 102–22). Asako Nakai points out that Bhabha elides the significance of the "ciphered marginalia" in the margins of that English book (Asako Nakai, *The English Book and its Marginalia* [Amsterdam: Rodopi, 2000], 27).

35. This is the focus of my 1995 book, *The Invention of the West.* Although the irony of Conrad's title remains as current as ever, given the ongoing permutations in the ideological formation and deformation of notions of "the West," this current project aims to undo the rhetorical power of this geopolitical term by turning attention to the phenomenon of "romanization," a phenomenon that has all the appearance of being synonymous with "westernization," but *also* reveals something more like its opposite.

36. Gelb, *A Study of Writing,* 240.

37. David Smith notes that "virtually every use of the word 'write' triggers" Conrad to write K in the margins of the manuscript (cited in Szczypien, "*Sailing Towards Poland,*" 206).

38. See Robert Hampson, "Conrad's Rites of Entry and Return" in *Migration, Modernity and Transnationalism,* ed. Kim Salmons and Tania Zulli (London: Bloomsbury, 2021), 17–34 (19).

39. Compare Bernhard Siegert's reading of this as part of a much broader "project designed by designs." As a part of what I am calling the chronotope of authorship, Conrad's cartographic design reveals that what Siegert labels "the projective recoding of the occidental subject as a design," is inextricably encoded in

the phenomenon of romanization. Bernhard Siegert, *Cultural Techniques: Grids, Filters, Doors, and Other Articulations of the Real*, trans. Geoffrey Winthrop-Young (New York: Fordham University Press, 2015), 131–32.

40. Agnieszka Adamowicz-Pośpiech, "From Berdyczów to Bishopsbourne: Conrad's real and imaginary journeys," in Salmons and Zulli, *Migration, Modernity and Transnationalism*, 51–71 (52).

41. There is an underlying pun on "sea" and "C" in the transposition from K to C, emphasized by the almost anagrammatical play on "letters" throughout (e.g. "the love of letters does not make a literary man, any more than the love of the sea makes a seaman" [*Record*, 108])—which is made almost explicit in the "Familiar Preface" comment on the design of the whole "bit of a psychological document" (*Record*, xx) as it moves toward "my first contact with the sea" (*Record*, xxi).

42. *Collected Letters*, Volume 8, 290.

43. Cf. Derrida's formulation of the term "mondialatinisation" in Jacques Derrida, *Foi et Savoir* (Paris: Editions de Seuil, 2000), translated as "globalatinization" in Gil Anidjar, *Acts of Religion: Jacques Derrida* (New York: Routledge, 2002).

44. Giorgio Agamben, "K," in *Nudities* trans. David Kishik and Stefan Pedatella (Redwood City: Stanford University Press, 2011), 20–36.

45. Yildiz, *Beyond the Mother Tongue*, 34.

46. Peter Hutchinson, "Kafka's Private Alphabet," *The Modern Language Review* 106 (3) (July 2011): 797–813 (801).

47. Tim Beasley-Murray, "German-Language Culture and the Slav Stranger Within" *Central Europe* 4 (2) (November 2006): 131–45.

48. Franz Kafka, *The Castle*, trans. Willa and Edwin Muir (New York: Penguin, 1977), 7–8.

49. Deleuze and Guattari, *Kafka*, 29.

50. Deleuze and Guattari, *Kafka*, 88.

51. Deleuze and Guattari, *Kafka*, 18.

52. Réda Bensmaïa, "Foreword" to Deleuze and Guattari, *Kafka*, xi.

53. Theodor Adorno, *Prisms*, trans. Samuel and Shierry Weber (Cambridge: MIT Press, 1997), 246.

54. Adorno, *Prisms*, 251; Theodor Adorno, *Prismen: Kulturkritik und Gesellschaft* (Berlin: Suhrkamp, 1976), 312.

55. I would further suggest comparing the way in which readers jump to the conclusion that Kafka's work is allegorical to the way in which so many readers assume that Conrad's "West" coincides with the term "the West" as used today.

56. Adorno, *Prisms*, 246.

57. Franz Kafka, *Sämtliche Erzählungen* (Frankfurt: Fischer, 1981), 107.

58. Kafka, *Sämtliche*.

59. Kafka, *Sämtliche*, 104.

60. Kafka, *Sämtliche*, 118.

61. Kafka, *Sämtliche*, 117.

62. Deleuze and Guattari, *Kafka*, 39.
63. Deleuze and Guattari, *Kafka*, 39–40.
64. Bensmaïa, "Foreword" to Deleuze and Guattari, *Kafka*, xi.
65. Bakhtin, *The Dialogic Imagination*, 250.
66. Deleuze and Guattari, *Kafka*, 16.
67. Deleuze and Guattari, *Kafka*.
68. Deleuze and Guattari, *Kafka*, 23–24.
69. Deleuze and Guattari, *Kafka*, 23.
70. Deleuze and Guattari, *Kafka*, 107.
71. Russell Samolsky, *Apocalyptic Futures: Marked Bodies and the Violence of the Text in Kafka, Conrad, and Coetzee* (New York: Fordham University Press, 2011), 55.
72. Yildiz, *Beyond the Mother Tongue*, 58.
73. Deleuze and Guattari, *Kafka*, 39.
74. Deleuze and Guattari, *Kafka*, 82.
75. Deleuze and Guattari, *Kafka*, 84.
76. Bakhtin, *The Dialogic Imagination*, 272.
77. Bakhtin, *The Dialogic Imagination*, 349.
78. Bakhtin, *The Dialogic Imagination*, 423.
79. Bakhtin, *The Dialogic Imagination*, 357.

Chapter 3. The Chinese Character of Romanization: Conrad and Lu Xun

1. Lydia Liu, *The Freudian Robot: Digital Media and the Future of the Unconscious* (Chicago: University of Chicago Press, 2010), 27.
2. As Derrida puts it, "The concept of Chinese writing . . . functioned as a sort of European hallucination." Jacques Derrida, *Of Grammatology* trans. Gayatri Chakravorty Spivak (Baltimore: Johns Hopkins University Press, 1976), 80.
3. Christopher Bush, *Ideographic Modernism: China, Writing, Media* (New York: Oxford University Press, 2010).
4. Bush, *Ideographic Modernism*, xxvii.
5. Jing Tsu, *Sound and Script in Chinese Diaspora* (Cambridge: Harvard University Press, 2010), 2 ff.
6. Jing Tsu, *Sound and Script*, 192–93.
7. Jing Tsu, *Kingdom of Characters: The Language Revolution that Made China Modern* (New York: Riverhead Books, 2022), 37.
8. Yurou Zhong, *Chinese Grammatology: Script Revolution and Literary Modernity, 1916–1958* (New York: Columbia University Press, 2019), 7.
9. Thomas Mullaney, *The Chinese Typewriter: A History* (Cambridge: MIT Press, 2018), 15.
10. Cited in Zhong, *Chinese Grammatology*, 2.
11. Cited in Mullaney, *The Chinese Typewriter*, 13.
12. Lu Xun, "Voiceless China," in *Jottings Under Lamplight*, ed. Eileen J. Cheng and Kirk Denton (Cambridge: Harvard University Press, 2017), 167.

13. See https://www.marxists.org/chinese/reference-books/luxun/12/023.htm.
14. Lu Xun, *Jottings Under Lamplight*, 169.
15. Zhong, *Chinese Grammatology*, 16.
16. Cited in Zhong, *Chinese Grammatology*, 16.
17. Zhong, *Chinese Grammatology*, 28.
18. Zhong, *Chinese Grammatology*, 73.
19. Zhong, *Chinese Grammatology*, 6–7 and passim.
20. Zhong, *Chinese Grammatology*, 18–19.
21. Zhong, *Chinese Grammatology*, 19.
22. Zhong, *Chinese Grammatology*, 37.
23. Tsu, *Kingdom of Characters*, 192.
24. Zhong, *Chinese Grammatology*, 28.
25. Tsu, *Kingdom of Characters*, see, in particular, Chapter 5.
26. One of the chapters of Jing Tsu's *Kingdom of Characters* is entitled "When 'Peking' became 'Beijing.'" It is in this chapter that Tsu discusses the moment, in 1958, that Zhong signals as the end (or containment) of the script revolution. Jing Tsu's account emphasizes the diasporic complexity of script reforms in giving rise to *pinyin*, focusing on the Central Asian, Dunganese experiments with romanization that influenced both Soviet and Chinese innovations. Tsu, *Kingdom of Characters*.
27. Cf. Friedrich Kittler, *Discourse Networks 1800/1900*, trans. Michael Metteer and Chris Cullens (Redwood City: Stanford University Press, 1990).
28. For an extensive discussion of the significance of the QWERTY keyboard in mediating Chinese characters, see Mullaney, *The Chinese Typewriter*, 239 ff.
29. Andrew Francis, "Languages in Conrad's Malay Fiction," in *Conrad and Language*, ed. Katherine Isobel Baxter and Robert Hampson (Edinburgh: Edinburgh University Press, 2016), 132–50, 133.
30. Cedric Watts, *The Deceptive Text: An Introduction to Covert Plots* (Hempstead: Harvester Press, 1984), esp. Chapter 5.
31. Benedict Anderson, *Imagined Communities: Reflections on the Origins and Spread of Nationalism*, revised edition (New York: Verso, 1991), 36–46.
32. Anderson, *Imagined Communities*, 43.
33. Anderson, *Imagined Communities*, 40–41.
34. Christopher GoGwilt, "Pramoedya's Fiction and History: An Interview with Indonesian Novelist Pramoedya Ananta Toer," *Yale Journal of Criticism* 9 (1) (1996): 147–64; 156.
35. One useful theoretical point of reference for the articulation of the relation between history and fiction may be found in Paul Ricoeur, *Time and Narrative*, Volume 1, trans. Kathleen McLaughlin and David Pellauer (Chicago: University of Chicago Press, 1984).
36. For an especially resonant rescripting of *Almayer's Folly*, see Julie Napolin's reading of the Chantal Ackerman film based on *Almayer's Folly*, *La folie Almayer*. Julie Napolin, *The Fact of Resonance: Modernist Acoustics and Narrative Form* (New York: Fordham University Press, 2020), 59–66.

37. For more on this, see my discussion in Christopher GoGwilt, *The Passage of Literature: Genealogies of Modernism in Conrad, Rhys, and Pramoedya* (New York: Oxford University Press, 2011), Chapter 2.

38. I am indebted to G. J. Resink for this insight. GoGwilt, *The Passage of Literature*, 52, 263.

39. Claudine Salmon, *Literature in Malay by the Chinese of Indonesia* (Montreal: Association Archipel, 1981); Henk Maier, "Boredom in Batavia: A Catalogue of Books in 1898," in *Text/Politics in Island Southeast Asia: Essays in Interpretation*, ed. D. M. Roskies (Athens: Ohio University Press, 1993), 131–56; Henk Maier, *We Are Playing Relatives: A Survey of Malay Writing* (Leiden: KITLV, 2004); James Siegel, *Fetish, Recognition, Revolution* (Princeton: Princeton University Press, 1997); Benedict Anderson, *Language and Power* (Ithaca: Cornell University Press, 1990); and Pramoedya Ananta Toer, *Tempo Doeloe: Antologi Sastra Pra-Indonesia* (Hasta Mitra, 1982).

40. Terry Collits, "Imperialism, Marxism, Conrad: A Political Reading of *Victory*." *Textual Practice* 3 (3) (1989): 1–18.

41. See Gene Moore on the ethnographic classification "Alfuro." The impossibility of determining what ethnographic group "Alfuro" refers to, stands in dialectical counterpoint to the way the term "Chinese" works in the novel. Gene Moore, "Who Are the Alfuros?" *Conradiana* 39 (3) (Fall 2007): 198–210.

42. Consider, further, the way that the narrator also emphasizes a contradiction in his own Chinese stereotyping of Davidson's owner: "He was small and wizened—which was strange, because generally a Chinaman, as he grows in prosperity, puts on inches of girth and stature." *Victory*, 30.

43. Peter Hitchcock, *The Long Space: Transnationalism and Postcolonial Form* (Redwood City: Stanford University Press, 2010).

44. See Fredric Jameson's *The Political Unconscious: Narrative as a Socially Symbolic Act* (Ithaca: Cornell University Press, 1981).

45. This is what I attempt to theorize in *The Passage of Literature* (especially in the final chapter "Postcolonial Philology and the Passage of Literature"). GoGwilt, *The Passage of Literature*.

46. Lydia Liu, *Translingual Practice: Literature, National Culture, and Translated Modernity—China, 1900–1937* (Redwood City: Stanford University Press, 1995), 47. My reading of Lu Xun's story follows that of Lydia Liu and Rey Chow. For another assessment of Lu Xun's place in Chinese modernism see Shu-Mei Shih, *The Lure of the Modern: Writing Modernism in Semicolonial China, 1917–1937* (Oakland: University of California Press, 2001), see especially 73–91. For contrasting perspectives on Lu Xun's importance for anglophone, Chinese writers in diaspora, see Ha Jin's "Introduction" to the Norton edition of *Selected Stories of Lu Hsun* (New York: W.W. Norton, 2003), and Yiyun Li's "Afterword" to the Penguin edition of Lu Xun, *The Real Story of Ah-Q and Other Tales of China: The Complete Fiction of Lu Xun*, trans. Julia Lovell (New York: Penguin, 2009).

47. Walter Benjamin, *Illuminations: Essays and Reflections*, trans. Harry Zohn (New York: Schocken, 1969), 219. The German reads (all in italics in the original): "*Um neunzehnhundert hatte die technische Reproduktion einen Standard erreicht, auf dem sie nicht nur die Gesamtheit der überkommenen Kunstwerke zu ihrem Objekt zu machen und deren Wirkung den tiefsten Veränderungen zu unterwerfen begann, sondern sich einen eigenen Platz unter den künstlerischen Verfahrungsweisen eroberte.*" (Walter Benjamin, *Illuminationen* (Berlin: Suhrkamp, 1977), 138–39.

48. Bush, *Ideographic Modernism*, 21–22.

49. See Arnold T. Schwab, "Conrad's American Speeches and His Reading from *Victory*," *Modern Philology* 62 (May 1965): 342–47, (345).

50. Schwab, "Conrad's American Speeches": 346.

51. The Chinese term for the technology is *dian ying* (电影), the term used today for "film." But in Lu Xun's time it likely meant something more like Conrad's "cinematograph" or a still-image slide projector.

52. Lu Xun, *The Real Story*, 17.

53. Lu Xun, *The Real Story*.

54. Liu, *Translingual Practice*, 63.

55. Rey Chow, *Primitive Passions: Visuality, Sexuality, Ethnography and Contemporary Chinese Cinema* (New York: Columbia University Press, 1995), 5.

56. Chow, *Primitive Passions*.

57. Chow, *Primitive Passions*, 10.

58. Chow, *Primitive Passions*, 14.

59. Chow, *Primitive Passions*. Lydia Liu also offers a brilliant, extended reading of this famous passage in Liu, *Translingual Practice*, 60–69.

60. Chow, *Primitive Passions*, 18.

61. Lu Xun, *The Real Story*, 18. In a more banal form of juxtaposing Chinese characters and roman letters, the "Preface" also uses the roman letter K to mark the Japanese medical school in Nanking—Kiangnan Naval Academy—where Lu Xun wanted to go.

62. This coincides, too, with what Yurou Zhong calls the emergence of "Chinese grammatology": "as a representative of nonalphabetic writing systems undergoing script reforms, the Chinese script ended up reconfiguring the basis of grammatology (the science of writing) as well as its politics in the short twentieth century." Zhong, *Chinese Grammatology*, 3.

63. Lu Xun, *The Real Story*, 17; my emphasis.

64. Benjamin, *Illuminations*, 226. The German text reads: "Sie fordern schon eine Rezeption in bestimmtem Sinne. Ihnen ist die freischwebende Kontemplation nicht mehr angemessen. Sie beunruhigen den Betrachter; er fühlt: zu ihnen muß er einen bestimmten Weg suchen. Wegweiser beginnen ihm gleichzeitig die illustrierten Zeitungen aufzustellen. Richtige oder falsche—gleichviel. In ihnen ist die Beschriftung zum ersten Mal obligat geworden. Und es ist klar, daß sie einen ganz anderen Charakter hat als der Titel eines Gemäldes. Die Direktiven, die der Betrachter von Bildern in der illustrierten Zeitschrift durch die Beschriftung erhält,

werden bald darauf noch präziser und gebieterischer im Film, wo die Auffassung von jedem einzelenen Bild durch die Folge aller vorangegangenen vorgeschrieben erscheint." Benjamin, *Illuminationen*, 148.

65. For an especially rich example of this kind of Conrad scholarship, see Stephen Donovan, *Joseph Conrad and Popular Culture* (London: Palgrave Macmillan, 2005), 20 and passim.

66. Liu, *Translingual Practice*, 75.

67. Liu, *Translingual Practice*.

68. Liu, *Translingual Practice*, 72.

69. Watts, *The Deceptive Text*, 109.

70. See in particular Fatimah Tobing Rony, *The Third Eye: Race, Cinema, and Ethnographic Spectacle* (Durham: Duke University Press, 1996).

71. Watts, *The Deceptive Text*, 109.

72. See Alfred Hitchcock's discussion of this montage-effect attributed to Kuleshov in François Truffaut, *Hitchcock*, revised edition (New York: Simon & Schuster, 1985), 214. See also the novel, *Disoriental*, whose narrator notes, "The years of the Russian Revolution were an opportunity for many filmmakers to experiment with, and theorize about, the art of cinematography. Around 1921 two of them, Lev Kuleshov and Vsevolod Pudovkin, carried out an experiment known as the Kuleshov effect, or K-effect, in an attempt to explain the crucial impact of film editing on the human mind." Négar Djavadi, *Disoriental*, trans. Tina Kover (Madrid: Europa, 2018), 135.

Chapter 4. Sanskritization, Romanization, Digitization

1. Sheldon Pollock, *The Language of the Gods and the World of Men: Sanskrit, Culture, and Power in Premodern India* (Oakland: University of California Press, 2006), 11 f.

2. Benedict Anderson, *Imagined Communities: Reflections on the Origin and Spread of Nationalism*, revised edition (New York: Verso, 1991), esp. 44 ff.

3. Pollock, *The Language of Gods*, 273.

4. Lydia Liu, *The Freudian Robot: Digital Media and the Future of the Unconscious* (Chicago: University of Chicago Press, 2010), 27

5. See Sanjay Krishnan, "Native Agent: Abdullah bin Abdul Kadir's Global Perspective," in *Reading the Global: Troubling Perspectives on Britain's Empire in Asia* (New York: Columbia University Press, 2007), 95–131. See also the parenthetical reference to Abdullah's work in Pramoedya Ananta Toer, *Realisme-Sosialis dan Sastra Indonesia* (Jakarta: Lentera Dipantra, 2003), 115.

6. Abdullah bin Abdul Kadir, *The Hikayat Abdullah*, trans. A. H. Hill, *Journal of the Malayan Branch of the Royal Asiatic Society* 28 (3:171) (June 1955): 147.

7. Cited in Sanjay Krishnan, *Reading the Global*, 116.

8. Ha Jin, *The Writer as Migrant* (Chicago: University of Chicago Press, 2008), 42.

9. Michel Foucault, *The Order of Things: An Archaeology of the Human Sciences* (New York: Vintage, 1973), especially Chapter 8; Edward Said, *Orientalism* (New

York: Vintage, 1979), 22 and passim. See also Vinay Dharwadker, "Orientalism and the Study of Indian Literatures," in *Orientalism and the Postcolonial Predicament*, ed. Carol Breckenridge and Peter van der Veer (Philadelphia: University of Pennsylvania Press, 1993), 158–83.

10. Pollock, *The Language of Gods*, 11.

11. Pollock, *The Language of Gods*, 273.

12. Pollock, *The Language of Gods*.

13. Pollock, *The Language of Gods*, 273–74.

14. See A. H. Hill's note #18, Abdullah bin Abdul Kadir, *The Hikayat Abdullah*, 305.

15. Wilhelm von Humboldt, *Über die Kawi-Sprache auf der Insel Java nebst einer Einleitung über die Verschiedenheit des menschlichen Sprachbaues und ihren Einfluß auf die geistige Entwickelung des Menschengeschlechts* (Berlin, 1836), x (my translation). Peter Heath translates this: "A true literature can arise, and this for internal reasons of linguistic culture itself, only with a script that is simultaneously given and comes into use" in Wilhelm von Humboldt, *On Language: The Diversity of Human Language-Structure and its Influence on the Mental Development of Mankind*, trans. Peter Heath (New York: Cambridge University Press, 1988), 17.

16. "Humboldt wished to show that, since grammatical structure is the criterion of linguistic affinity, the Kawi language was Malayan in spite of its Indian vocabulary. It did not, therefore, as was maintained by some, stand in the same intimate relationship to Sanskrit as the Pali language. But seen in larger perspective, it was important by virtue of its geographical location, which linked it to practically all the known languages of the globe, from the African shores of the Indian Ocean to the west across the great archipelago in the middle to the Americas in the east and to China and India on the Asian mainland. In the Kawi he had late in life found the global vantage point that would enable him to achieve the synthesis he had always aimed for." Hans Aarsleff's, "Introduction" to Humboldt, *On Language*, xii.

17. My translation. Peter Heath's translation substitutes "On Language" for the original book's focus on the Kawi language in part because it is a translation only of the introduction to the longer work.

18. For an illuminating discussion of the ambitions—and limitations—of Humboldt's book, see Haun Saussy, *Great Walls of Discourse and Other Adventures in Cultural China* (Cambridge: Harvard University Press, 2001), Chapter 4. See also Hans Aarsleff's introduction to Peter Heath's translation in Humboldt, *On Language*, vii–lxv.

19. Humboldt, *Über die Kawi-Sprache*, x. For Peter Heath's translation, see Humboldt, *On Language*, 17.

20. Humboldt, *Über die Kawi-Sprache*, liv. For Heath's translation, see Humboldt, *On Language*, 47.

21. Humboldt, *Über die Kawi-Sprache*, xii–xvi; Humboldt, *On Language*, 7–9.

22. Humboldt, *Über die Kawi-Sprache*, see especially x, lxii, and cii.

23. Humboldt, *Über die Kawi-Sprache*, clii. For Heath's translation see Humboldt, *On Language*, 111.

24. In the early pages of the study of Kawi proper, Humboldt discusses the relation between the "Kawi-Alphabet" and *"Dêwanâgarî,"* naming the script, described in the preface on transliteration, simply as the "Sanskrit-Alphabet." See Humboldt, *Über die Kawi-Sprache*, 43. The preface explaining the system used to transliterate from the "Sanskrit-Alphabet" and "Javanese Alphabet," states that "Words like Java, Sanskrit, Pandit and others, that have appeared regularly in our print usage, I have neither altered nor burdened with additional diacritics." ("Wörter, die, wie Java, Sanskrit, Pandit und andere, schon völlig in unsren Büchergebrauch übergegangen sind, habe ich weder in ihrer Schreibung verändert, noch mit Zeichen überladen" [xi]). For Heath's translation see Humboldt, *On Language*, 7.

25. Jacques Derrida, *Of Grammatology*, translated by Gayatri Chakravorty Spivak (Baltimore: Johns Hopkins University Press, 1976), 75 ff.

26. Derrida, *Of Grammatology*, 33; Jacques Derrida, *De la Grammatologie* (Paris: Editions de Minuit, 1967), 48.

27. Ferdinand de Saussure, *Cours de linguistique géneral*e, ed. Tullio de Mauro (Paris: Payot, 1986), 48. My translation. Compare Wade Baskin's translation in Ferdinand de Saussure, *Course in General Linguistics*, trans. Wade Baskin, ed. Charles Bally and Albert Sechehaye (New York: Philosophical Library, 1959), 27.

28. Saussure, *Cours*, 64; Saussure, *Course*, 39.

29. In a footnote, special attention is made to some exceptions, and especially to the multiple problems posed by the letter K that crisscrosses Greek and Latin, but whose effect is described as a kind of back-formation. Another K-effect of romanization. See Saussure, *Cours*, 64–65; Saussure, *Course*, 39.

30. Humboldt already foreshadows Saussure's bracketing of Sanskrit as being too distant in historical time: "India, for us, recedes into too dark a distance for us to be capable of passing a judgement on its prehistory." (Humboldt, *On Language*, 40); "Indien geht für uns in zu dunkler Ferne hinauf, also daß wir über seine Vorzeit zu urtheilen im Stande wären." (Humboldt, *Über die Kawi-Sprache*, xliv)

31. Derrida, *Of Grammatology*, 71, 84; Derrida, *De la Grammatologie*, 99, 120. In the original French there is no grave accent on the final "e" of "gramme."

32. For the anusvari, however, the OED places a dot below the first "m" of *saṃskṛta* whereas the Tenth International Congress of Orientalists proposed a dot above the letter "m." See "Tenth International Congress of Orientalists, Held at Geneva," *The Journal of the Royal Asiatic Society of Great Britain and Ireland* (October 1895): 879–92; https://www.jstor.org/stable/25207765).

33. For a glimpse of the significance of English in mediating the politicization of Devanagari as an Indian (Hindi) nationalist script, see Arundhati Roy, "In What Language Does Rain Fall Over Tormented Cities," in *Azadi: Freedom, Fascism, Fiction* (Chicago: Haymarket, 2020).

34. Pramoedya Ananta Toer, *The Mute's Soliloquy: A Memoir* (New York: Hyperion East, 1999), 251; *Nyanyi Sunyi Seorang Bisu: Catatan-catatan dari Buru*, 2 Volumes (Jakarta: Lentera, 1995), Volume 1 (39). My translation.

35. For a discussion of language and caste in Pramoedya's *Arok Dedes*, see Annette Damayanti Lienau, "The Ideal of Casteless Language in Pramoedya's *Arok Dedes*," *Comparative Studies of Southeast Asia, Africa and the Middle East*, 32 (3) (2012): 591–603.

36. Pramoedya Ananta Toer, *House of Glass*, trans. Max Lane (New York: Penguin, 1992), iv.

37. Benedict Anderson, *The Spectre of Comparisons: Nationalism, Southeast Asia and the World* (New York: Verso, 1998), 293.

38. Haun Saussy, *Great Walls of Discourse*, 83.

39. N. Katherine Hayles, *How We Became Posthuman* (Chicago: University of Chicago Press, 1999), 43. The word "flicker," which Conrad's *Heart of Darkness* uses to mark the perspectival shift from Romanization to romanization—"We live in the flicker . . ." (*Heart*, 106)—acquires the technical, technological sense associated with cinematography (the "flicker effect") precisely over this period: see the OED, and note the first appearance of the word as related to cinematography in the 1933 Supplement. See also Garrett Stewart, "Modernism and the Flicker Effect," in *Between Film and Screen: Modernism's Photo Synthesis* (Chicago: University of Chicago Press, 1999), Chapter 7.

40. Leonard Bloomfield, *Language* (Austin: Holt, Rinehart & Winston, 1961), 208–9.

41. Cited in Ranajit Guha, *Elementary Aspects of Peasant Insurgency in Colonial India* (New York: Oxford University Press, 1994), 46.

42. The OED cites Bloomfield as a point of reference for the linguistic sense of the term "zero." Bloomfield, *Language*.

43. James Joyce, *Finnegans Wake* (London: Faber and Faber, 1979), 346.

44. Bloomfield's discussion of the "special accusative case-form" in the English use of "personal-definite substitutes" notes that some of the "possessive adjectives" derived from them "have a special form for zero anaphora" (Bloomfield, *Language*, 256). His analysis continues to focus on the grammatical forms *within* a language (English, French) rather than—as romanization demands we do here—across languages and scripts. Nonetheless, Bloomfield has just referred to the fact that, "Some languages, such as Japanese and Malay, distinguish several substitutes for both first and second persons, according to deferential relations between speaker and hearer" (Bloomfield, *Language*, 256) before he moves to the use of "a kind of closed system of *personal-definite* substitutes" in the cases of English and French. The juxtaposition calls out for consideration of what happens when the "deferential relations" collide with a "closed system of *personal-definite* substitutes." Perhaps "Kaspar! Makan!" is just such an example.

45. Christopher GoGwilt, *The Passage of Literature: Genealogies of Modernism in Conrad, Rhys, and Pramoedya* (New York: Oxford University Press, 2011), Chapter 6.

46. Pramoedya Ananta Toer, *This Earth of Mankind*, trans. Max Lane (New York: Penguin, 1996), 54; *bumi manusia*, 44.

47. Pramoedya Ananta Toer, *Tales from Djakarta: Caricatures of Circumstances and Their Human Beings* (Southeast Asia Program, Cornell University, 1999), 17. For an alternative translation, see James T. Siegel, *Fetish, Recognition, Revolution* (Princeton: Princeton University Press, 1997), 233.

48. Guha, *Elementary Aspects of Peasant Insurgency*, 46 ff.

49. Guha, *Elementary Aspects of Peasant Insurgency*, 47.

50. Arundhati Roy, *The Ministry of Utmost Happiness* (New York: Knopf, 2017), 8.

51. Roy, *The Ministry*.

52. See also Roy's own meditation on the "complicated map of languages that underpins" *The Ministry of Utmost Happiness* in Arundhati Roy, *Azadi: Freedom. Fascism. Fiction.* (Chicago: Haymarket, 2020), 32.

53. Christina Sharpe, *In the Wake: On Blackness and Being* (Durham: Duke University Press, 2016), 76–77.

54. As with Roy's novel, Sharpe's "wake" work seeks to theorize a "trans" experience that is not limited to "transgender," although it repeatedly involves "Euro-Western gender's dismantling" (Sharpe, *In the Wake*, 30). She marks the "trans" with an asterisk: "trans*"—"the asterisk after the word functions as the wildcard"—perhaps we might think of that affix, like the prefix "ana-" as the "zero anaphora" (this is Bloomfield's improvisation on the Sanskrit "lopa"), generated through the transcription, transliteration, and translation work of sanskritization, romanization, and digitization.

Bibliography

Abdullah bin Abdul Kadir. *The Hikayat Abdullah*. Translated by A. H. Hill. *Journal of the Malayan Branch of the Royal Asiatic Society*, Vol. 28 (3:171) (June 1955).
Aboulela, Leila. *The Translator*. Shelter Island: Black Cat, 1999.
Achebe, Chinua. *Hopes and Impediments: Selected Essays*. Albany: Anchor, 1989.
Adorno, Theodor. *Prismen: Kulturkritik und Gesellschaft*. Berlin: Suhrkamp, 1976.
———. *Prisms*. Translated by Samuel and Shierry Weber. Cambridge: MIT Press, 1997.
Agamben, Giorgio. *Homo Sacer: Sovereign Power and Bare Life*. Translated by Daniel Heller-Roazen. Redwood City: Stanford University Press, 1998.
———. *Karman: A Brief Treatise on Action, Guilt, and Gesture*. Translated by Adam Kotsko. Redwood City: Stanford University Press, 2018.
———. *Nudities*. Translated by David Kishik and Stefan Pedatella. Redwood City: Stanford University Press, 2011.
———. *The Time That Remains: A Commentary on the Letter to the Romans*. Translated by Patricia Dailey. Redwood City: Stanford University Press, 2005.
Anderson, Benedict. *Imagined Communities: Reflections on the Origin and Spread of Nationalism*, revised edition. New York: Verso, 1991.
———. *Language and Power*. Ithaca: Cornell University Press, 1990.
———. *The Spectre of Comparisons: Nationalism, Southeast Asia and the World*. New York: Verso, 1998.
Apter, Emily. *Against World Literature: on the Politics of Untranslatability*. New York: Verso, 2013.
———. *The Translation Zone: A New Comparative Literature*. Princeton: Princeton University Press, 2006.
Aristotle. *On the Art of Poetry*. Translated by S. H. Butcher. Indianapolis: Bobbs-Merrill, 1981.

Aytürk, İlker. "Introduction: Romanisation in Comparative Perspective." *Journal of the Royal Asiatic Society*, Third Series, Vol. 20 (1) (January 2010): 1–9.

———. "Script Charisma in Hebrew and Turkish: A Comparative Framework for Explaining Success and Failure of Romanization." *Journal of World History*, Vol. 21 (1) (2010): 97–130.

Bakhtin, Mikhail. *The Dialogic Imagination: Four Essays*. Translated by Caryl Emerson. Edited by Michael Holquist. Austin: University of Texas Press, 1981.

———. *Problems of Dostoevsky's Poetics*. Edited and translated by Caryl Emerson. Minneapolis: University of Minnesota Press, 1984.

Baldwin, Debra Romanick. "Simple Ideas and Narrative Solidarity in 'Prince Roman.'" *Conradiana*, Vol. 35 (1) (Spring 2010): 17–27.

Baxter, Katherine Isobel, and Robert Hampson, eds. *Conrad and Language*. Edinburgh: Edinburgh University Press, 2016.

Beasley-Murray, Tim. "German-Language Culture and the Slav Stranger Within." *Central Europe*, Vol. 4 (2) (November 2006): 131–145.

Benjamin, Walter. *Illuminationen: Ausgewählte Schriften*. Berlin: Suhrkamp, 1977.

———. *Illuminations: Essays and Reflections*. Translated by Harry Zohn. New York: Schocken, 1969.

———. *Reflections: Essays, Aphorisms, Autobiographical Writings*. New York: Schocken, 1978.

Berry, John D. *Language Culture Type: International Type Design in the Age of Unicode*. Zürich: Graphis, 2002.

Bhabha, Homi. *The Location of Culture*. New York: Routledge, 1994.

Bloomfield, Leonard. *Language*. Austin: Holt, Rinehart & Winston, [1933] 1961.

Borsuk, Amaranth. *The Book*. Cambridge: MIT Press, 2018.

Bush, Christopher. *Ideographic Modernism: China, Writing, Media*. New York: Oxford University Press, 2010.

Busza, Andrzej. "Conrad's Polish Literary Background and Some Illustrations of the Influence of Polish Literature on His Work." *Antemurale*, Vol. 10 (1966): 109–255.

———. "Rhetoric and Ideology in Conrad's *Under Western Eyes*." In *Joseph Conrad: A Commemoration*. Edited by Norman Sherry. New York: Macmillan, 1976.

Carabine, Keith. *The Life and the Art: A Study of Conrad's Under Western Eyes*. Amsterdam: Rodopi, 1996.

Caserio, Robert. "*The Rescue* and the Ring of Meaning." In *Conrad Revisited: Essays for the Eighties*. Edited by Ross C. Murfin. Tuscaloosa: University of Alabama Press, 1985, 125–49.

Cezair-Thompson, Margaret. "The Blank Spaces of *Heart of Darkness*." *Conradiana*, Vol. 48 (2-3) (Fall/Winter 2016).

Chambers, Helen. *Conrad's Reading: Space, Time, Networks*. London: Palgrave Macmillan, 2018.

Chow, Rey. *Primitive Passions: Visuality, Sexuality, Ethnography, and Contemporary Chinese Cinema*. New York: Columbia University Press, 1995.

Collits, Terry. "Imperialism, Marxism, Conrad: A Political Reading of *Victory*." *Textual Practice*, Vol. 3, (3) (1989): 1–18.
Conrad, Joseph. *The Collected Letters of Joseph Conrad*, 9 volumes. Edited by Frederick Karl and Laurence Davies. New York: Cambridge University Press, 1983–2008.
———. *The Collected Works*. 26 Volumes. New York: Doubleday, 1926.
———. "Geography and Some Explorers" in *Last Essays: The Cambridge Edition of the Works of Joseph Conrad*. Edited by Harold Ray Stevens and J. H. Stape. New York: Cambridge University Press, 2011.
Coulmas, Florian. *An Introduction to Multilingualism: Language in a Changing World*. New York: Oxford University Press, 2018.
———. *Writing Systems: An Introduction to Their Linguistic Analysis*. New York: Cambridge University Press, 2003.
Crowley, Tony. *Standard English and the Politics of Language*, second edition. London: Palgrave Macmillan, 2003.
Dalby, Andrew. *Dictionary of Languages: The Definitive Reference to More Than 400 Languages*. New York: Columbia University Press, 2004.
Damrosch, David. "Scriptworlds: Writing Systems and the Formation of World Literature." *Modern Language Quarterly*, Vol. 68 (2) (June 2007): 195–219.
Daniels, Peter, and William Bright. *The World's Writing Systems*. New York: Oxford University Press, 1996.
Darvay, Daniel. "The Politics of Gothic in Conrad's *Under Western Eyes*." *Modern Fiction Studies*, Vol. 55 (4) (Winter 2009): 693–715.
Davies, Laurence. "Afterword." In *Conrad and Language*. Edited by Katherine Baxter and Robert Hampson. Edinburgh: Edinburgh University Press, 2016.
DeFrancis, John. *Nationalism and Language Reform in China*. Princeton: Princeton University Press, 1950.
Deleuze, Gilles, and Félix Guattari. *Kafka: Toward a Minor Literature*. Translated by Dana Polan. Minneapolis: University of Minnesota Press, 1986.
Derrida, Jacques. *Acts of Religion*. Edited by Gil Anidjar. New York: Routledge, 2002.
———. *The Beast and the Sovereign*. Volume I. Translated by Geoffrey Bennington. Chicago: University of Chicago Press, 2009.
———. *De la Grammatologie*. Paris: Editions de Minuit, 1967.
———. *Foi et Savoir: suivi de Le Siècle et le Pardon*. Paris: Editions de Seuil, 2000.
———. *Of Grammatology*. Translated by Gayatri Chakravorty Spivak. Baltimore: Johns Hopkins University Press, 1976.
Dharwadker, Vinay. "Orientalism and the Study of Indian Literatures." In *Orientalism and the Postcolonial Predicament*. Edited by Carol Breckenridge and Peter van der Veer. Philadelphia: University of Pennsylvania Press, 1993.
Djavadi, Négar. *Disoriental*. Translated by Tina Kover. Madrid: Europa, 2018.
Dodd, W. J. *Kafka and Dostoevsky: The Shaping Influence*. London: Palgrave Macmillan, 1992.

Donovan, Stephen. *Joseph Conrad and Popular Culture*. London: Palgrave Macmillan, 2005.
Feldman, Leah. *On the Threshold of Eurasia: Revolutionary Poetics in the Caucasus*. Ithaca: Cornell University Press, 2018.
Ferrara, Silvia. *The Greatest Invention: A History of the World in Nine Mysterious Scripts*. New York: Farrar, Straus and Giroux, 2022.
Fleishman, Avrom. *Conrad's Politics: Community and Anarchy in the Fiction of Joseph Conrad*. Baltimore: Johns Hopkins University Press, 1967.
Foucault, Michel. *The Order of Things: An Archaeology of the Human Sciences*. New York: Vintage, 1973.
Francis, Andrew. *Culture and Commerce in Conrad's Asian Fiction*. New York: Cambridge University Press, 2015.
———. "Languages in Conrad's Malay Fiction." In *Conrad and Language*. Edited by Katherine Isobel Naxter and Robert Hampson. Edinburgh: Edinburgh University Press, 2016.
Gelb, I. J. *A Study of Writing*, revised edition. Chicago: University of Chicago Press, 1963.
Gilroy, Paul. *The Black Atlantic: Modernity and Double Consciousness*. Cambridge: Harvard University Press, 1993.
Gitelman, Lisa. *Always Already New: Media, History, and the Data of Culture*. Cambridge: MIT Press, 2006.
Gold, Moshe. "Printing the Dragon's Bite: Joyce's Poetic History of Thoth, Cadmus, and Gutenberg in *Finnegans Wake*." *James Joyce Quarterly*, Vol. 42/3 (1/4) (Fall 2004–Summer 2006): 269–296.
GoGwilt, Christopher. "Afterword: How Black lives matter for Conrad's personal record of migration and transnationalism." In *Migration, Modernity and Transnationalism in the Work of Joseph Conrad*. Edited by Kim Salmons and Tania Zulli. London: Bloomsbury, 2021.
———. *The Invention of the West: Joseph Conrad and the Double-Mapping of Europe and Empire*. Redwood City: Stanford University Press, 1995.
———. *The Passage of Literature: Genealogies of Modernism in Conrad, Rhys, and Pramoedya*. New York: Oxford University Press, 2011.
———. "Postcolonial Philology and the Transposition of 'Western consciousness'." In *Transposing the West*. Edited by Christopher GoGwilt, Holt Meyer, and Vasilios Makrides. Forthcoming, de Gruyter.
———. "Pramoedya's Fiction and History: An Interview with Indonesian Novelist Pramoedya Ananta Toer." *Yale Journal of Criticism*, Vol. 9, (1) (1996): 147–64.
Gottlieb, Nanette. "The Romaji Movement in Japan." *Journal of the Royal Asiatic Society*, Third Series, Vol. 20 (1) (January 2010): 74–88.
Guha, Ranajit. *Elementary Aspects of Peasant Insurgency in Colonial India*. New York: Oxford University Press, [1983] 1994.
Ha Jin. "Introduction to Lu Hsun." In *Selected Stories of Lu Hsun*. New York: W.W. Norton, 2003.

———. *War Trash*. New York: Pantheon, 2004.
———. *The Writer as Migrant*. Chicago: University of Chicago Press, 2008.
Hamner, Robert, ed. *Joseph Conrad: Third World Perspectives*. Washington, D.C.: Three Continents, 1990.
Hampson, Robert. *Cross-Cultural Encounters in Joseph Conrad's Malay Fiction*. London: Palgrave Macmillan, 2000.
Hay, Eloise Knapp. *The Political Novels of Joseph Conrad: A Critical Study*. Chicago: University of Chicago Press, 1963.
Hayles, N. Katherine. *How We Became Posthuman*. Chicago: University of Chicago Press, 1999.
———. *My Mother Was a Computer: Digital Subjects and Literary Texts*. Chicago: University of Chicago Press, 2005.
Hayot, Eric. *The Hypothetical Mandarin: Sympathy, Modernity, and Chinese Pain*. New York: Oxford University Press, 2009.
Hill, Michael Gibbs. "New Script and a New 'Madman's Diary.'" *Modern Chinese Literature and Culture*, Vol .27 (1) (Spring 2015): 75–104.
Hillis, Faith. *Children of Rus': Right-Bank Ukraine and the Invention of Russia*. Ithaca: Cornell University Press, 2013.
Hitchcock, Peter. *The Long Space: Transnationalism and Postcolonial Form*. Redwood City: Stanford University Press, 2010.
Humboldt, Wilhelm von. *On Language: The Diversity of Human Language-Structure and its Influence on the Mental Development of Mankind*. Translated by Peter Heath. New York: Cambridge University Press, 1988.
———. *Über die Kawi-Sprache auf der Insel Java nebst einer Einleitung über die Verschiedenheit des menschlichen Sprachbaues*. Berlin, 1836.
Hutchison, Peter. "Kafka's Private Alphabet." *The Modern Language Review*, Vol. 106 (3) (July 2011): 797–813.
Israel, Nico. *Outlandish: Writing Between Exile and Diaspora*. Redwood City: Stanford University Press, 2000.
Jaffe, Alexandra, Jannis Androutsopoulos, Mark Sebba, and Sally Johnson, eds. *Orthography as Social Action: Scripts, Spelling, Identity and Power*. Berlin: De Gruyter Mouton, 2012.
Jakobson, Roman. *Slavic Languages: A Condensed Survey*, second edition. New York: King's Crown Press, 1955.
Jameson, Fredric. *The Political Unconscious: Narrative as a Socially Symbolic Act*. Ithaca: Cornell University Press, 1981.
Jany, Christian. "Schriftkerben//Kerfs of Writing: A Phenomenology of Kafka's Stylus." *Monatsheft*, Vol. 103 (3) (Fall 2011): 396–415.
Jean-Aubry, G. *Joseph Conrad: Life and Letters*, 2 Volumes. New York: Doubleday, 1927.
Joyce, James. *Finnegans Wake*. London: Faber and Faber, [1939] 1979.
———. *Ulysses*. New York: Vintage, 1961.
Kafka, Franz. *America*. Translated by Willa and Edwin Muir. New York: Penguin, 1967.

———. *The Castle*. Translated by Willa and Edwin Muir. New York: Penguin, 1977.
———. *The Complete Stories*. Edited by Nahum N. Glatzer. New York: Schocken, 1983.
———. *The Diaries of Franz Kafka*. Edited by Max Brod. New York: Penguin, 1982.
———. *Sämtliche Erzählungen*. Frankfurt: Fischer, 1981.
———. *The Trial*. Translated by Willa and Edwin Muir. New York: Penguin, 1962.
Kamusella, Tomasz. *The Politics of Language and Nationalism in Modern Central Europe*. London: Palgrave Macmillan, 2008.
Kirschner, Paul. "Topodialogic Narrative in *Under Western Eyes* and the Rasoumoffs of 'La Petite Russie.'" In *Conrad's Cities: Essays for Hans van Marle*. Edited by Gene M. Moore. Amsterdam: Rodopi, 1992.
Kittler, Friedrich. *Discourse Networks, 1800/1900*. Translated by Michael Metteer and Chris Cullens. Redwood City: Stanford University Press, 1990.
———. *Literature, Media, Information Systems*. Edited by John Johnston. Geneva: Overseas Publishers Association, 1997.
Krenn, Heliéna. *Conrad's Lingard Trilogy: Empire, Race, and Women in the Malay Novels*. New York: Garland, 1990.
Krishnan, Sanjay. *Reading the Global: Troubling Perspectives on Britain's Empire in Asia*. New York: Columbia University Press, 2007.
Lawtoo, Nidesh, ed. *Conrad's Heart of Darkness and Contemporary Thought: Revisiting the Horror with Lacoue-Labarthe*. London: Bloomsbury, 2012.
———. *Conrad's Shadow: Catastrophe, Mimesis, Theory*. East Lansing: Michigan State University Press, 2016.
Lienau, Annette Damayanti. "The Ideal of Casteless Language in Pramoedya's *Arok Dedes*." *Comparative Studies of Southeast Asia, Africa and the Middle East*, Vol. 32 (3) (2012): 591–603.
Liu, Lydia. *The Freudian Robot: Digital Media and the Future of the Unconscious*. Chicago; University of Chicago Press, 2010.
———. *Translingual Practice: Literature, National Culture, and Translated Modernity –China, 1900–1937*. Redwood City: Stanford University Press, 1995.
Livy. *The History of Rome*. Books V, VI and VII with an English translation. Edited by Benjamin Oliver Foster. Portsmouth: Heinemann, 1924.
Lothe, Jakob. *Conrad's Narrative Method*. Oxford: Clarendon Press, 1989.
Love, Harold. "Early Modern Print Culture: Assessing the Models." *Parergon*, Vol. 20 (1) (2003): 45–64.
Lu Xun. *Jottings Under Lamplight*. Edited by Eileen J. Cheng and Kirk Denton. Cambridge: Harvard University Press, 2017.
———. *The Real Story of Ah-Q and Other Tales of China: The Complete Fiction of Lu Xun*. Translated by Julia Lovell. New York: Penguin, 2009.
Maier, Henk. "Boredom in Batavia: A Catalogue of Books in 1898." In *Text/Politics in Island Southeast Asia: Essays in Interpretation*. Edited by D. M. Roskies. Athens: Ohio University Press, 1993.
———. *We Are Playing Relatives: A Survey of Malay Writing*. Leiden: KITLV, 2004.

Mallios, Peter Lancelot. *Our Conrad: Constituting American Modernity.* Redwood City: Stanford University Press, 2010.
Marsden, William. *Dictionary of the Malayan Language.* London: Black, Parry, and Kingsbury, 1812.
McLuhan, Marshall. *Understanding Media: The Extensions of Man.* Berkeley: Gingko Press, 2003.
Mecsnóber, Tekla. "Diacritic Aspirations and Servile Letters: Alphabets and National Identities in Joyce's Europe." *European Joyce Studies*, Vol. 23 (2014): 167–188.
———. *Rewriting Joyce's Europe: The Politics of Language and Visual Design.* The Florida James Joyce Series. Gainesville: University of Florida Press, 2021.
Merriam-Webster Dictionary. https://www.merriam-webster.com/dictionary/.
Milesi, Laurent. "Metaphors of the Quest in *Finnegans Wake.*" In *Finnegans Wake: Fifty Years.* Edited by Gert Lernout. Amsterdam: Rodopi, 1990.
Moore, Gene, ed. *Conrad's Cities: Essays for Hans van Marle.* Amsterdam: Rodopi, 1992.
———. "Who Are the Alfuros?" *Conradiana*, Vol. 39 (3) (Fall 2007): 198–210.
Mullaney, Thomas. *The Chinese Typewriter: A History.* Cambridge: MIT Press, 2018.
Murray, James A. H., et al, eds. *A New English Dictionary on Historical Principles* [O.E.D.], 13 Volumes. New York: Oxford University Press, 1884–1928, Supplement 1933.
Mustafa, Fawzia. "Gurnah and Naipaul: Intersections of *Paradise* and *A Bend in the River.*" *Twentieth-Century Literature*, Vol. 61 (2) (June 2015): 232–263.
Najder, Zdzislaw. *Conrad's Polish Background: Letters to and from Polish Friends.* New York: Oxford University Press, 1964.
———. *Joseph Conrad: A Chronicle.* New Brunswick: Rutgers University Press, 1983.
Nakai, Asako. *The English Book and Its Marginalia.* Amsterdam: Rodopi, 2000.
Napolin, Julie Beth. *The Fact of Resonance: Modernist Acoustics and Narrative Form.* New York: Fordham University Press, 2020.
Nazareth, Peter. "Conrad's Descendants." *Conradiana*, Vol. 22 (2) (Summer 1990).
North, Michael. *The Dialect of Modernism: Race, Language, and Twentieth-Century Literature.* New York: Oxford University Press, 1994.
Ogilvie, Sarah. *Words of the World: A Global History of the Oxford English Dictionary.* New York: Cambridge University Press, 2012.
Ong, Walter. *Orality and Literacy: The Technologizing of the Word* [1982]. New York: Routledge, 2002.
Oxford English Dictionary. [1884–present]. http://www.OED.com. (see also Murray).
Pollock, Sheldon. *The Language of the Gods in the World of Men: Sanskrit, Culture, and Power in Premodern India.* Oakland: University of California Press, 2006.
Pramoedya Ananta Toer. *Arok Dedes.* Edited by Joesoef Isak. Hasta Mitra, 1999.
———. *Arus Balik.* Hasta Mitra, 1995.
———. *Child of All Nations.* Translated by Max Lane. New York: Penguin, 1996.
———. *House of Glass.* Translated by Max Lane. New York: Penguin, 1992.

———. *The Mute's Soliloquy: A Memoir.* Translated by Willem Samuels. New York: Hyperion East, 1999.

———. *Nyanyi Sunyi Seorang Bisu: Catatan-catatan dari Buru*, 2 Volumes. Jakarta: Lentera Dipantara, 1995, 1997.

———. *Realisme-Sosialis dan Sastra Indonesia.* Jakarta: Lentera Dipantara, 2003.

———. *Tales from Djakarta: Caricatures of Circumstances and Their Human Beings.* Southeast Asia Program, Cornell University, 1999.

———. *Tempo Doeloe: Antologi Sastra Pra-Indonesia.* Hasta Mitra, 1982.

———. *This Earth of Mankind.* Translated by Max Lane. New York: Penguin, 1996.

Remy, Johannes. "The Ukrainian Alphabet as a Political Question in the Russian Empire Before 1876." *Ab Imperio*, Vol. 2 (2005): 167–190.

Renner, Andreas. "Defining a Russian Nation: Mikhail Katkov and the 'Invention' of National Politics." *SEER* Vol. 81 (4) (October 2003): 659–682.

Ricoeur, Paul. *Time and Narrative.* Volume I. Translated by Kathleen McLaughlin and David Pellauer. Chicago: University of Chicago Press, 1984.

Rony, Fatimah Tobing. *The Third Eye: Race, Cinema, and Ethnographic Spectacle.* Durham: Duke University Press, 1996.

Roy, Arundhati. *Azadi: Freedom. Fascism. Fiction.* Chicago: Haymarket, 2020.

———. *The God of Small Things* [1997]. New York: Penguin, 2002.

———. *The Ministry of Utmost Happiness.* New York: Knopf, 2017.

Rushdie, Salman. *Joseph Anton: A Memoir.* New York: Random House, 2012.

Said, Edward. *Orientalism.* New York: Vintage, 1979.

Salmon, Claudine. *Literature in Malay by the Chinese of Indonesia.* Montreal: Association Archipel, 1981.

Salmons, Kim and Tania Zulli, eds. *Migration, Modernity and Transnationalism in the Work of Joseph Conrad.* London: Bloomsbury, 2021.

Samolsky, Russell. *Apocalyptic Futures: Marked Bodies and the Violence of the Text in Kafka, Conrad, and Coetzee.* New York: Fordham University Press, 2011.

Saussure, Ferdinand de. *Cours de linguistique Générale.* Edited by Tullio de Mauro. Paris: Payot, 1986.

———. *Course in General Linguistics.* Translated by Wade Baskin. Edited by Charles Bally and Albert Sechehaye. New York: Philosophical Library, 1959.

Saussy, Haun. *Great Walls of Discourse and Other Adventures in Cultural China.* Cambridge: Harvard University Press, 2001.

Schwab, Arnold T. "Conrad's American Speeches and His Reading from *Victory*." *Modern Philology*, Vol. 62 (May 1965): 342–7.

Sharpe, Christina. *In the Wake: On Blackness and Being.* Durham: Duke University Press, 2016.

Shih, Shu-Mei. *The Lure of the Modern: Writing Modernism in Semicolonial China, 1917–1937.* Oakland: University of California Press, 2001.

Siegel, James. *Fetish, Recognition, Revolution.* Princeton: Princeton University Press, 1997.

Siegert, Bernhard. *Cultural Techniques: Grids, Filters, Doors, and Other Articulations of the Real*. Translated by Geoffrey Winthrop-Young. New York: Fordham University Press, 2015.

Smith, David R., ed. *Joseph Conrad's Under Western Eyes: Beginnings, Revisions, Final Forms*. North Haven: Archon Books, 1991.

———. "The Hidden Narrative: The K in Conrad." In *Joseph Conrad's Under Western Eyes: Beginnings, Revisions, Final Forms*. Edited by David Smith. North Haven: Archon Books, 1991.

Snyder, Timothy. "The War in Ukraine Has Unleashed a New Word." *The New York Times*. April 22, 2022.

Stewart, Garrett. *Between Film and Screen: Modernism's Photo Synthesis*. Chicago: University of Chicago Press, 1999.

———. *Reading Voices: Literature and the Phonotext*. Oakland: University of California Press, 1990.

Szczypien, Jean. "Joseph Conrad's *A Personal Record*: Composition, Intention, Design: Polonism." *Journal of Modern Literature*, Vol. 16 (1) (Summer 1989): 3–30.

———. *"Sailing Towards Poland" With Joseph Conrad*. Lausanne: Peter Lang, 2017.

———. "Untyrannical Copy-Texts for the Prefatory Essays to Joseph Conrad's *A Personal Record*." *Conradiana*, Vol. 9 (2) (1984): 81–9.

Tenth International Congress of Orientalists, Held at Geneva. *The Journal of the Royal Asiatic Society of Great Britain and Ireland* (October 1895). 879–892. https://www.jstor.org/stable/25207765.

Towheed, Shafquat. "Geneva v. St. Petersburg: Two Concepts of Literary Property and the Material Lives of Books in *Under Western Eyes*." *Book History*, Vol. 10 (2007): 169–191.

Tran, Ben. *Post-Mandarin: Masculinity and Aesthetic Modernity in Colonial Vietnam*. New York: Fordham University Press, 2017.

Truffaut, François. *Hitchcock*, revised edition. New York: Simon & Schuster, 1985.

Tsu, Jing. *Kingdom of Characters: The Language Revolution that Made China Modern*. New York: Riverhead, 2022.

———. "Romanization without Rome: China's Latin New Script and Soviet Central Asia." In *Asia Inside Out: Connected Places*. Edited by Eric Tagliacozzo et al. Cambridge: Harvard University Press, 2015.

———. *Sound and Script in Chinese Diaspora*. Cambridge: Harvard University Press, 2010.

Uzman, Mehmet. "Romanisation in Uzbekistan Past and Present." *Journal of the Royal Asiatic Society*, Third Series, Vol. 20 (1) (Jan 2010): 49–60.

Warodell, Johan Adam. *Conrad's Decentered Fiction*. Cambridge: Cambridge University Press, 2022.

Watt, Ian. *Conrad in the Nineteenth Century*. Oakland: University of California Press, 1979.

Watts, Cedric. *The Deceptive Text: An Introduction to Covert Plots*. Hempstead: Harvester, 1984.
Wisnicki, Adrian. "Victorian Field Notes from the Lualaba River, Congo." *Scottish Geographical Journal*, Vol. 129 (3–4) (2013): 210–239. http://dx.doi.org/10.1080/14702541.2013.826378.
Woolf, Virginia. *Mr. Bennett and Mrs. Brown*. London: Hogarth Press, 1924. http://www.columbia.edu/~em36/MrBennettAndMrsBrown.pdf.
Yefimov, Vladimir. "Civil Type and Kis Cyrillic." In *Language, Culture, Type: International Type Design in the Age of Unicode*. Edited by John Berry. Zürich: Graphis, 2002.
Yeow, Agnes S. K. *Conrad's Eastern Vision: A Vain and Floating Appearance*. London: Palgrave Macmillan, 2009.
Yildiz, Yasemin. *Beyond the Mother Tongue: The Postmonolingual Condition*. New York: Fordham University Press, 2012.
Zhong, Yurou. *Chinese Grammatology: Script Revolution and Literary Modernity, 1916–1958*. New York: Columbia University Press, 2019.

Index

10th International Congress of Orientalists (1893), 174, 213n32
1911, 23, 24
27th letter of the English alphabet, 66, 70, 126, 182

Aarsleff, Hans, 167, 212n16, 212n18
Abdulla (*Almayer's Folly*), 47, 48, 54, 131, 132; *A Personal Record* [spelled Abdullah], 95, 97
Abdullah bin Abdul Kadir, 159–68, 170
Aboulela, Leila, 14, 202n46
accusative case, 51–60, 66, 93, 98, 100, 128–29, 143, 153, 178–79, 184–86, 214n44; self-accusative, 93, 98, 100, 102, 137, 143, 184
Achebe, Chinua, 5, 14, 61, 69
Ackerman, Chantal, 208n36
Adamowicz–Pospiech, Anieszka, 97
Adorno, Theodor, 105–6, 112
Africa, 5, 15, 19, 26, 32, 36–37, 51, 60–61, 66, 68–70, 89, 97, 181–82. *See also* African languages; blank space; central Africa
African languages, 5, 37, 69. *See also ajami*
Agamben, Giorgio, 102–3
Agencement. See assemblage
ajami (Arabic script), 69
Alfuros (*Victory*), 136–38, 142–43, 153, 209n41
Almayer's Folly, 8–10, 27, 41, 47–49, 51, 53–54, 57–58, 94, 96–97, 128, 131–34, 138–39, 143–44, 162, 164, 184, 189. *See also* "Kaspar! Makan!" (opening words)
alphabet, 1–10, 12–13, 15–18, 28, 31–41, 45, 60, 62, 64, 65–74, 101–2, 124, 126–27, 130, 163, 166–72, 174, 182; claims to singularity of, 1, 8, 32, 35–36, 37, 40, 78, 101, 171, 196n10; English 4, 7, 13, 15–16, 24, 26, 32–35, 39–41, 64, 66, 70–71, 92, 117, 126, 182, 197n20; Greek, 171–72, 203n6; Indian, 167–69, 172, 174; International Phonetic, 1, 64, 199n2; rival national variants, 63–4; roman, passim; Russian, 72–116; in relation to Sanskrit, 163, 166–72; Ukrainian, 80–81
alphabetic universalism, 123–25
alphanumerical digital coding, 2, 13, 26, 29, 32, 65–66, 71, 117, 126, 158, 182
The Americans (TV series), Figure 10, 180
Amerika (Kafka), 22, 112
anagrammatical, 18–19, 21, 187–89, 206n41; anagrammatical Blackness, 18–19, 187, 188. *See also* Sharpe, Christina
Anderson, Benedict, 27, 76, 129–30, 134, 141, 146, 157, 175, 177, 197n21
anti-colonial nationalism, 26, 33, 40, 46, 59, 133–34, 136, 141, 175, 156
Apter, Emily, 3, 196n7
Arab (people), 48, 54, 97, 175, 185
Arab (language), 52, 56, 132, 175
Arab (script), 2, 5, 6, 8–12, 16, 20–21, 28, 33, 37, 39, 43–59, 69–70, 81, 97, 128–32, 134, 146, 159–62, 164, 166, 174–79. *See also ajami; jawi;* Perso-Arabic script
Aristotle, 53, 129
Arok Dedes (Pramoedya), 176, 179
Arrival (film), Figure 11, 146, 180–82
Arus Balik (Pramoedya), 176
ASCII, 126

assemblage (Deleuze and Guattari), 76, 103–6, 108–9, 111–13, 116; and chronotope, 105, 109, 113–16
Atatürk, Mustafa Kemal, 2, 33, 46.
Auerbach, Erich, 3
Austro-Hungarian Empire, 75–76, 110, 114
"Author and Cinematograph" (1923 Conrad lecture), 147, 153
Aytürk, İlker, 31, 38–39, 44, 46, 200n18

Babalatchi (*Almayer's Folly, An Outcast of the Islands*), 129, 131, 133–35, 138
bahasa Indonesia (Indonesian language), 5, 33, 39–40, 46, 134, 159, 175–76, 179
baihua (plain speech, Chinese), 121
Bakhtin, Mikhail, 9–10, 12, 19, 47, 74, 84, 109–10, 113–16, 129, 181, 188–89; *The Dialogic Imagination*, 114; "Discourse in the Novel," 113, 115. *See also* chronotope; novelization
Balinese, 97, 129, 131, 133
Barthes, Roland, 186
Beasley-Murray, Tim, 103
Beijing (Peking), 6, 126, 208n26
Benjamin, Walter, 76, 105–6, 109, 112, 146–51, 154, 197n21, 210n47, 210n64
Bensmaïa, Réda, 109
Berdychiv, 204n10
Berlin, 196n9
betrayal, 12–15, 17, 145, 152, 198n29
Bhabha, Homi, 205n34
bismillah, 131–32, 164
Black Atlantic, The (Paul Gilroy), 12, 19
Blade Runner (film), 146
blank space, 26, 32, 51, 61, 66, 68–71, 89, 95, 97, 107, 126, 181–84, 188
Bloomfield, Leonard, 183–84, 214n42, 214n44, 215n54
Bopp, Franz, 165
Borges, Jorge Luis, 14
Borneo, 97
Borsuk, Amaranth, 197n21, 197n22, 202n48
Brahmi script, 166
Brahminic, 177
British Empire, 46, 66, 69, 101, 132, 159, 162
British Merchant Marine, 4, 93
Brox, Max, 23, 103
Buddhist, 177
Bugis (people, language, script), 55, 58, 97, 129, 133
Burmese, 166
Buru Island prison camp (Indonesia), 176, 186
Buru tetralogy (Pramoedya), 176–77, 185–86; *House of Glass*, 176–77

Bush, Christopher, 28, 117–18, 122, 141, 147, 149, 196n7. *See also* ideographic modernism

C (letter), 6,7, 67, 73, 92, 98, 113, 180, 182, 206n41
Cambodian, 12
cartography, 61, 66, 69–70, 89, 97, 181–82, 205n39
caste, 176, 179, 185–86
Castle, The (Kafka), 23, 103–4, 112
Central Africa, 66, 69, 70
Central Asia, 5, 33, 125, 208n26
Central Europe, 5, 16, 27, 72–73, 75, 78, 81–82, 102, 113, 116, 124
Cezair-Thompson, Margaret, 202n45
character (ambiguous designation for script and people), 21, 23, 25, 27, 53–54, 57, 127, 129
Chassé, Charles, 101
Chekhov, 6, 78, 92
Chernihiv, 204n10
Chiang, Ted, 146, 180
China, 2, 5, 17, 28, 40, 118–23, 130, 141, 145, 147, 149, 153, 212n16
Chinese languages, 2, 4–5, 16, 23, 119, 120–27, 142–43, 178
Chinese modernism, 4, 149
Chinese people, 13, 20, 24, 27–28, 46, 54, 129–55, 160–61, 166, 185
Chinese Postal Map Romanization System (1906), 126
Chinese script, 2, 5–13, 16, 20–21, 24, 27–28, 32, 38, 40, 45, 58, 68, 81, 117–56, 120–61, 166, 171; calls to abolish characters, 118–22, 146
Chow, Rey, 148–50, 152, 196n7, 209n46
Christian, 177
chronotope, 9–10, 12, 19, 21; of Arabic, 162, 164; of authorship, 98; and Chinese, 118, 127–28, 132, 135, 139–40, 143–44, 146, 154; of Cyrillic, 74, 77, 80, 83, 85, 89–94, 97, 102, 106–8; of digital romanization, 180–81, 188; as itself a chronotope, 114, 189; in Joyce, 60–70, 179; and Kafka's "assemblage," 105, 109, 113–16; in Lu Xun, 146, 149, 179; in Pramoedya, 176–77, 179, 185; of romanization in Conrad, 26, 29, 32, 47–49, 51–52, 58–63, 158, 179, 184; in Arundhati Roy, 186–87. *See also* assemblage; Bakhtin, Mikhail; novelization; romanization
Church Slavonic, 77, 204n10
civil type (*grazhdanskiy shrift*), 77
Collits, Terry, 137–38, 153–54
colonization, 11, 47, 106–7, 131, 133, 144–46, 159, 163, 175–76, 182, 185

INDEX

computer coding, 13, 16–17, 26, 28, 60–64, 66, 67, 71, 109, 113, 117, 119, 157–58, 182, 183, 197n20
Congo, 74, 107
Conrad, Joseph, 2ff.; appearance in OED, 32, 41, 42, 47, 50, 201n39; authorial signature, 8, 14–15, 18, 22–23, 25, 67, 73–76, 81–82, 94, 98 100–104, 112–13, 189; and Joyce, 16, 23–26, 32, 59–71, 126, 179, 182, 184, 189; and Kafka, 16, 23–27, 72–73, 76–77, 81–82, 102–16, 179, 189; and Lu Xun, 16, 23–26, 118, 122, 145–56, 179, 189; and Pramoedya Ananta Toer, 20, 129–36, 141, 144, 174–79, 185–87; and racism, 19, 51, 61, 127–28, 130, 137, 153; and romanization, 4–6, 8–19, 22–29, 31ff. passim. *See also specific works and characters*; chronotope; K-effect
coolie labor, 27, 127, 135–37, 139, 143–44, 154, 186
Coulmas, Florian, 11–12, 33–35, 195n2, 199n2, 200n27
Cunninghame Graham, R. B., 53, 56, 58, 103
Cyrillic, 3, 6, 10–12, 16, 19–21, 26–27, 33, 72–74, 77–92, 98–102, 106–7, 114–16, 180, 203n6, 204n25; relation to roman alphabet, 73–74, 78–79, 82–83, 90, 92, 115–16; and Ukrainian, 79–81
Czech, 16, 23, 76, 78, 110–12, 116

Damrosch, David, 11, 45, 161, 197n16
Darfur, 202n46
Davies, Laurence, 204n10
decolonization, 11, 46–47, 131, 133–34, 144–46, 175–76, 185–86
delayed decoding, 9, 15, 54, 128, 143, 154, 185, 198n27
Deleuze, Gilles, and Félix Guattari, 23, 76, 103–4, 106, 109–12, 114, 116, 198n40. *See also* assemblage; minor literature
Derrida, Jacques, 3, 18, 37, 59, 60, 62–63, 155, 169–72, 174, 178–79, 195n5, 196n6, 198n31, 200n26, 206n43; *Of Grammatology*, 3, 18, 171. *See also* globalatinization; *différance*; *espacement*
Devanagari, 12, 16, 158, 161, 168, 169, 170, 171, 174, 179, 213n24, 213n33
diacritical marks, 62–64, 112, 169, 174–75, 213n24, 213n32
dialogized interior monologue (Bakhtin), 84–86, 91
Dictionary of the Malayan Languages, 43. *See also* Marsden, William
différance (Derrida), 18, 37, 60, 62, 178–79

digitization, 11, 13, 16, 21, 28, 50, 60, 62, 70, 117, 127, 157–59, 179, 181–82, 184–86, 188, 197n20, 215n54. *See also* alphanumerical digital coding; computer coding
Djavadi, Négar, 211n72
Donovan, Stephen, 211n65
Dostoevsky, Fyodor, 79, 84–85, 114–15
Douglass, Frederick, 19
Dunganese (language), 125, 208n26
Dutch East Indies, 28, 33, 46, 59, 136, 159
Dutch language, 97, 129, 131, 133, 177

Egyptian, 65
Einstein, Albert, 115, 181
Emerson, Caryl, 114
Ems decree (1876), 80
English language: English–language bias, 4, 39; standardization of, 5, 13, 16, 31–32, 39, 40–41, 47, 58; pidgin, 141–43, 153
English people, 16, 21, 25, 41–42, 47–51, 55–57, 73, 77, 82–89, 93–97, 129, 135
English print, passim. *See also* alphabet; print; Standard English
espacement (Derrida), 18, 37, 60
Esperanto, 120
ethno-nationalist imperative, 74–76, 80–81, 91–93, 113–14, 116, 168

fangyan (language variants in Chinese), 124
film, 13, 118, 122, 146, 148–56, 179–80, 210n51; and captions, 148, 150–52, 155. *See also* ideographic modernism; montage
Finnegans Wake (Joyce), 12, 26, 32, 60, 62–66, 69–71, 126, 182, 184. *See also* iSpace (Joyce); Joyce, James
Fleishman, Avrom, 85
flickering signification, 62–63, 66–67, 158, 180, 182, 214n39. *See also* Hayles, N. Katherine
Ford, Ford Madox, 103
Formosa, 137
Foucault, Michel, 165
Fraktur script (German), 112
Francis, Andrew, 129
French, 4, 62, 78, 95, 99, 101, 109, 120, 125, 175, 177, 204n10

Gaelic, 64, 65
Galsworthy, John, 73
García Márquez, Gabriel, 14
Garnett, Edward, 72–73, 76, 103
Gaul, 36
Gelb, I. J., 3, 18, 35, 78, 92, 113, 195n1, 199n8
Geneva, 83, 86, 175

"Geography and Some Explorers" (Conrad essay), 181
German language, 16, 23, 24, 62, 64, 76, 78–79, 110–12, 116, 125, 175. See also *Fraktur* script (German)
Germany, 75
Gide, André, 14
Gilroy, 12, 19
globalatinization (Derrida, *mondialatinisation*), 18, 57, 58, 59, 195n5, 198n31, 206n43
Gobard, Henri, 110
Gottlieb, Nanette, 200n20
grammar, 19, 21, 51–52, 54, 58, 101, 164, 167, 173–74, 178–79, 182–86, 214n44. See also anagrammatical; Pāṇini; zero degree
grammatology, 3, 18, 28, 35, 68, 119, 122–24, 170–73, 210n62. See also Derrida, Jacques; Gelb, I. J.; Zhong, Yurou
Greek, 6, 19, 35, 40, 52, 57, 65, 114–15, 172–73, 184, 203n6, 213n29; alphabet, 171–73
gu wen (古文), 121–22
Guha, Ranjit, 186
Gurnah, Abdulrazak, 14–15, 17
Gwoyeu Romatzyh (National Language Romanization script), 40, 123, 125

Ha Jin, 13–18, 25, 146, 162; on Lu Xun, 209n46; *War Trash*, 198n29
Habsburg Empire (Austro-Hungarian Empire), 75–76, 110, 114
Hayles, N. Katherine, 61–63, 66–67, 182, 197n21, 202n48, 214n39
Heart of Darkness (Conrad), 5, 10, 15, 26, 36, 51, 61, 66–67, 154, 182; Cyrillic script in, 73–74, 82, 89–90, 94, 100–102, 107; and Kafka's "The Penal Colony," 107–8; McLuhan on, 68–69; and *A Personal Record*, 97
Heath, Stephen, 70
Hebrew (language and script), 23, 80–81, 110–12, 198n42, 204n10
Heidegger, Martin, 148
Hepburn romanization system (Japanese), 33, 38
Heptapod-B (language and script, *Arrival*), 181
Heyst, Axel (*Victory*), 135–44, 153–55
hieroglyph, 68
Hikayat Abdullah, 159–65, 175–76, 180. See also Abdullah bin Abdul Kadir
Hillis, Faith, 75, 77, 79
Hitchcock, Alfred, 211n72
Hitchcock, Peter, 144–5
Holquist, Michael, 144

House of Glass, 176–77. See also Buru tetralogy (Pramoedya)
"Houseboy + Maid" (Pramoedya), 185–86
Humboldt, Wilhelm, 28, 165, 167–76, 178, 183, 212n16, 212n18, 213n24, 213n30
Hungarian (language and script), 62, 64
Huters, Theodore, 122

ideographic, 28, 32, 60, 63, 65–66, 68, 70, 117–18, 120, 122–23, 141, 147, 149–50, 152, 158, 171, 181, 197n20. See also ideographic modernism; ideographic turn
ideographic modernism, 28, 122, 141, 147, 149
ideographic turn, 28, 60, 63–66, 70, 117–18, 120, 141, 150, 152, 158, 181, 197n20
Indo-European, 168, 170
Indonesia, 2, 4–5, 20–21, 26, 28, 33, 39–40, 46, 129, 131, 133–36, 141, 144, 154, 159, 174–78, 185–86, 200n19
International Phonetic Alphabet, 1, 199n2
Ireland, 65
Islam, 15, 17, 52–53, 96–97, 133, 175, 177. See also Muslim
iSpace (Joyce), 26, 32, 60–64, 66, 70–71, 126, 182, 184, 188, 202n55
Istanbul, 3, 4, 196n9
Italian, 57

Jakobson, Roman, 19, 186, 203n6
Jameson, Fredric, 145
Japan, 2, 8, 32–33, 38–39, 148, 150–52, 155; language, 32–33, 38, 39; writing systems, 8, 38, 39, 150, 152, 155, 200n20
Javanese (language), 58, 166–69, 171, 175–79, 185–86. See also Kawi
jawi (Arabic Malay script), 5, 9, 20, 43, 44, 46, 59, 128, 159, 160, 162–64, 175
Jewish, 23, 76, 80, 110–11
Jim-Eng (*Almayer's Folly*), 131–34
Joyce, James, 3, 12, 16, 23–26, 32, 59–67, 69–71, 126, 179, 182, 184, 202n56. See also iSpace; *Finnegans Wake*; *Ulysses*
Judea ("Youth: A Narrative"), 19, 58

K (letter), 2ff. passim; and Conrad's authorial signature, 8, 14–15, 18, 22, 23, 25, 67, 73–76, 81–82, 94, 98, 100–105, 112–13, 115–16, 189; in Kafka, 16, 76, 81, 102–5, 112–16. See also K-effect
K-effect, of OED, 6ff.; in Conrad, 8–28, 40, 45, 66–71, 73, 76–82, 92, 101–4, 112–13, 126, 147, 154–55, 158–59, 182, 184, 188–89; and the K–function in Kafka, 81ff.; 103,

INDEX 231

112–13; and the Kuleshov effect, 154, 211n72
Kadugli, 202n46
Kafka, Franz, 3, 16, 23–25, 27, 72–73, 76–77, 81–82, 102–16, 179, 189; authorial signature, 81–82, 102–4, 112–13, 116; on "minor literature," 23–24, 110–11, 198n40. See also specific works
kalumnia, 102–3
Karain, 8
Karima, 202n46
Kaspar Almayer (Almayer's Folly), 8, 9, 20, 21, 47, 51, 57. See also Almayer's Folly
"Kaspar! Makan!" (opening words, Almayer's Folly), 8–11, 16, 20–21, 47, 51, 54, 57–58, 96–97, 128, 130, 134, 143, 154, 162, 184, 196n14, 214n44
Kassala, 202n46
Katkov, Mikhail Nikiforovich, 79
Kawi (Old Javanese language and script), 166–69, 175, 213n24
Kay, Jackie, 14
Kayerts, 8
Keating, George T., 72
ketchup, 1–2
Khartoum, 6
Khlebnikov, Velimir, 12
Khmer, 166
Kirilyo Sidorovich Razumov (Under Western Eyes), 8, 73, 82–93, 98, 106. See also Under Western Eyes
Kirschner, Paul, 205n32
Kittler, Friedrich, 197n21
knight (silent K in), 66, 126, 154–55, 182
Korean, 12
Korzeniowski, Józef, 8, 74, 94, 112–13. See also Conrad, Joseph
Krishnan, Sanjay, 161
Krom, N. J., 166
Kruchenykh, Aleksei, 12
Kuleshov, Lev, 154, 211n72
kulishivka, 80. See also Ukrainian (script)
Kunrei-shiki romanization system (Japan), 38
Kurtz (Heart of Darkness), 8, 51, 61, 94
Kyiv (Kiev), 204n25

language, and script, hierarchies of, 8–10, 13, 21–22, 27, 34, 39, 42–47, 50, 53, 59, 71, 120, 123–24, 143, 147, 151, 156, 158, 172, 175–76, 179, 186, 189. See also individual languages and scripts; scriptworld; worldscript
lantern slide, 149–50, 210n51

Lao, 166
Latin language and script, 6, 331, 34–36, 40, 45, 50, 52, 57, 59, 65, 77–78, 81, 99, 110, 114–15, 130, 158, 165, 171, 175, 177, 204n10, 213n29. See also alphabet; romanization
Latin alphabet fetishism, 3, 35, 37, 78, 125, 172, 199n8
Latin America, 53, 56–57; Latin Americanization, 57
Latinization movement (China), 123–25
Latinxua Sin Wenz (new script, China), 123, 125
Lawrence, D. H., 24
Lena/Alma (Victory), 136–37, 140–43, 153–54
Leopold Bloom (Ulysses), 65, 67
lexis, 51–53, 56– Kafka's "The Penal Colony," 107–8;8, 102, 129, 156. See also Aristotle
Li, Yiyun, 209n46
Lingard (Almayer's Folly, An Outcast of the Islands, The Rescue), 10, 47, 49, 51–52, 54–58, 129, 132; decaying letters of sign "Office: Lingard and Co.," 10, 48–49, 55, 132, 138–39
linguistic turn, 167, 171–74
linguistics, 2, 3, 29, 167, 171–74, 181–83; sociolinguistics, 2, 26, 38, 40, 44, 53, 70–71, 77–78, 116, 124, 126, 144; and literary form, 109, 110, 116; and structural linguistics, 171, 173–74, 183. See also philology
lithography, 146, 149, 159
Lithuanian press ban (1865–1904), 80
Liu, Lydia, 23, 28, 60, 62–63, 65, 67, 70, 117–18, 120, 145, 148, 150, 152, 196n7, 197n20, 197n21, 209n46; on Lu Xun, 145, 148, 150, 152, 209n46. See also ideographic turn
logocentrism, 37, 200n26. See also Derrida, Jacques
lopa, 183–86. See also zero degree
Lord Jim (Conrad), 14, 26, 41, 43, 47, 51, 53–58, 67, 93, 128, 143, 185. See also Tuan
Lothe, Jakob, 85
Love, Harold, 197n21
Lu Xun, 3, 16, 23–24, 28, 118, 121–24, 145–51, 153, 155–56, 179, 189, 209n46, 210n51, 210n61. See also specific works
Lynd, Robert, 72

Macassar, 129
Maier, Henk, 134
Malay language and script, 2, 4, 5, 8–11, 16, 26, 41–59, 66, 97, 127–35, 141–53, 153–55, 161–62. See also Kawi; jawi; rumi
Malay (OED entry), Figure 4, 44, 45, 118

Malay people, 27, 41–42, 47–49, 52, 54–56, 66, 97, 129, 131, 133, 161. *See also* Bugis; Indonesian; *peranakan* (Indonesian-born) Chinese
Malay romanized print form, 4, 8–9, 11, 15–16, 20–21, 26, 28, 33, 39, 45, 45, 50, 59, 66, 132, 134, 141, 144, 159, 162. *See also* pre-Indonesian; revolutionary Malay
Mallarmé, Stéphane, 18
Mann, Thomas, 14
Marsden, William, 43
May Fourth Movement (China), 121, 145
McLuhan, Marshall, 36–37, 50, 59, 60, 63, 65, 68–69, 78, 172
Mecsnóber, Tekla, 62–64
Mencken, Henry Louis, 72, 76
Milesi, Laurent, 63, 70
minor literature (Kafka), 23–24, 110–11, 198n40. *See also* Deleuze, Gilles, and Félix Guattari; Kafka, Franz
modernism, 2ff.; transnational, 3–6, 12, 22–23, 27, 144–45, 147, 158, 188; Chinese, 4, 23, 145; Creole, 20; Czech-German, 23; English, 20–25, 31–71; European, 73, 103, 117, 141; Irish, 23
monolingual paradigm, 75–78, 81–82, 91, 102–3, 110–16, 119. *See also* Yildiz, Yasemin
montage, 147, 154–55, 211n72
Moore, Gene, 209n41
Morse code, 66–67
Moscow, 4, 79, 80, 196n9
Moten, Fred, 18
Muhammad, 6
Mullaney, Thomas, 119–22, 124
multilinguistic, 3–5, 8–14, 21, 29, 39, 41, 70–71, 75, 76, 78, 158
multimedia, 3, 5, 10, 16, 28–29, 68, 71, 117, 120, 122
multiscript, 8, 10–11, 21, 27, 29, 39, 41, 70–71, 75, 78, 114, 123, 158, 164, 196n7
Murakami, Haruki, 146
Muslim, 15, 17, 52–53, 96–97, 133, 175, 177. *See also* Islam
Mustafa, Fawzia, 15

Nabokov, Vladimir, 13–14, 17
Naipaul, V. S., 14–15, 17
Nakai, Asako, 205n34
Nan-Shan ("Typhoon"), 19, 135
Napolin, Julie Beth, 196n14, 208n36
narrative form, 5, 8, 10, 12, 53, 57, 58, 109, 128, 133, 134, 156, 186; micro-narrative, 51–53, 57–58; "long space," 145–46, 186–8; short passage, 20, 145ff. *See also* Aristotle; Bakhtin, Mikhail; chronotope; novelization; parable
Nazareth, Peter, 14, 15
Ngugi Wa Thiong'o, 14
Nicholas I, 99
The Nigger of the 'Narcissus' (Conrad), 19, 51, 128
Nile, 69, 70, 182
Nostromo (Conrad), 26, 51, 53, 56–58
novelization, 110, 115–16, 188. *See also* Bakhtin, Mikhail; chronotope; narrative form
Numb3rs (TV series), 180, Figure 9
nyai, 185–86; grammatical counterpart to Tuan, 185–86. *See also* Pramoedya Ananta Toer; Tuan

Oath of Youth (*sembah sumpah*), 33, 39
Ogden, Charles Kay, 65
ogham (script), 65
Ogilvie, Sarah, 41, 196n13, 201n32
Old Church Slavonic, 77
Olmeijer, Charles William, 95
Ong, Walter, 35–37, 59, 60, 63–65, 171–72, 196n10, 203n6; *Orality and Literacy*, 35; insistence on "one alphabet," 35–37, 64–65, 171, 196n10
Orientalism, 44, 45, 50, 52–53, 133, 150, 165, 175–7. *See also* Said, Edward; philology
orthography, 7, 13, 17–18, 39, 40, 67, 75, 77, 80, 100–101, 169, 175, 180–81; non-linear, 180–81
Orzeszkowa, Eliza, 13
Ottoman script. *See* Perso-Arabic script
Outcast of the Islands, An (Conrad), 41, 47, 133
Oxford English Dictionary (OED), 6ff., 31–71; changing archive of, 21, 39, 44–45, 48–52, 69; Conrad's appearance in, 41–43, 47, 50, 54; definition of romanization, 33–34, 38, 39; disappearance of Arabic script from, 44–46, 48–50, 69; entry on Sanskrit, 174–75, 178–79; entry on Tuan, Figure 2, 41–49, 54, 56, 175; entry on zero, 182–83, 214n42; K-effect in, 6–8

Pāṇini, 178, 182–83, 186
parable, 105–8, 165
Patna (*Lord Jim*), 14, 19, 58
Peirce, Charles Sanders, 67
Peking (Beijing), 6, 126, 208n26
"Penal Colony, The" (Kafka), 82, 103, 106–11
peranakan (Indonesian-born) Chinese, 28, 134, 137, 144, 154
Persian, 8
Perso-Arabic script, 2, 33, 44

INDEX

Personal Record, A (Conrad), 22, 72–75, 79–80, 82, 88, 93–102, 104–5, 108, 113, 181, 206n41; 1911 Familiar Preface, Figure 7, 73, 94–95, 98, 100–102, 105, 113, 206n41
Peter I (Russian Tsar), 77; Petrine reforms, 77
Phillips, Caryl, 14
philology, 3, 28, 44, 45, 50, 145, 163–74, 177–79, 183, 186; German, 3, 165; Orientalist, 44–45, 50; European comparative philology, 163–74, 178, 183; Sanskrit, 186. *See also* linguistics; *Oxford English Dictionary* (OED)
Phoenician, 6, 40
phonetic, 1–2, 6, 8, 10, 18, 32, 35–37, 42, 45, 60, 62, 64–65, 68–69, 117, 119, 122–24, 155, 170–74, 182–83; alphabet, 1, 35–37, 68–69. *See also* alphabet; phonocentrism
phonocentrism, 18, 37, 123–25, 141, 155, 169, 170, 173, 200n26. *See also* Derrida, Jacques; Zhong, Yurou
phonograph, 117, 147
photography, 117–18, 146, 147, 149–50, 154
pinyin, 5, 38, 120, 124, 126, 208n26
plot, 10, 53, 102, 129, 132, 154; covert plot, 129, 131–33, 135, 138–39, 141, 154; *mythos*, 53, 129. *See also* Aristotle; chronotope; narrative form
Poland, 14, 17, 72, 75–76, 79–80, 99; 1831 uprising, 99; 1863 uprising 75, 79–80
Polish, 4, 8, 13–17, 22, 25, 76, 78–80, 82, 93, 95, 98–102, 108–9, 113, 125, 204n10
Pollock, Sheldon, 28, 157–58, 163, 165–66, 168; "Sanskrit cosmopolis," 28, 157–58
Polustav type, 77
Portuguese, 176–77
Prague, 76, 110–11, 114, 196n9
Pramoedya Ananta Toer, 14, 20, 129, 131–34, 136, 141, 144, 174–77, 179, 185–86, 189. *See also specific works*; pre-Indonesian
Pre-Indonesian, 20, 46, 129, 134, 141, 144, 154, 178, 185
Prince K (*Under Western Eyes*), 8, 92
"Prince Roman" (Conrad), 74, 83, 98–100, 102, 108–10
print, 1ff.; print culture, 1, 5, 13, 35, 157, 197n21; print media, 1, 2, 5–11, 17ff.; transformations of, 16–17, 26, 29, 32, 36, 46, 59–66, 70, 117, 146, 158, 179, 189, 197n20, 197n21. *See also* digitization; Malay (romanized print form); romanization
print-capitalism (Anderson), 27–28, 101, 130–31, 134, 144–46, 154, 157, 197n21
Prussia, 75

Q (letter), 16, 24, 145, 146–47, 149, 152; and K-effect, 198n42
QWERTY keyboard, 38, 126–27, 208n28

racialization, 8, 11, 17, 21–24, 27, 51, 57, 119, 127–28, 130–31, 133, 136–37, 142–43, 153, 184
racism, 51, 61, 127–28, 130, 133, 137, 153.
Raffles, Sir Stamford, 160, 164–65
Rajah (title), 55–56
rattan (OED entry), Figure 5, 44
"Real Story of Ah Q, The" (Lu Xun), 16, 23, 145, 148–49, 152
remediation, 13, 62, 197n22, 202n48
Remy, Johannes, 80
Renner, Andreas, 79
Rescue, The (Conrad), 9, 53, 55–56, 133, 201n38
Resink, G. J., 209n38
revolutionary Malay, 28, 46, 129, 132, 134, 141, 144, 154, 177, 179
Romanian, 97
romanization, 1ff. passim; Chinese character of, 117–23, 126, 130, 135–44, 147, 152, 155–56; definitions, 33, 38–39, 195n1; double-effect of, 6–10, 47, 59 and passim; global turn toward, 1, 7, 16, 40, 59, 78; lowercase vs. uppercase, 7, 16, 37, 40–41, 45, 50, 28, 34–36, 65–68, 100, 106, 115, 158; lowercase romanization, 53, 60, 62, 64, 89, 102, 116, 157, 159; and novelization, 115, 188; Russian face of, 81, 102, 106–7, 114–16; and sanskritization, 170, 172, 174, 179, 183–88, 215n54; uppercase Romanization, 7, 16, 28, 31, 59, 157
Romanization movement (China), 123–25. *See Gwoyeu Romatzyh*
Rome, 31, 34, 36, 165; Roman law, 102, 103
Rony, Fatimay Tobing, 211n70
Roy, Arundhati, 14, 186–87, 213n33, 215n52, 215n54
rumi (Malay Roman script), 5, 9, 20, 59, 128, 162. *See also* Kawi; jawi
Rushdie, Salman, 14–15, 17
Russia, 4–5, 17, 33, 72–78, 80, 98–102, 204n25
Russian formalism, 4, 19
Russian language, 4–5, 8, 10, 13, 15–16, 22, 24, 26, 72–81, 83, 99, 106, 108–9, 113, 117, 125, 152, 155, 188, 204n10; language reforms, 74–81. *See also* Cyrillic (script)
Russification, 74–75, 77, 79, 80–81, 124
Russo-Japanese war, 148, 151
Ruthenian. *See* Ukrainian

Said, Edward, 165
Salih, Tayeb, 14

Salmon, Claudine, 134
Samburan (*Victory*), 135, 141–42
Samolsky, Russell, 111
Sanskrit, 9, 16, 28–29, 157–58, 163–86; 213n24, 213n30, 213n32; European colonial appropriation of Sanskrit, 165, 171, 189; and lowercase romanization, 166, 168, 170–72, 174–75, 178–79, 182–86, 215n54; lowercase sanskritization, 21, 28, 157, 166, 168, 170–71; Sanskrit cosmopolis, 28, 157–58, 163–69, 172, 175–76
Saussure, Ferdinand de, 18, 28, 67, 171–73, 183, 186, 213n29, 213n30
Saussy, Haun, 178, 195n5, 212n18
Schlegel, Friedrich, 165
script, 2ff. passim; definition, 12. *See also individual scripts*; scriptworld; worldscript
script charisma, 31, 44, 200n19
script conversion, 2, 33, 37, 46, 126–27, 134, 146, 162, 176, 200n19; in Indonesia, 2, 33, 39, 46, 134; in Turkey, 2, 3, 33, 39, 46
script reforms, 2–3, 5, 9, 27, 33, 35, 46, 81, 114, 116, 118, 145; China, 2, 40, 118–25, 208n26, 210n62; Indonesian, 2, 4, 33, 39, 40; Japan, 2, 4, 33, 39; Russia, 4, 5, 27, 33, 74–81; Turkish, 2–4, 33, 39
scriptworld, 3f.; and Conrad's fiction, 52–59; defined, 11–12, 21, 45, 81–82, 158–59, 161; and mediating role of Chinese, 117, 125–26, 129, 132, 144, 146, 151–52; and mediating role of English, 34–35, 45–49, 52–53, 55–59, 66, 70–71; and mediating role of Russian, 73, 75, 77, 81–83, 91–92, 97–101, 108–9, 116; and Sanskrit model, 157–58, 161–66, 175–77, 179, 182, 197n16
Sebald, W. G., 14
Semitic languages and scripts, 6, 35, 40, 65
Sennar, 202n46
Shanghai, 196n9
Shannon, Claude, 60, 65–66, 70, 182, 197n20
Sharpe, Christina, 18–19, 187–88, 215n54. *See also* anagrammatical: anagrammatical Blackness
sheng (voice, speech sound), 123–24
Shih, Shu-Mei, 209n46
Shklovsky, Viktor, 19; *fabula* and *sjuzet* (story and plot); *ostranenie* (estrangement); *priem* (device), 19
Siegel, James, 134
Siegert, Bernhard, 205n39
Sin Wenz. *See Latinxua Sin Wenz*
Singapore, 137, 139, 159–61, 167
Slav, 22, 25, 72–73, 76, 81–82, 101–3, 113, 116; Sclavonism, 72–73, 76, 102; Slavonism, 101. *See also* Polish; Russian

Smith, David R., 203n8, 205n37
Surabaya, 136
South Asia, 157–58, 165–66, 169, 175
Southeast Asia, 27–28, 125, 136, 144, 157–58, 165–67, 169, 175
Soviet Union, 33. *See also* Russia
Spanish, 53, 56–57, 176; Spanish-American, 56–57
Spanish-American war, 53
Spillers, Hortense, 18
Spitzer, Leo, 3
St. Petersburg, 83, 86
Standard English, 7, 32, 40, 117
standardization, 2ff.; of Chinese script, 5, 27, 40, 124–27; of English, 5, 7, 13, 27–31, 39–41, 47, 58, 67, 71, 158; Japanese, 38; and OED, 42, 47, 71; and print media, 11, 16, 41, 63; of Russian script, 5, 74–79, 80–81; Southeast Asia, 5; Ukrainian, 80. *See also individual languages and scripts*; Standard English
Stanley Falls, 96, 181
Stephen Dedalus (*Ulysses*), 65, 67
Stewart, Garrett, 214n39
Stimilli, Elettra, 103
subaltern, 186
Sulu, 9, 97, 133
Swedish, 135, 140
Szczypien, Jean, 203n8

Tanganyika, 69, 181
technolinguistic, 119–20, 127
telecommunications, 59–60, 65
telegraph, 59, 65, 119, 147
telephone, 59
television, 13, 179–80
Thai, 166, 199n2
Tirto Adi Suryo, 177
titles, 41–43, 47–49, 52–58, 66, 132, 124
Tokyo, 4, 33, 39, 196n9
Tolstoy, Leo, 115
Torah, 111
Towheed, Shafquat, 205n30
transcription, 1–2, 7–8, 16–17, 19, 29, 38–39, 41–43, 46–49, 51–52, 55, 57, 59, 89, 98, 128, 134, 142, 144–45, 151, 162, 164, 174–75, 177–78, 184, 187–88, 200n27, 215n54
translation, 9, 13–14, 17, 24, 39, 41–43, 46–49, 51–52, 55, 59, 90, 128, 145, 162, 174, 184, 215n54
transliteration, 1–2, 6, 9, 17–18, 24, 33, 36–37, 39, 41–43, 46–56, 59–61, 66, 68, 70, 84, 90, 95, 101, 128, 145, 162, 170, 173–74, 177–78, 183–84, 215n54
Trial, The (Kafka), 23, 104, 112

INDEX   235

Tsu, Jing, 118–22, 124–26, 196n7, 208n26
Tuan, 41–51, 54–55, 58, 70–71, 128, 143, 174–75, 184–86; in Conrad's fiction, 41–51, 53–56, 93, 128, 143, 184–86; as grammatical counterpart to *nyai*, 185–86; in Joyce's *Finnegans Wake*, 70–71, 184; Marsden *Dictionary* definition in *jawi* script, Figure 3, 43; OED entry on, 41–44, 46–50, 70, 174–75, 184
Turgenev, Ivan, 115
Turkey, 2, 3, 33, 39, 200n19; and script reforms of 1928, 2, 3, 39
Turkish, 8, 44–45, 62, 125
typewriter, 59, 119, 147
Typhoon (Conrad), 127, 135
typography, 36–37, 48, 50, 60, 67, 71, 74, 77

Ukraine, 4, 76, 79, 80, 97, 204n10, 204n25
Ukrainian language and script, 79–81, 101, 204n25; Kulishivka alphabet, 80–81
Ulysses (Joyce), 63–67
Under Western Eyes (Conrad), 10, 14, 22, 72–74, 77, 80, 82–94, 98, 100, 102, 106–8; chronotope of Cyrillic script contrasted to *Heart of Darkness*, 89, 100, 102, 107; comparison to Kafka's work, 102, 106–8
Unicode, 126

V.-David, Madeleine, 3, 170
Valuev circular (1863), 80
Vergil, 165
Victoria Nyanza, 69, 181
Victory (Conrad), 10, 28, 127, and the effacement of Chinese characters, 135–44, and film, 153–55, 185. See also Heyst, Axel; Wang
Vietnamese, 199n2
Villeneuve, Denis, 180
"Voiceless China" (Lu Xun), 121–23

Wang (*Victory*), 127, and effacement of Chinese character, 135–44, and film, 153–55; as problem of reading, 139–43, 153, 155
Warodell, Adam, 203n8
Watt, Ian, 198n27
Watts, Cedric, 129, 131, 153–54. *See also* plot: covert plot
Wau, 202n46
Weber, Max, 31
West, the, 90–91, 150, 205n35, 206n55
Westernization, 11, 31
Wiener, Norbert, 60
Wisnicki, Adrian S., 69
Woolf, Virginia, 12, 14, 23–25
world literature, 29, 81, 132, 157–59
worldscript, 11, 12, 15–17, 21, 24–25, 29, 31, 34–37, 44–59, 64–66, 69–71, 73, 75, 81–82, 89, 91, 99, 102, 108, 116, 125, 130, 144, 152, 156–59, 161–62, 164, 166, 169–70, 174–79, 182
writing systems. *See individual scripts*; alphabet; script

Xu Bing, 146

Yefimov, Vladimir, 77
Yiddish, 23, 79–80, 110–12, 204n10
Yildiz, Yasemin, 75–76, 78, 81, 102–3, 110–12, 114–16, 196n7. *See also* monolingual paradigm
"Youth: A Narrative" (Conrad), 51, 58, 67

zaum, 12
zero degree, 181–86, 214n42, 214n44, 215n54. *See also* lopa
Zhong, Yurou, 35–36, 119–25, 196n7, 210n62
Zhou Enlai, 120
Zhytomyr, 204n10

Christopher GoGwilt is Professor of English and Comparative Literature at Fordham University. He is the author of *The Passage of Literature: Genealogies of Modernism in Conrad, Rhys, and Pramoedya* (Oxford University Press, 2011. Winner, Modernist Studies Association Book Prize); *The Fiction of Geopolitics: Afterimages of Culture from Wilkie Collins to Alfred Hitchcock* (Stanford University Press, 2000); and *The Invention of the West: Joseph Conrad and the Double-Mapping of Europe and Empire* (Stanford University Press, 1995).

www.ingramcontent.com/pod-product-compliance
Lightning Source LLC
Chambersburg PA
CBHW020404080526
44584CB00014B/1171